# graphis annual 77|78

W9-AJN-230

*Edited by Walter Herdeg*

This is the 26th annual edition of the original cornerstone of the "Graphis trilogy" which has richly earned its world-wide reputation as the standard work reflecting the latest international trends in all design fields. This year's collection continues its survey of graphics in advertisements, annual reports, booklets, book jackets and magazine covers, trademarks, letterheads, packaging, record covers, film and television, and editorial design. Here is an endless source of ideas and a perfect "swipe file" for art directors, illustrators and designers, keeping them up-to-date as well as offering new ideas and solutions to graphic arts problems.

The Two Companion Annuals, Edited by Walter Herdeg:

## GRAPHIS POSTERS
### The International Annual of Poster Art

"As with all the *Graphis* publications, this is an outstanding state-of-the-art commentary... technically and artistically excellent."—*Communication Arts Magazine*. "Filled to the brim with an excellent panoply of poster art... beautifully designed."—*Art Direction*. "A superb book, suitable for art teachers in senior high school or college; also, professionals in advertising and graphics."—*School Arts*. Each edition offers visual evidence of the world's best posters arranged in four major categories: Advertising posters, Cultural posters, Social posters, Decorative posters.

Published each year in early Spring.

## PHOTOGRAPHIS
### The International Annual of Advertising, Editorial and Television Photography

Presented here are outstanding photographic achievements from around the world in Advertising; Annual Reports; Book Jackets; Editorial Photography; Magazine Covers; Packaging; Calendars; House Organs; Booklets; Television. "The definitive recap of what's been going on in the wonderful world of photography."—*Publishers Weekly*. "The most comprehensive, eclectic compilation of the world's most successful photography."—*PhotoGraphic*. "An excellent idea book."—*Photomethods*.

Published each year in late Spring.

Other Graphis Books, Edited by Walter Herdeg:

*"Square Books" format (9½" × 9⅜")*

## FILM AND TV GRAPHICS 2
### An International Survey of the Art of Film Animation

## GRAPHIS / DIAGRAMS
### The Graphic Visualization of Abstract Data

## GRAPHIS / RECORD COVERS
### The Evolution of Graphics in Record Packaging

*In 9½" × 12" format:*

## GRAPHIS / ANNUAL REPORTS
*Text by Richard A. Lewis*

## GRAPHIS / PACKAGING 3

*Write for a complete catalogue:*

## VISUAL COMMUNICATION BOOKS

Hastings House, Publishers, 10 East 40th Street, New York, N.Y. 10016

# graphis annual 77|78

# 77\78 graphis annual

The International Annual of Advertising and
Editorial Graphics

Das internationale Jahrbuch der Werbegraphik und der redaktionellen Graphik

Le répertoire international de l'art graphique
publicitaire et rédactionnel

Edited by / Herausgegeben von / Réalisé par:

Walter Herdeg

Walter Herdeg, The Graphis Press, Zurich

Distributed in the United States by

**Hastings House**
Publishers
10 East 40th Street, New York, N.Y. 10016

PUBLICATION No. 149     [ISBN   0–8038–2687–7]

# Contents　　　Inhalt　　　Sommaire

# Abbreviations     Abkürzungen     Abréviations

| | | | | | |
|---|---|---|---|---|---|
| Argentina | ARG | Argentinien | ARG | Afrique du Sud | SAF |
| Australia | AUS | Australien | AUS | Allemagne occidentale | GER |
| Austria | AUT | Belgien | BEL | Allemagne orientale | GDR |
| Belgium | BEL | Brasilien | BRA | Argentine | ARG |
| Brazil | BRA | Deutschland (Ost) | GDR | Australie | AUS |
| Canada | CAN | Deutschland (West) | GER | Autriche | AUT |
| Cuba | CUB | Finnland | FIN | Belgique | BEL |
| Czechoslovakia | CSR | Frankreich | FRA | Brésil | BRA |
| Finland | FIN | Grossbritannien | GBR | Canada | CAN |
| France | FRA | Hongkong | HKG | Cuba | CUB |
| Germany (East) | GDR | Israel | ISR | Espagne | SPA |
| Germany (West) | GER | Italien | ITA | Etats-Unis | USA |
| Great Britain | GBR | Japan | JPN | Finlande | FIN |
| Hong Kong | HKG | Jugoslawien | YUG | France | FRA |
| Hungary | HUN | Kanada | CAN | Grande-Bretagne | GBR |
| Israel | ISR | Kuba | CUB | Hongkong | HKG |
| Italy | ITA | Niederlande | NLD | Hongrie | HUN |
| Japan | JPN | Norwegen | NOR | Israël | ISR |
| Netherlands | NLD | Oesterreich | AUT | Italie | ITA |
| Norway | NOR | Polen | POL | Japon | JPN |
| Poland | POL | Schweden | SWE | Norvège | NOR |
| South Africa | SAF | Schweiz | SWI | Pays-Bas | NLD |
| Spain | SPA | Spanien | SPA | Pologne | POL |
| Sweden | SWE | Südafrika | SAF | Suède | SWE |
| Switzerland | SWI | Tschechoslowakei | CSR | Suisse | SWI |
| Uruguay | URU | Ungarn | HUN | Tchécoslovaquie | CSR |
| USA | USA | Uruguay | URU | Uruguay | URU |
| Yugoslavia | YUG | USA | USA | Yougoslavie | YUG |

Cover/Umschlag/Couverture: Jean Lagarrigue

■ With this issue GRAPHIS ANNUAL begins its second quarter-century of gathering for the delight and instruction of the contemporary reader and observer the most significant works of the past year in international graphic design. Leo Lionni has said for us in his thoughtful and penetrating preface why this exercise is worth while. To do it well, we need the support of graphic designers the world over, and this note says our thanks to them for their continued contributions. We cannot help feeling that this volume is once more a tribute to their profession, to the great skill, empathy and imagination they are capable of putting into their job.

■ Ein Vierteljahrhundert ist vergangen, seit GRAPHIS ANNUAL erstmals dem interessierten zeitgenössischen Beobachter der internationalen Design-Szene die hervorragendsten Arbeiten des vergangenen Jahres vorstellte. In seinem gehaltvollen und scharfsinnigen Vorwort zu diesem Band streicht Leo Lionni die Bedeutung eines solchen Unternehmens heraus. Um diese Aufgabe wie bis anhin weiterzuführen, sind wir auf die Mitarbeit der Graphik-Designer aus der ganzen Welt angewiesen, welchen wir mit diesen Zeilen unseren herzlichsten Dank für ihre Mitarbeit aussprechen. Wir sind überzeugt, dass auch dieser Band das Können, die Einfühlungsgabe und das schöpferische Vorstellungsvermögen, die sie in ihre Arbeit investieren, unter Beweis stellt.

■ Voici la 26e fois que GRAPHIS ANNUAL présente les meilleures réalisations internationales de l'année écoulée en un ouvrage que le lecteur intéressé se plait à feuilleter pour s'informer ou pour le seul plaisir des yeux. Dans sa préface perspicace, Leo Lionni met en évidence l'importance de tels ouvrages. Pour pouvoir les compiler, nous dépendons de la coopération des designers du monde entier, et ces quelques lignes s'adressent à eux pour leur remercier sincèrement de leur concours continu. Nous sommes convaincus que ce volume rend hommage à leur profession, ainsi qu'au talent, à l'empathie et à l'imagination dont bénéficient leurs travaux.

JEAN LAGARRIGUE painted our cover, paying homage in it to Caravaggio, Hokusai, Edvard Munch and Walt Disney. After moving for some time between the USA and France, he settled in Paris, where he teaches at the Ecole des arts décoratifs and recently did a large mural for the Centre Beaubourg.

JEAN LAGARRIGUE huldigt in unserem Umschlag Caravaggio, Hokusai, Munch und Disney. Nachdem er einige Zeit zwischen den USA und Frankreich pendelte, liess er sich in Paris nieder, wo er an der Ecole des arts décoratifs lehrt. Kürzlich vollendete er ein Wandgemälde für das Centre Beaubourg.

JEAN LAGARRIGUE, qui à réalisé la peinture de notre couverture, y rend hommage à Caravage, Hokusaï, Edvard Munch et Walt Disney. Après des voyages réitérés entre les Etats-Unis et la France, il s'est installé à Paris où il enseigne à l'Ecole des arts décoratifs. Récemment il a réalisé une grande peinture murale pour le Centre Beaubourg.

*Leo Lionni*

# Introduction

LEO LIONNI, though of Italian parentage, was born in Amsterdam and spent over twenty years in the USA, where he was among other things art director of *Fortune*. Living in Italy since 1960, he has distinguished himself as a writer and illustrator of children's books and has devoted himself primarily to the fine graphic arts and sculpture. His long familiarity with the design scene, however, eminently qualifies him to review its achievements against a wider cultural background, as he does with such sagacity in these paragraphs.

In the twenty-five previous volumes of GRAPHIS ANNUAL the praises of advertising in general and of its visual aspects in particular have been voiced and echoed from all points of our cultural panorama. At this juncture there would seem to be little to add to these explanations of the economic, sociological, historical, political and even moral significance of our endeavours in this field. Its merits and faults have been analysed and judged, its results statistically researched and measured. One would think, in fact, that with all the knowledge and wisdom thus accumulated advertising would have been able to deliver foolproof techniques and foreseeable results—that, as in cooking, its processes could be codified and trusted to tested recipes, enriched perhaps with occasional advice from an old aunt.

Indeed, many of us remember the times when, against our intuitive judgements and personal inclinations, we were given rigid prescriptions. We were told that kittens and babies were sure bait for a woman's attention but that humour was strictly a man's business. We were shown how eyes travel on the printed page and where, in the geography of pictures and words, they were bound to stop. We were confronted with figures and charts. But as the kittens and the babies grew, and the turmoil of competition grew wilder and more complex, one ingredient, unmeasurable, unpredictable and capricious, was to take on an increasingly important role in the advertising kitchen: the ingredient of surprise. And so against all odds, while the words seemed to become more and more the regimented slaves of a prescribed rhetoric, commercial graphics, during the first half-century of their adult life, assumed more and more the lively function of "advertising the advertisement", so to speak, through the flamboyant agressiveness of their means.

The things that happen to the results and teachings of research when they are forced through the filters of personal passion, imagination and creative drive constitute a fascinating process which, to my knowledge, has never been convincingly analysed. But then again, it is perhaps too early to understand fully the factors which have determined the evolution of commercial graphics and their gradual acquisition of independence from the pressure of business *realpolitik.* Perhaps, as in all human history, it is the very unpredictability which in nature characterizes man alone that has diverted the course of a development which only a few decades ago seemed to be headed in the opposite direction.

What we do know is that the proliferation of individual styles, manners and mannerisms has produced a new language, enormously varied, ambiguous and seductive, and apparently quite independent of the restrictive demands of mass communication. Often surreal, sometimes on the verge of a happy madness, much of its imagery, if isolated from its context and seen through the eyes of the uninitiated, would surely fail to betray its utilitarian origins and motivations.

Parallel to, but only at arm's length from the fast-moving world of op and pop, of happenings, Neo-Dada and New Reality, graphics have been in constant motion, exploding from pages and walls with a wild vitality and a freedom of inventiveness which are perhaps unprecedented in the history of communication. Today their joyful anarchy, daring acrobatics and playful creativeness, which in the early days we had to fight for every inch of the way, are being accepted, even demanded by some of the stodgiest, most pedantic members of the advertising community. Whether the reasons are fully understood or not, no one seems to doubt any longer the ability of our visual media to appeal to the emotions, to stimulate the imaginative processes, to animate the slower, more constricted modes of verbal intercourse, and no one seems to be shocked if the form and contents of the illustrations often totally elude the laws of rational interpretation.

It is not surprising that the vigour of this new language can be felt best in its recent influence on the fine arts. The inclusion of advertisements in collages, prints and paintings (Rauschenberg), the exploitation of special techniques and forms (Lichtenstein), the manipulation of commercial posters (Rotella), the elaboration of symbols (Chryssa) are the most blatant examples of the direct use of advertising in the fine arts. Far indeed are the days when "The Use of the Fine Arts in Advertising" was a provocative subject for discussion and the title of many an article. By now the increasing frequency of reciprocal incursions as between Art and art has created a vast area of visual expression where the forms and symbols are difficult to assign to one side or the other of the museum wall. A surprising aspect of this trading and raiding is that while in the beginning it was graphic design that borrowed the forms from its more respectable neighbour, we now find the content and symbology of graphic language as a "play within a play" in painting and even in sculpture.

It is true that advertising is sometimes lifted out of its context, much as in Warhol's tomato soup can, to denounce the vulgarities of our consumer society in the realm of social or cultural criticism. But even so there can be little doubt that we are faced with a new language which has greatly enriched our stock of symbols, has extended our means of self-expression, sensitized our imagination and, last but not least, moved things from shelves into our homes.

Folon, who like many artists of today is as much at home in the museum as on the market-place, has demonstrated that even one of the most banal of graphic devices, the arrow, is in reality a highly ambiguous symbol, powerfully charged with poetic content. Here, I believe, we are close to the one quality of graphics which is beginning to emerge more clearly in our understanding. Much of the enormous volume of visual material which bombards our retinas from walls, pages and screens seems to bypass the pedantic mechanisms of primary communication, to penetrate that zone of our mind in which we are capable of making new and adventurous connections between symbols and feeling, where the vague boundaries of meaning allow us to invent a new imagery, unpolluted by the verifiable realities we are forced to deal with for physical survival, where we can play an ambiguous game of fictions in which the aims and rules are more akin to poetry than to prose.

Certainly one can object that graphics of this sort are only the small, visible part of the iceberg—that the great mass which floats hidden in the contaminated waters of our culture is trite, vulgar and, worse perhaps, unforgivingly boring. Sceptics might also be tempted, in a similar order of thought, to dismiss the contents of this Annual as the refined choice of an elite, naively unaware of the banal realities of our visual landscape. I would like to remind them of the functions of our museums. No one believes that what they show should represent the actual status of painting and sculpture. Surely their function is not to inventorize but rather to discover and reveal what is *significant* in the development of art today. This Annual in the same way gathers what is *significant* in today's graphics. And it does so with the only possible criterion: a severe critical selection of the most surprising, the most inventive, the most original—the *best* of the year.

*Leo Lionni*

# Vorwort

LEO LIONNI ist italienischer Abstammung, wurde jedoch in Amsterdam geboren. Er verbrachte mehr als 20 Jahre in den USA, wo er unter anderem als Art Director der Zeitschrift *Fortune* tätig war. 1960 kehrte er nach Italien zurück. Er schuf sich grosse Anerkennung als Autor und Illustrator von Kinderbüchern, sein Hauptinteresse gilt jedoch der freien Graphik und der Bildhauerei. Dank seiner langjährigen Tätigkeit und seinen fundierten Kenntnissen der Design-Szene ist er zweifellos wie kaum ein anderer qualifiziert, die heutige Gebrauchsgraphik in einen weiten kulturellen Zusammenhang zu stellen und ihre Leistungen entsprechend zu würdigen.

In den fünfundzwanzig vorhergehenden Bänden von GRAPHIS ANNUAL ist das Lob der Anzeigenwerbung im allgemeinen und seiner visuellen Aspekte im besonderen besungen und von allen Seiten unseres Kulturpanoramas bekräftigt worden. An dieser Stelle ist diesen Erklärungen der wirtschaftlichen, soziologischen, historischen, politischen und sogar moralischen Bedeutung unserer Bestrebungen auf diesem Gebiet anscheinend wenig hinzuzufügen. Ihre Verdienste und Fehler sind analysiert und beurteilt, ihre Ergebnisse statistisch untersucht und gemessen worden. Man möchte in der Tat glauben, dass mit all der so angesammelten Kenntnis und Erkenntnis die Anzeigenwerbung in der Lage sein müsste, narrensichere Techniken und vorhersehbare Resultate zu liefern – dass die einzelnen Arbeitsgänge wie beim Kochen in erprobten und vertrauenswürdigen Rezepten aufgeschrieben werden könnten, angereichert vielleicht noch mit gelegentlichen Ratschlägen einer guten alten Tante.

Viele von uns erinnern sich noch an die Zeiten, da man uns gegen unsere intuitive Beurteilung und persönliche Neigung strenge Vorschriften machte. Man brachte uns bei, dass Kätzchen und Babies sichere Köder für Frauen seien, dass Humor jedoch nur etwas für Männer sei. Man zeigte uns, wie die Augen über bedrucktes Papier wandern und wo sie unwillkürlich in der Bilder- und Wortlandschaft Halt machen müssen. Man konfrontierte uns mit Zahlen und Tabellen. Doch während die Kätzchen und Kinder heranwuchsen und der Wettbewerb aufreibender und vielschichtiger wurde, sollte ein Grundbestandteil, unmessbar, unvorhersehbar und kapriziös, eine immer bedeutendere Rolle im Arsenal der Werbeküche einnehmen: das Ingredienz der Überraschung. Und während die Wörter mehr und mehr zu konventionellen Sklaven einer vorgeschriebenen Rhetorik zu werden schienen, übernahm die Werbegraphik im ersten halben Jahrhundert ihres Erwachsenwerdens trotz aller Widrigkeiten mehr und mehr die lebendige Funktion der «Werbung für die Anzeigenwerbung» mit der auffallenden Aggressivität ihrer Methoden.

Was aus den Resultaten und Lehren der Forschung wird, wenn sie die Filter persönlicher Leidenschaften, Phantasie und schöpferischen Dranges passieren müssen, ist ein faszinierender Prozess, der meines Wissens noch nie überzeugend analysiert wurde. Aber vielleicht ist es noch zu früh, um ganz jene Faktoren zu verstehen, die für die Entwicklung der Werbegraphik und ihre schrittweise Lösung aus der Abhängigkeit von den Zwängen wirtschaftlicher Realpolitik bestimmend waren. Wie stets in der Menschheitsgeschichte, ist es vielleicht gerade das Unberechenbare, das allein den Menschen in der Natur charakterisiert, das den Lauf der Entwicklung, die noch vor wenigen Jahren in die entgegengesetzte Richtung zu führen schien, umgekehrt hat.

Wir wissen jedoch, dass die Verbreitung individueller Lebensweisen, Manieren und Manierismen eine neue, äusserst variantenreiche, vieldeutige und verführerische Sprache hervorgebracht hat, die offensichtlich auch völlig unabhängig ist von den restriktiven Forderungen der Massenkommunikation. Oft surrealistisch, manchmal am Rand glückseliger Verrücktheit balancierend, dürfte ein grosser Teil ihrer Bildersprache, wenn man sie von ihrem Umfeld isoliert und mit den Augen des Uneingeweihten sieht, gewiss nichts von ihren utilitaristischen Ursprüngen und Motivationen verraten.

Parallel dazu, aber nur um Armeslänge von der rasch bewegten Welt von Op und Pop, von Happenings, von Neo-Dada und New Reality entfernt, befindet sich auch die Graphik in ständiger Bewegung, explodiert aus Zeitungs- und Zeitschriftenseiten und von Wänden herab mit einer unbezähmbaren Vitalität und einer freien Erfindungsgabe, wie sie in der Geschichte der Kommunikation wohl noch nie dagewesen sind. Ihre fröhliche Anarchie, wagemutige Akrobatik und verspielte Kreativität, für die wir in der Anfangszeit auf jedem Zoll des Weges kämpfen mussten, sind heute akzeptiert und werden sogar von einigen der Schwerfälligsten und pedantischsten Angehörigen der werbungtreibenden Wirtschaft gefordert. Ob man die Gründe dafür ganz versteht oder nicht, niemand scheint mehr die Fähigkeit unserer visuellen Medien zu bezweifeln, an die Emotionen zu appellieren, die Phantasie zu stimulieren, den langsameren und eingeengteren Weg der Wortwerbung zu beleben; und niemand scheint mehr schockiert zu sein, wenn Form und Inhalt der Illustrationen oft völlig die Gesetze rationaler Interpretation ignorieren.

Es überrascht nicht, dass man die Durchschlagskraft dieser neuen Sprache am besten an ihrem derzeitigen Einfluss auf die schönen Künste spüren kann. Die Einbeziehung von Anzeigen in Collagen, Photos und Malereien (Rauschenberg), die Ausnutzung besonderer Techniken und Formen (Lichtenstein), die geschickte Handhabung von Reklameplakaten (Rotella), die Ausarbeitung von Symbolen (Chryssa) sind die marktschreierischsten Beispiele der direkten Anwendung von Reklame in den schönen Künsten. Fern sind in der Tat die Tage, da «Die Anwendung der Schönen Künste in der Reklame» ein Reizthema in der Diskussion und der Titel so manches Artikels war. Inzwischen hat die zunehmende Häufigkeit gegenseitiger Durchdringung, wie zwischen Kunst und Kunsthandwerk, ein unermessliches Feld visueller Ausdrucksmöglichkeiten geschaffen, wo sich die Formen und Symbole schwer der einen oder anderen Seite der Museumstür zuordnen lassen. Dieses Geben und Nehmen hat einen überraschenden Aspekt: während anfangs die Graphik ihre Formen von den respektablen Nachbarn auslieh, finden wir heute den Inhalt und die Symbolik der graphischen Sprache wie ein «Theater im Theater» in der Malerei und sogar in der Bildhauerei wieder.

Es stimmt, dass Reklame manchmal aus ihrem Zusammenhang gerissen wird, wie etwa bei Warhols Tomatensuppendose, um die vulgären Seiten unserer Konsumgesellschaft mit den Mitteln sozialer oder kultureller Kritik blosszustellen. Doch selbst da kann es kaum Zweifel geben, dass wir mit einer neuen Sprache konfrontiert sind, die unseren Bestand an Symbolen sehr bereichert, unsere Mittel der Selbstverwirklichung vermehrt, unsere Vorstellungskraft sensibilisiert und, last but not least, Dinge von den Ladenregalen in unsere Wohnungen gebracht hat.

Folon, der wie viele moderne Künstler genauso im Museum wie auf dem Markplatz zu Hause ist, hat demonstriert, dass selbst eines der banalsten graphischen Zeichen, der Pfeil, in Wahrheit ein sehr vieldeutiges Symbol ist, kräftig mit poetischem Gehalt befrachtet. Hier, so glaube ich, kommen wir jener Qualität der Graphik nahe, die wir immer klarer zu verstehen beginnen. Viel von der gewaltigen Flut visuellen Materials, das unsere Netzhaut von Wänden, Druckseiten und Bildschirmen bombardiert, scheint an dem pedantischen Mechanismus primärer Kommunikation vorbeizustreben und in jene Zone unseres Gehirns zu dringen, in der wir neue und abenteuerliche Verbindungen zwischen Symbolen und Emotionen knüpfen, wo die unbestimmten Grenzen der Auslegung uns erlauben, eine neue Bildersprache zu erfinden, unbeeinträchtigt von jenen Tatsachen, mit denen wir täglich um unser physisches Überleben ringen müssen, wo wir ein schillerndes Spiel mit Fiktionen treiben können, bei dem die Ziele und Regeln mehr denen der Poesie als denen der Prosa ähneln.

Gewiss kann man einwenden, dass Graphik dieser Art nur der kleine, sichtbare Teil des Eisberges ist – dass die grosse Masse, die unter der Oberfläche in den verseuchten Wassern unserer Kultur schwimmt, trivial, vulgär und, vielleicht schlimmer noch, unverzeihlich langweilig ist. Skeptiker mögen auch versucht sein, in einem ähnlichen Gedankengang den Inhalt dieses Jahrbuchs als die feingesiebte Auswahl einer Elite abzutun, die eine naive Ahnungslosigkeit von den banalen Realitäten unserer visuellen Landschaft verrät. Diese Leute möchte ich an die Funktion unserer Museen erinnern. Niemand glaubt doch, dass deren Schaustücke den tatsächlichen jeweiligen Stand von Malerei und Bildhauerei repräsentieren. Gewiss ist es nicht ihre Funktion, Bestandesaufnahme zu machen, sondern vielmehr das zu entdecken und zu zeigen, was für die Entwicklung der heutigen Kunst *kennzeichnend* ist. Dieses Jahrbuch versammelt auf gleiche Weise, was für den heutigen Stand der Graphik *kennzeichnend* ist. Und es tut dies nach dem einzig möglichen Massstab: einer strengen, kritischen Auswahl der überraschendsten, der einfallsreichsten, der originellsten – der *besten* Beispiele des Jahres.

*Leo Lionni*

# Préface

LEO LIONNI, Italien d'origine, est né à Amsterdam. Il a passé plus de 20 années aux Etats-Unis, où il assuma la direction artistique de *Fortune.* Installé en Italie depuis 1960, il s'est fait un nom en tant qu'auteur et illustrateur de livres d'enfant. Cependant, c'est le graphisme, la peinture et la sculpture auxquels il se consacre principalement. Ses connaissances approfondies de tout ce qui se passe dans le domaine du design le qualifient au mieux de discuter les tendances nouvelles qu'il sait mettre en rapport avec la situation culturelle de l'époque.

Dans les vingt-cinq volumes précédents de GRAPHIS ANNUAL, les avantages inhérents à la publicité en général et à ses aspects visuels en particulier ont été mis en évidence et examinés de tous les points de vue imaginables de notre univers culturel. En abordant le vingt-sixième, il semble que l'on ne puisse guère renchérir sur tout ce qui a déjà été dit quant aux implications économiques, sociologiques, historiques, politiques, voire morales des efforts entrepris dans ce domaine. Nous en connaissons pleinement les aspects positifs et négatifs par l'analyse et l'appréciation qui en ont été faites, les résultats par la recherche et mesure statistiques auxquelles la publicité visuelle a donné lieu. Au vu de la somme de connaissances et d'expériences réunie, on serait porté à croire qu'en publicité, les techniques sont assurées, les résultats acquis sans marge d'erreur, tout comme, pour prendre un exemple trivial, un corpus de recettes codifiées, mille fois testées met la cuisinière expérimentée à l'abri de toute surprise, quitte à s'inspirer de temps à autre des conseils éclairés d'un vieux cordon-bleu.

En fait, nous sommes certainement nombreux à nous rappeler l'époque où, en dépit de notre intuition et de nos préférences personnelles, nous étions obligés de nous soumettre bon gré, mal gré à des normes précises en matière de création publicitaire. Les chatons et les bébés étaient censés captiver l'attention d'une femme, l'humour restant strictement réservé au public masculin. On nous enseignait la manière dont l'œil balaie la page en s'arrêtant à telle aspérité du relief que tissaient les mots et les images. On nous bourrait le crâne de chiffres et de graphiques. Pourtant, le nombre croissant des chatons et des bébés d'une part, la complexité et l'acharnement croissants de la concurrence, de l'autre, ont progressivement donné le rôle de vedette à un facteur non mesurable, imprévisible et capricieux: l'effet de surprise. De la sorte, l'art publicitaire en est venu, au cours de son premier demi-siècle d'existence adulte, à assumer de plus en plus la fonction sémillante d'un art appliqué «faisant de la publicité pour la publicité», grâce à la mise en œuvre de moyens agressifs et hauts en couleur qui juraient avec le caractère guindé et corseté des mots employés conformément à une rhétorique bien réglée.

L'inflexion que subissent les résultats et enseignements de la recherche au passage du prisme de la passion, de l'imagination et de la créativité personnelles est un phénomène fascinant qui n'a jamais été, à ce que je sache, analysé de manière convaicante. Peut-être est-il encore trop tôt pour saisir pleinement les causes profondes de l'évolution qu'a subi l'art publicitaire et son émancipation progressive par rapport aux pressions implacables de la «realpolitik» en affaires. Après tout, c'est peut-être, comme dans toute l'Histoire des hommes, l'imprévisibilité inhérente à la nature humaine qui est à l'origine de l'inversion d'une tendance jugée inéluctable il y a quelques décennies à peine.

Ce qui est certain, c'est que la prolifération des styles, modes et maniérismes individuels a été à la source d'un nouveau langage extrêmement varié, ambigu et séduisant, qui semble se jouer des restrictions imposées à la communication de masse. L'imagerie employée, souvent surréelle, parfois frisant la folie communicative, renie en apparence son origine et ses motivations utilitaires, surtout si on l'isole du contexte et l'observe par le bout profane de la lorgnette.

Suivant une évolution parallèle, à courte distance, à celle de l'univers kaléidoscopique de l'op et du pop, du happening, du néo-dadaïsme et du nouveau réalisme, l'art graphique appliqué est soumis à des mutations constantes qui le font jaillir des pages imprimées et des murs dans un feu d'artifice dont la vitalité et la liberté d'invention sont probablement sans égales dans l'histoire de la communication. De nos jours, la joyeuse anarchie, les périlleuses acrobaties et la créativité ludique qui y règnent sont non seulement acceptées, mais encore réclamées à cor et à cri par les représentants les plus compassés et les plus pédants de la communauté des annonceurs, alors qu'il nous a fallu à l'époque conquérir de haute lutte chaque pouce de terrain artistique. Que la raison en soit comprise ou non, personne ne semble plus douter de ce que nos médias visuels sont capables d'éveiller les émotions, de stimuler le processus imaginatif, de donner vie et entrain à l'échange verbal au cours trop lent et trop canalisé, et personne non plus ne semble choqué de voir la forme et le contenu d'une illustration échapper souvent totalement aux lois de l'interprétation rationnelle.

Il n'est pas étonnant que la vigueur de ce nouveau langage déborde sur les arts majeurs; c'est ainsi que l'inclusion d'annonces dans les collages, les gravures et les peintures (Rauschenberg), la mise à contribution de techniques et formes publicitaires spéciales (Lichtenstein), la manipulation d'affiches commerciales (Rotella) et l'élaboration de symboles (Chryssa) sont représentatives de l'incursion de l'art publicitaire dans les beaux-arts, juste retour des choses après l'époque révolue où «l'emploi des beaux-arts en publicité» constituait un thème de discussion et de publication particulièrement provocateur. L'interpénétration du grand art et de l'art appliqué en est désormais à un stade où il paraît difficile d'attribuer à chacun son dû, de part et d'autre des murs ségrégationnistes du Musée. Si l'art graphique appliqué pillait sans vergogne son grand frère à l'origine, le contraire est vrai aujourd'hui, où l'on voit le contenu et le symbolisme du langage graphique investir la peinture et même la sculpture sous la forme d'un «jeu à l'intérieur du jeu».

Il est vrai que la publicité est parfois extraite de son contexte — comme dans la boîte de soupe à la tomate de Warhol — pour stigmatiser les aspects vulgaires de notre société de consommation du point de vue de la critique sociale et de la critique de la civilisation. Même en nous rangeant à ce genre d'arguments, force nous est de reconnaître que nous avons affaire à un nouveau langage qui a fourni du sang frais à notre fonds ancien de symboles, élargi notre champ d'expression, sensibilisé notre imagination et — last, but not least — garni nos foyers d'objets longtemps admirés à distance dans les vitrines.

Folon qui, à l'instar de beaucoup d'artistes contemporains, se meut comme un poisson dans l'eau des musées et le sillage du marché, a démontré que même le plus banal des signes graphiques, la flèche, est en réalité un symbole très ambigu qui dégage un énorme pouvoir poétique. Nous rencontrons là, à ce que je crois, l'une des vertus de l'art graphique qui commencent à s'imposer à notre compréhension. Une grande partie de l'énorme avalanche de matériaux visuels qui bombardent sans répit nos rétines impressionnées par les affiches, les imprimés et la publicité sur écran semblent être capable de court-circuiter les mécanismes obtus et simplistes de la communication primaire et de pénétrer dans cette zone de notre esprit où nous sommes à même d'établir des connexions nouvelles et audacieuses entre les symboles et l'affectivité et où la relative dissolution des barrières délimitant le sens des mots nous permet d'inventer des images neuves, pas encore polluées par le réel vérifiable, par cette réalité physique contraignante à laquelle nous devons bien nous adapter pour survivre. Dans cette zone, nous sommes libres de jouer à un jeu ambigu de créations fictives dont le but et les règles relèvent de la poésie plutôt que de la prose.

On pourra certes objecter que la création graphique telle que nous venons de la décrire ne représente que la petite partie émergée de l'iceberg et que l'énorme masse invisible flottant dans les eaux contaminées de notre civilisation se présente sous un jour trivial, vulgaire ou, pis encore, inexorablement ennuyeux. Les esprits sceptiques pourront tout aussi bien récuser le contenu du présent annuaire comme représentant le choix raffiné d'une élite inconsciente des réalités banales de notre environnement visuel. J'aimerais rappeler à ces incrédules la fonction de nos musées. Personne ne croit que ce qui s'y trouve incarne l'état actuel de la peinture et de la sculpture. Leur fonction véritable, c'est assurément non pas l'inventaire total de ce qui est, mais la découverte et la révélation de ce qui est *significatif* pour l'orientation de l'art contemporain. Le présent annuaire réunit de la même manière ce qui est *significatif* de l'art graphique appliqué de nos jours. Ce faisant, il s'inspire du seul critère imaginable: une rigoureuse sélection critique des créations les plus surprenantes, les plus inventives et les plus originales — une sélection du *meilleur* de l'année.

# Index to Artists and Designers
# Verzeichnis der Künstler und Gestalter
# Index des artistes et maquettistes

# Index to Art Directors
# Verzeichnis der künstlerischen Leiter
# Index des directeurs artistiques

# Index to Agencies, Studios and Producers
# Verzeichnis der Agenturen, Studios und Produzenten
# Index des agences, studios et producteurs

# Index to Publishers
# Verzeichnis der Verleger
# Index des éditeurs

# Index to Advertisers
# Verzeichnis der Auftraggeber
# Index des clients

ERRATA – GRAPHIS ANNUAL 76/77

■ Pages 162/163, Figs. 492, 497: The attribution of these illustrations to the magazine *Record* was incorrect. They were published in *Okapi*, another French magazine for young people (Bayard Presse, Paris). The designer was Michel Rémondière.
■ Page 204, Figs. 637/638: World rights on the environmental books of Etienne Delessert are held by Middelhauve Verlag, Cologne. The original title was *Die Maus und die Giftchen*, the book appeared in an environmental series for children. We reproduced in Fig. 637 the cover of the French edition published under licence by Gallimard, Paris.

■ Seiten 162/163, Abb. 492 und 497: In den Legenden schrieben wir irrtümlicherweise, diese Illustrationen seien in der Zeitschrift *Record* erschienen. Sie wurden jedoch im französischen Jugendmagazin *Okapi* (Bayard Presse, Paris) veröffentlicht. Als Gestalter zeichnete Michel Rémondière.
■ Seite 204, Abb. 637/638: Die Weltrechte an den Umweltbüchern von Etienne Delessert liegen beim Middelhauve Verlag, Köln; der Originaltitel lautet *Die Maus und die Giftchen*, das Buch erschien in der Reihe «Umweltbücher für Kinder». Wir haben auf diesen Seiten die bei Gallimard, Paris, erschienene französische Lizenzausgabe abgebildet.

■ Pages 162/163, fig. 492 et 497: Contrairement à nos légendes, ces deux illustrations n'ont pas paru dans le magazine *Record*, mais dans le magazine des jeunes *Okapi* (Bayard Presse, Paris). Maquettiste responsable: Michel Rémondière.
■ Page 204, fig. 637/638: Les droits universels des «Petits Fables Ecologiques» d'Etienne Delessert se trouvent auprès des Editions Middelhauve, Cologne; le titre original allemand est *Die Maus und die Giftchen*, le livre a paru dans la série intitulée «Umweltbücher für Kinder». Nous avons reproduit la couverture de l'édition française, parue chez les Editions Gallimard, Paris.

■ Entry instructions will be mailed to anyone interested in submitting samples of outstanding graphics or photography for possible inclusion in our annuals. No fees involved. Closing dates for entries:
GRAPHIS ANNUAL (Advertising and editorial graphics): 15 December
PHOTOGRAPHIS (Advertising and editorial photography): 30 June
GRAPHIS POSTERS (International annual on poster art): 30 March
Write to: The Graphis Press, Dufourstr. 107, 8008 Zurich, Switzerland.

■ Einsendebedingungen können von jedermann angefordert werden, der uns Beispiele hervorragender Graphik oder Photographie zur Auswahl für unsere Jahrbücher unterbreiten möchte. Es werden keine Gebühren erhoben.
Einsendetermine:
GRAPHIS ANNUAL (Werbe- und redaktionelle Graphik): 15. Dezember
PHOTOGRAPHIS (Werbe- und redaktionelle Photographie): 30. Juni
GRAPHIS POSTERS (Internationales Jahrbuch der Plakatkunst): 30. März
Adresse: Graphis Verlag, Dufourstr. 107, 8008 Zürich, Schweiz.

■ Tout intéressé à la soumission de travaux graphiques et photographiques est prié de nous demander les informations nécessaires. Sans charge de participation.
Dates limites:
GRAPHIS ANNUAL (art graphique publicitaire et rédactionnel): 15 décembre
PHOTOGRAPHIS (photographie publicitaire et rédactionnelle): 30 juin
GRAPHIS POSTERS (répertoire international de l'art de l'affiche): 30 mars
S'adresser à: Editions Graphis, Dufourstr. 107, 8008 Zurich, Suisse.

Editor, Art Director: Walter Herdeg
Assistant Editor: Stanley Mason
Project Manager: Vreni Monnier
Designers: Ulrich Kremmner, Klaus Schröder
Art Assistants: Martin Byland, Willy Müller, Peter Wittwer

# 1

Magazine Advertisements

Newspaper Advertisements


Zeitschriften-Inserate

Zeitungs-Inserate


Annonces de revues

Annonces de presse

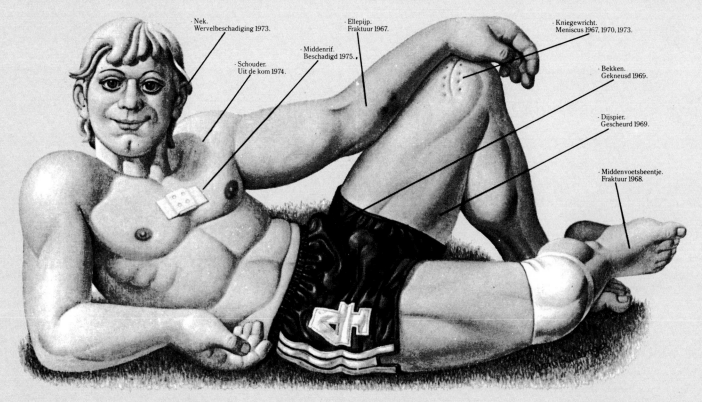

# Het grootste mannenblad van Nederland gaat toevallig niet over sex en sensatie.

Nek.
Wervelbeschadiging 1973.

Schouder.
Uit de kom 1974.

Middenrif.
Beschadigd 1975.

Ellepijp.
Fraktuur 1967.

Kniegewricht.
Meniscus 1967, 1970, 1973.

Bekken.
Gekneusd 1969.

Dijspier.
Gescheurd 1969.

Middenvoetsbeentje.
Fraktuur 1968.

Wekelijks bereik: 431.000 mannen, verdeeld over alle welstandsgroepen (NOP '75). Een oplage van 190.694 (NOD '76).

**Voetbal International.**
Een familieblad zou er jaloers op zijn.

1

---

ARTIST / KÜNSTLER / ARTISTE:

1, 2  Hans Reizinger
3  Jeff Witchel
4  Roger Hill
5  Gene Calogero
6, 7  Uwe Duvendack/Mane Weigand (Photo)

DESIGNER / GESTALTER / MAQUETTISTE:

1, 2  Pim van der Meer/
Jan van Lieshout
3  Jeff Witchel/Steve Kasloff
4  David Purser

ART DIRECTOR / DIRECTEUR ARTISTIQUE:

1, 2  Pim van der Meer
3  Jeff Witchel/Steve Kasloff
4  David Purser
5  Hy Varon
6, 7  Uwe Duvendack

AGENCY / AGENTUR / AGENCE – STUDIO:

1, 2  Trend Communications BV
3  Young & Rubicam
4  McCann-Erickson
5  Warwick, Welsh & Miller, Inc.
6, 7  TBWA GmbH

**Advertisements**

**Inserate**

**Annonces**

## FILL OUT THIS TOMATO AND WE'LL SEND YOU 25 WAYS TO EAT IT.

# FREE!

4

### Our Philosophy.

**Only V.O. is V.O. The First Canadian.**

5

26

**1, 2** Magazine advertisements for *Voetbal International,* which describes itself as the largest men's magazine in the Netherlands, and one that is not concerned with sex and sensation. (NLD)
**3** Magazine ad as an invitation to *Young & Rubicam* "reel of the month" shows. (USA)
**4** Newspaper ad offering a free book with 25 tomato recipes from *Del Monte.* (USA)
**5** Full-colour magazine advertisement for a Canadian whisky made by *Seagram's.* (USA)
**6, 7** Magazine advertisements from a campaign to introduce and popularize *Beck's,* a German beer, in France. (FRA)

**1, 2** Zeitschriftenanzeigen aus einer Serie für ein Magazin für Männer, das sich weder mit Sex noch mit Sensationen befasst. (NLD)
**3** Anzeige als Einladung zur monatlichen Dia-Show über die neuesten Arbeiten der Werbeagentur *Young & Rubicam.* (USA)
**4** Zeitungsanzeige für ein Gratisbuch mit 25 Tomaten-Rezepten von *Del Monte.* (USA)
**5** Mehrfarbiges Zeitschrifteninserat für einen kanadischen Whisky. (USA)
**6, 7** Zeitschriftenanzeigen aus einer Werbekampagne, die zum Ziel hat, das deutsche *Beck's* Bier in Frankreich einzuführen und bekannt zu machen. (FRA)

**1, 2** Annonces de magazine d'une série pour la promotion d'un magazine masculin qui ne s'interesse ni à la sexualité, ni aux sensations. (NLD)
**3** Annonce sous forme d'invitation à une présentation mensuelle de diapos sur les travaux les plus récents de l'agence publicitaire *Young & Rubicam.* (USA)
**4** Annonce de presse offrant un livre gratuit contenant 25 recettes. (USA)
**5** Annonce de magazine polychrome pour un whisky canadien. (USA)
**6, 7** Annonces de magazine figurant dans une campagne pour introduire et populariser la bière allemande *Beck's* en France. (FRA)

8　　9

## Advertisements / Inserate / Annonces

**8, 9** From a series of full-colour magazine advertisements for *Evian* mineral water. That in Fig. 8 says that the water facilitates the digestion of milk and is therefore good for babies, while Fig. 9 is a "history" of this mineral water. (FRA)
**10** Magazine advertisement in the form of an old embroidered "text", in colour on black, for *Johnnie Walker* Scotch whisky. (USA)
**11** Magazine advertisement for sandwich meats marketed by Leo's Quality Foods, Inc., with full-colour illustration. (USA)
**12** "*Lanitex* follows the evolution of fashion, joining threads of friendship." Magazine advertisement in full colour for a textile manufacturer. (SPA)
**13–15** From a long series of magazine advertisements for soy sauce made by Kikkoman Shoyu Co. Ltd. Fig. 14 in yellow-green shades, Fig. 15 pink on white. (JPN)

**8, 9** Aus einer Serie von mehrfarbigen Anzeigen für das Mineralwasser *Evian*. Abb. 8 weist darauf hin, dass dieses Mineralwasser, weil es sehr leicht verdaulich ist, auch Kleinkindern gegeben werden kann; Abb. 9 erzählt die Geschichte des Mineralwassers von Evian, das in den Alpen mit Kalzium und Magnesium angereichert wird. (FRA)
**10** Zeitschriftenanzeige für einen Whisky. Blumen in Lila- und Rosatönen. (USA)
**11** Mehrfarbige Zeitschriftenanzeige für Fleisch- und Wurstwaren, die bereits in Tranchen geschnitten sind und sich besonders für Sandwiches eignen. (USA)
**12** «*Lanitex* folgt den Modeströmungen, indem sie Fäden der Freundschaft knüpft.» Mehrfarbiges Zeitschrifteninserat für eine Textilfirma. (SPA)
**13–15** Aus einer langjährigen Serie von Zeitschriftenanzeigen, vorwiegend mit Gemüsemotiven, für Sojasauce. Abb. 14: grüne Erbse auf hellgrünem Grund; Abb. 15: Langouste in Rosa- und Rottönen. (JPN)

**8, 9** Exemples figurant dans une série d'annonces de magazines en couleurs pour la promotion de l'eau minérale d'*Evian*. Grâce à sa légèreté et sa pureté, l'eau d'*Evian* facilite la digestion du lait et peut donc être mélangée au biberon (fig. 8). La fig. 9 raconte l'histoire de l'eau d'*Evian*. (FRA)
**10** Annonce de magazine pour une marque de whisky. Texte évoquant une ancienne broderie. En polychromie sur fond noir. (USA)
**11** Annonce de magazine en couleurs pour des produits de boucherie en tranches qui se prêtent excellemment à la préparation de sandwiches. (USA)
**12** «*Lanitex* suit l'évolution de la mode en unissant les fils de l'amitié.» Annonce pleine page pour un fabricant de tissus à la mode. En polychromie. (SPA)
**13–15** Extraits d'une longue série d'annonces de magazines pour la promotion d'une marque de sauce soja. Fig. 14: en vert jaunâtre; fig. 15: teintes roses. (JPN)

10

**Leo's sandwich meats will give your family something to roar about.**
They'll love Leo's sliced beef, breast of turkey, corned beef, ham, pastrami, dark turkey, spicy beef, chicken and jalapeno beef. And that's no baloney.
©1976 Leo's Quality Foods, Inc.

11

ARTIST / KÜNSTLER / ARTISTE:

8, 9  E. Delessert
10  Gallardo
11  Sharleen Pederson
12  Enric Huguet
13–15  Tadashi Ohashi

DESIGNER / GESTALTER:

10  Stuart Pittman
11  Dennis McKaylian
12  Enric Huguet
13–15  Tadashi Ohashi

ART DIRECTOR:

10  Murray Klein
11  Dennis McKaylian
12  Enric Huguet
13–15  Tadashi Ohashi

AGENCY / AGENTUR / AGENCE:

8, 9  TBWA
10  Smith/Greenland, Inc.
11  Klein Medberry Advertising
12  Impact-Publicidad

13

# LANITEX
*sigue la evolución de la moda uniendo hilos de amistad*

**LANITEX, S.A.** - SABADELL - ESPAÑA
Fábrica de hilados,tejidos de estambre y sus mezclas

Artículos para caballero en Pura Lana,
en Lana - Trevira, y en Mohair - Trevira.

12

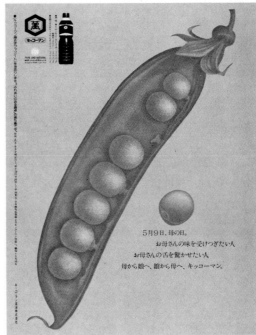

14

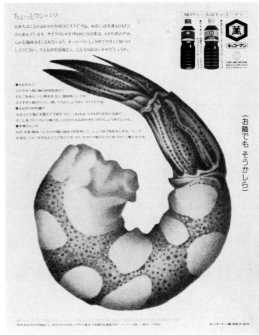

15

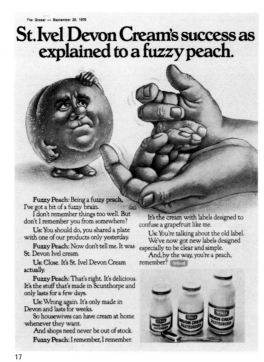

The Grocer — September 20. 1975

# St.Ivel Devon Cream's success as explained to a fuzzy peach.

**Fuzzy Peach:** Being a fuzzy peach, I've got a bit of a fuzzy brain. I don't remember things too well. But don't I remember you from somewhere?

**Us:** You should do, you shared a plate with one of our products only yesterday.

**Fuzzy Peach:** Now don't tell me. It was St. Devon Ivel cream.

**Us:** Close. It's St. Ivel Devon Cream actually.

**Fuzzy Peach:** That's right. It's delicious. It's the stuff that's made in Scunthorpe and only lasts for a few days.

**Us:** Wrong again. It's only made in Devon and lasts for weeks. So housewives can have cream at home whenever they want. And shops need never be out of stock.

**Fuzzy Peach:** I remember, I remember.

It's the cream with labels designed to confuse a grapefruit like me.

**Us:** You're talking about the old label. We've now got new labels designed especially to be clear and simple. And, by the way, you're a peach, remember? St.Ivel

17

16–18 Two complete advertisements and detail of an illustration from a campaign for *St. Ivel* products, here for Devon cream and chilled desserts. Copy in the form of a dialogue with the peach, pudding, etc. (GBR)
19–21 From a long series of advertisements for *Bonduelle* tinned vegetables. The green wheelbarrow is used to suggest fresh vegetables straight from the garden. The illustrations are in full colour. (GER)
22–25 Full-page and double-page advertisements from a campaign launched by the weekly magazine *Grit,* which claims to be "a big frog in small towns". Numbers of illustrators have been invited to contribute their own colourful specimens of frogs as the eye-catchers of this series. (USA)

16–18 Beispiele aus einer mehrfarbigen Anzeigenkampagne für *St.-Ivel*-Produkte, hier für Desserts und pasteurisierten Vollrahm. Der Text besteht jeweils aus einem Dialog von *St. Ivel* mit dem abgebildeten Motiv. (GBR)
19–21 Aus einer umfangreichen Anzeigenserie für *Bonduelle*-Gemüse aus der Dose. Der als Grundmotiv der Serie erscheinende grüne Schubkarren soll beim Leser die Assoziation mit frischem Gemüse aus dem Garten hervorrufen. Die Illustrationen sind alle mehrfarbig. (GER)
22–25 «Der grosse Frosch in kleinen Städten.» Aus einer Kampagne von ein- und doppelseitigen Anzeigen für eine amerikanische Wochenzeitschrift, die vor allem in Kleinstädten gelesen wird. Verschiedene Künstler wurden beauftragt, an dieser Kampagne mitzuarbeiten. Mehrfarbige Frösche. (USA)

16–18 Annonces polychromes figurant dans une campagne en faveur des produits *St. Ivel.* Fig. 17: «Le succès de la crème *St. Ivel Devon* expliqué à une pêche un peu confuse». Tous les textes sont conçus sous forme de dialogues. (GBR)
19–21 Exemples d'une longue série d'annonces de magazine pour les conserves de légumes *Bonduelle.* Le motif central — la brouette verte — devrait évoquer l'association avec des légumes frais du jardin. En polychromie. (GER)
22–25 «La grosse grenouille des petites villes.» Annonces simple et double page tirées d'une campagne promotionnelle destinée aux annonceurs de l'hebdomadaire *Grit* qui se vend surtout dans les petites villes. On a demandé à divers artistes de créer une grenouille pour illustrer cette série. En couleurs. (USA)

# St.Ivel chilled dessert's success as explained to a stodgy pudding.

**Stodgy Pudding:** I'm all steamed up!
**Us:** So what's new about that? Surely that's why people like you.
**Stodgy Pudding:** I'm not so sure. Just recently everyone seems to have taken a fancy to your St. Ivel chilled desserts.
**Us:** We noticed that. Last year in a market which grew by 16% our brand share grew from 20% to 26%.
**Stodgy Pudding:** It must be this hot weather I hate it. All the public want are nice chilled St. Ivel desserts.
It makes me sticky just thinking about it.
**Us:** Your time will come. Why don't you go away and hibernate under your blanket of custard until then?
**Stodgy Pudding:** I can't, I'm stuck to the plate. St.Ivel

16

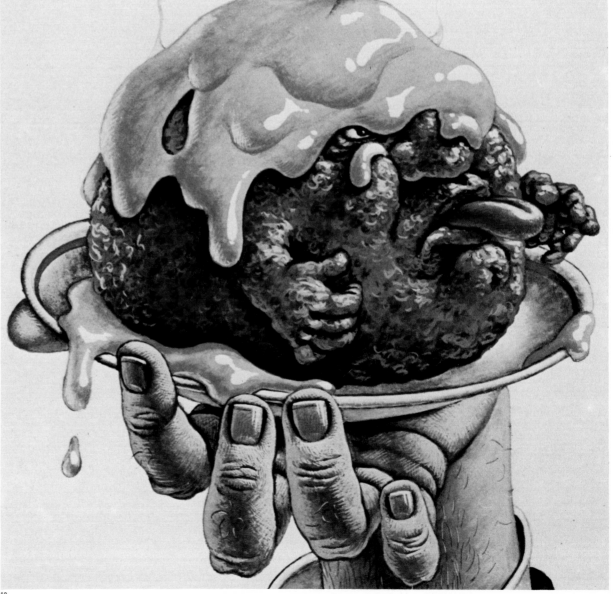

18

19

20

21

22

23

24

25

ARTIST / KÜNSTLER / ARTISTE:

16–18 Michael Terry/Peter Barbieri (Photo)
19–21 Tomi Ungerer
22–25 Tony Chen

DESIGNER / GESTALTER / MAQUETTISTE:

19–21 Tomi Ungerer
22–25 Elmer Pizzi

ART DIRECTOR / DIRECTEUR ARTISTIQUE:

16–18 David Christensen
19–21 Tomi Ungerer
22–25 Elmer Pizzi

AGENCY / AGENTUR / AGENCE – STUDIO:

16–18 Boase Massimi Pollitt
19–21 Robert Pütz GmbH
22–25 Gray & Rogers, Inc.

26

Prosit and cheers to the next 200 years.

27

ARTIST / KÜNSTLER / ARTISTE:

26, 27  Ruppi Schneider
28  Axel Vasco Gnad
29  Lenacdu
30  Diane Kavelaras
31  Gerry Embleton
32  Sean Early/Don Grimes/Greg King/Woody Pirtle/
Larry Sons/Ron Sullivan/Jack Summerford/
Mike Washlesky
33, 34  Etienne Delessert

DESIGNER / GESTALTER / MAQUETTISTE:

32  Woody Pirtle
33, 34  Paul Amar

28

Happy birthday from the star of German magazines.

(We're going to celebrate America's bicentennial in our special 100 page magazine in our April 9, 1976 magazine.)

# Arrivano i topi!

Ricordate l'amabile distinzione fra topo di campagna e topo di città? Superata.

Oggi, per topo, s'intende soprattutto il ratto di chiavica, che si moltiplica incontrollato ovunque. Negli edifici, nelle cantine, nelle stalle. Come nelle fogne, nei campi, lungo i canali. Grosso, grasso, feroce, resistente a tutto, anche ai veleni. E senza nemici naturali.

Perché i falchi, le poiane, le civette, i gufi, sono quasi spariti, mentre la marea di scarichi e rifiuti rende sempre più facile la vita ai topi.

In Italia si uccidono ogni anno 150 milioni di uccelli. C'è una legge al Parlamento che propone, fra l'altro, la regolamentazione della caccia.

Per evitare la sparizione di specie che hanno una precisa funzione in natura.

Per migliorare, almeno in parte, un ambiente che sta diventando favorevole solo ai nemici dell'uomo.

Lega nazionale contro la distruzione degli uccelli.
Lungarno Guicciardini 9, Firenze

Se volete saperne di più sullo sterminio dell'avifauna in Italia, scriveteci. Vi manderemo opuscoli e materiale informativo.

Nome
Cognome
Indirizzo
C.A.P.        Città

29

**26–28** Illustration and two complete double-spread advertisements placed in American magazines by the German weekly *Stern* on the occasion of the Bicentennial. Fig. 26 shows famous figures of American and German history from Lincoln to Muhammad Ali, from Goethe to Marlene Dietrich. In Fig. 28 the stars are those of the *Stern*. (USA)
**29** "The rats are coming!" Magazine advertisement from a campaign to stop the large-scale destruction of birds. (ITA)
**30** Black-and-white magazine ad for CCA "all-star" packaging. (USA)
**31** Double-spread ad with a colour rendering of the *Ovaltine* girl. (GBR)
**32** First page of a four-page ad for the TM company, offering broadcasting services. Colour illustration. (USA)
**33, 34** "Only ignoramuses know everything…the others go to SICOB." Illustration and ad for a communications exhibition in Paris. (FRA)

ART DIRECTOR / DIRECTEUR ARTISTIQUE:

26–28 Thomas Rempen
29 Bob Elliott
30 Diane Kavelaras
31 John Hegarty
32 Woody Pirtle
33, 34 Serge de Filippi

AGENCY / AGENTUR / AGENCE – STUDIO:

26–28 Hildmann, Simon, Rempen & Schmitz
29 Promos
31 TBWA
32 The Richards Group
33, 34 Publicis Conseil

**Advertisements
Inserate
Annonces**

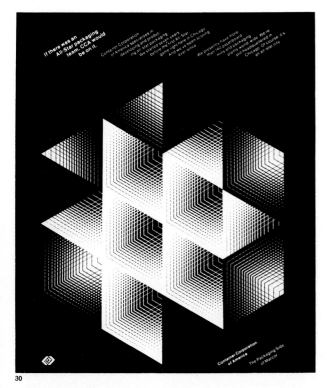

30

31

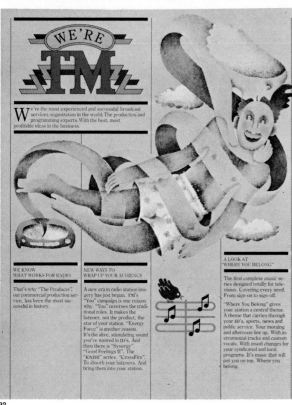

32

33

34

26–28 Illustration und doppelseitige Anzeigen, die das Wochenmagazin *Stern* als Eigenwerbung in amerikanischen Zeitschriften publizierte. Die Kampagne lief während den 200-Jahr-Feierlichkeiten mit einem gleichzeitigen Hinweis auf ein 100seitiges Magazin über die USA, das einer Ausgabe des *Stern* beigelegt wurde. Mehrfarbig. (USA)
29 Schwarzweisses Inserat für CCA-«All-Star»-Packungen. (USA)
30 Schwarzweisses Inserat für CCA-«All-Star»-Packungen. (USA)
31 Anzeige mit Farbillustration des *Ovomaltine*-Mädchens. (GBR)
32 Anzeige einer Firma, die sich auf Programme für Radio- und Fernsehanstalten spezialisiert hat. Mehrfarbig. (USA)
33, 34 Illustration und vollständige Anzeige für eine Ausstellung über Informatik, Kommunikationstechnik und Betriebsorganisation. (FRA)

26–28 Illustration et annonces figurant dans une série autopromotionnelle de l'hebdomadaire *Stern* publiée dans les magazines américains. La fig. 26 présente des personnages célèbres de l'histoire américaine et allemande, de Lincoln à Muhammed Ali, de Goethe à Marlène Dietrich. Fig. 28: les étoiles sont celles du magazine *Stern*. Série publiée à l'occasion du Bicentenaire des E.-U. (USA)
29 «Les rats arrivent!» Annonce de magazine pour une campagne de protection des oiseaux. (ITA)
30 Annonce noir-blanc pour les emballages «vedettes» CCA. (USA)
31 Annonce avec une illustration servant de symbole à *Ovaltine*. (GBR)
32 Annonce de quatre pages pour la TM Company. (USA)
33, 34 Illustration et annonce complète pour SICOB, une exposition d'informatique, de communication et d'organisation. (FRA)

If people saw a marriage counselor before they got married, there might be fewer divorces.

That's not a bad idea for corporations that are merger-minded, either.

Consider: of the 16,000 mergers since World War II, nearly a third have been fiscal fiascos.

Why? The companies involved never really took a good look at themselves, let alone their intended.

They never really had an organized plan to follow, but rather ran helter-skelter into what they thought was opportunity.

If you're thinking merger, the chances are

Irving Trust can help you keep on the long-lasting and happy side of the statistical picture.

Our Corporate Financial Counseling Department acts as merger counselor for many companies.

We help them in drawing up an effective acquisition program.

Play matchmaker by identifying potential sellers.

Act as a confidential intermediary. And advise on pricing and financing.

In short, when we play cupid for you, the odds are better than you'll enjoy the benefits of your merger happily ever after.

**The Corporate Marriage. 1 out of 3 ends up on the rocks.**

At IRVING TRUST COMPANY we back you up with more than money.
One Wall Street
© A Charter New York Bank. Member F.D.I.C.

35

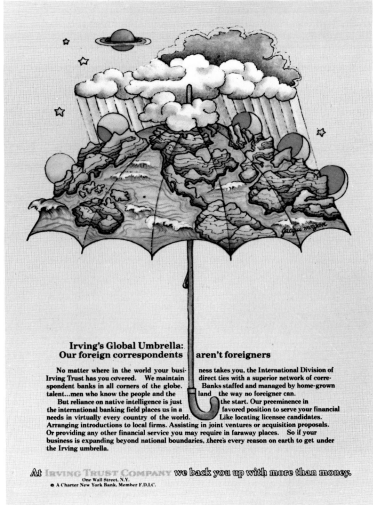

**Irving's Global Umbrella: Our foreign correspondents aren't foreigners**

No matter where in the world your business takes you, Irving Trust has you covered. We maintain correspondent banks in all corners of the globe. The International Division of direct ties with a superior network of correspondent talent...men who know the people and the Banks staffed and managed by home-grown land the way no foreigner can.

But reliance on native intelligence is just the international banking field places us in a the start. Our preeminence in favored position to serve your financial needs in virtually every country of the world. Like locating licensee candidates.

Arranging introductions to local firms. Assisting in joint ventures or acquisition proposals. Or providing any other financial service you may require in faraway places. So if your business is expanding beyond national boundaries, there's every reason on earth to get under the Irving umbrella.

At IRVING TRUST COMPANY we back you up with more than money.
One Wall Street, N.Y.
© A Charter New York Bank. Member F.D.I.C.

36

---

Advertisements / Inserate / Annonces

**35, 36** From a campaign for the Irving Trust Company, here offering advice on business mergers and financial services in faraway places. (USA)
**37** Newspaper advertisement in which *Swissair* offers to help Americans to enjoy their holidays in Europe more by "thinking like a European". (USA)
**38** Advertisement in which Second National Bank offers its credit card to simplify Christmas shopping by having everything put on one bill. (USA)
**39** Advertisement in Art Nouveau style for North Carolina National Bank, which calls itself "Chapel Hill's oldest bank". (USA)
**40, 41** "Remake the world with Concorde." — "Europe begins here." From a series of double-spread full-colour magazine advertisements for *Air France*, featuring the first Concorde flight to Rio and the new Roissy airport (with a map of Europe in the clouds). (FRA)

**35, 36** Aus einer Anzeigen-Serie mit mehrfarbigen Illustrationen für ein Finanzinstitut, das die Kunden «nicht nur mit Geld unterstützt». (USA)
**37** «Sobald Sie mal wie ein Europäer denken, werden Sie Europa mehr geniessen mit weniger Geld.» Zeitungsanzeige der *Swissair* für Europaflüge. (USA)
**38** Anzeige einer Bank, die zu Weihnachten eine spezielle Kreditkarte herausgab, die das Einkaufen erleichtert, weil der Inhaber nur eine einzige Rechnung präsentiert bekommt. (USA)
**39** Anzeige des ältesten Bankinstituts in Chapel Hill. (USA)
**40, 41** «Macht die Welt neu mit der Concorde.» – «Hier beginnt Europa.» Aus einer Serie von doppelseitigen, mehrfarbigen Zeitschrifteninseraten der *Air France*. Sie erschienen anlässlich des ersten Fluges der Concorde auf der Strecke Paris–Rio (Abb. 40) und der Eröffnung des neuen Pariser Flughafens Roissy–Charles de Gaulle (Abb. 41), mit einer aus Wolken gebildeten Europakarte. (FRA)

**35, 36** Annonces avec illustrations en couleurs figurant dans la série d'un établissement financier spécialisé aux services dans des pays lointains. (USA)
**37** «Aussitôt que vous pensez à l'européenne, vous vous sentirez plus à l'aise avec moins d'argent.» Annonce de journal de *Swissair* en faveur des vols à destination de l'Europe. (USA)
**38** Annonce d'une banque pour une carte de crédit spéciale issue avant Noël, carte qui facilite beaucoup les achats de Noël, car le client n'a qu'une facture à régler. (USA)
**39** Annonce de la banque la plus ancienne de Chapel Hill. (USA)
**40, 41** Exemples figurant dans une série d'annonces sur page double de la compagnie aérienne *Air France*. Elles ont été publiées à l'occasion de l'inauguration de la route Paris–Rio avec la Concorde (fig. 40) et de l'ouverture de l'aéroport parisien Roissy–Charles de Gaulle (fig. 41, avec des nuages représentant l'Europe). En polychromie. (FRA)

**34**

The 27,000 shareholders and 13,700 employees of Swissair believe that the more you know about travel the better it is for you. And us.

# Once you start thinking like a European, Europe will cost you less and you'll enjoy it more.

SWISSAIR

37

ART DIRECTOR / DIRECTEUR ARTISTIQUE:

35, 36  Santo Pulise
37  Howard Title
38  David Perkins
39  Steven D. Clark
40, 41  Claude Parvaix

AGENCY / AGENTUR / AGENCE – STUDIO:

35, 36  J. Walter Thompson
37  Waring & La Rosa
38  Johnson & Dean
39  NCNB Advertising
40, 41  Havas Conseil

38

40

39

41

ARTIST / KÜNSTLER / ARTISTE:

35, 36  Jacqui Morgan
37  Tom Daly/Norman Green/Rick Myerowitz
38  James Johnson
39  Marcus Hamilton
40, 41  Michel Dubré

DESIGNER / GESTALTER / MAQUETTISTE:

37  Howard Title
38  David Perkins
39  Marcus Hamilton

**42** "A big step" in the manufacture of sewage conduits—the use of the more ductile nodular cast iron—is featured in this advertisement for the *Pont-à-Mousson* foundries. (FRA)
**43** Magazine ad for *Olivetti* equipment as a means of preventing companies being strangled by their own accounting systems. (USA)
**44** Advertisement for television sets. (GER)
**45** Full-colour magazine ad for a *Fender* amplifier. Also available as a poster. (USA)
**46** Advertisement for IBM, offering thought on the use of human resources—here water. (JPN)
**47** Newspaper advertisement in colour for fibreboard supplied by Bowater Packaging Ltd. (GBR)
**48–50** Advertisements from a series for Typographic Innovations, Inc. (examples of word emphasis, comparisons of serif faces and of serif condensed faces). (USA)

## un grand pas

Oui, nous avons franchi un grand pas dans l'art de fabriquer des canalisations. Ces progrès sont le résultat d'une découverte métallurgique révolutionnaire : celle de la **fonte ductile** où le graphite est cristallisé sous forme de robustes petites sphères au lieu de fines lamelles. Cette nouvelle structure a bouleversé les propriétés de la fonte, au point d'en faire un métal **incassable**, qui se laisse tordre et plier. Le monde entier l'a adopté et sa production dépasse aujourd'hui **2.000.000 de tonnes.** La Société des Fonderies de Pont-à-Mousson, la première, a réussi industriellement à adapter la fonte ductile aux canalisations. Elle a déjà livré **10.000 kilomètres de tuyaux** de ce type pour l'équipement des villes, des campagnes, et des usines. Le tuyau en fonte ductile transporte à forte pression et à longue distance l'eau, le gaz, les hydrocarbures, les saumures et tous les effluents industriels.

**PONT·A·MOUSSON S.A.**

42

olivetti

43

*Found in virtually all musical environments, the Precision Bass is by far the most prolific of the species Basso Electrica. The frequency of the sighting reflects upon the enormous range of the Precision Bass's moods for it roars rhythmically like a lion and purrs melodically like a pussycat with equal ease.*

*Its versatile antics affect humans as well, causing almost uncontrollable rhythmic motions of the lower extremities and banging of the palms in thunderous blows.*

*For further reference, see Fender, Authorized Dealer.*

*Pick the live one*

**Fender**
CBS Musical Instruments

For full-color poster of this ad, send $2 to Fender, Box 3410, Dept. 270, Fullerton, CA 92634.

*Entertainers know the "King of the Jungle" as a quick and lively performer sure to draw crowds. Stimulated by large audiences, the Precision Bass inspires its playmates to its own unique level of frenzy when in close proximity to the rocking Bassman Amp and other Amplifiers Fender.*

*The Hearty-Roaring, Wide-Ranging Precision Bass®*
*(Bassis Fender).*

45

IBM

水産.

46

**42** «Ein grosser Schritt...» Anzeige eines Hütten- und Giesswerkes, das Kanalisationsrohre aus einem duktilen Gusseisen herstellt. (FRA)
**43** «Wird Ihre Firma durch das eigene Buchungssystem stranguliert?» Anzeige für *Olivetti*-Computer und elektronische Buchungsanlagen. (USA)
**44** Zeitschriftenanzeige für Fernsehgeräte von *Main Radio*. (GER)
**45** Ganzseitige Zeitschriftenanzeige für Verstärker. Mehrfarbige Illustration auf mattgelbem Grund. (USA)
**46** Zeitschrifteninserat für IBM-Computer, die z.B. auch zur Lösung von Problemen auf dem Gebiet der Oekologie eingesetzt werden. (JPN)
**47** Anzeige einer Verpackungsfirma. Verschiedene Brauntöne. (GBR)
**48–50** Aus der Anzeigenkampagne einer Schriftgiesserei mit Textbeispielen in verschiedenen Schrifttypen und -grössen. (USA)

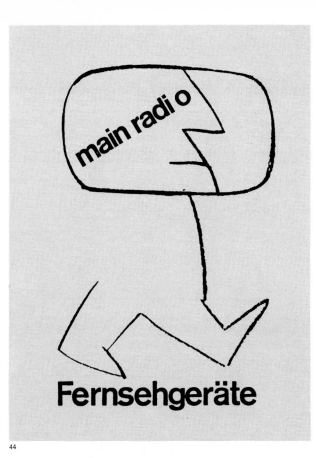

44

48

49

47

50

42 Annonce de la Société des Fonderies de Pont-à-Mousson qui a introduit la fonte ductile pour les canalisations. (FRA)
43 «Votre entreprise, sera-t-elle étranglée par le propre système de comptabilité?» Annonce pour les ordinateurs et machines *Olivetti*. (USA)
44 Annonce de magazine pour des appareils de télévision. (GER)
45 Annonce de magazine pleine page pour des amplificateurs. Illustration en couleurs sur fond en jaune atténué. (USA)
46 Annonce de magazine en faveur des ordinateurs IBM. Le texte traite des ressources naturelles et de la résolution de problèmes écologiques. (JPN)
47 Annonce d'une fabrique de conditionnement. Divers tons bruns. (GBR)
48–50 Annonces figurant dans la série d'un atelier de composition avec présentation de textes en divers caractères. (USA)

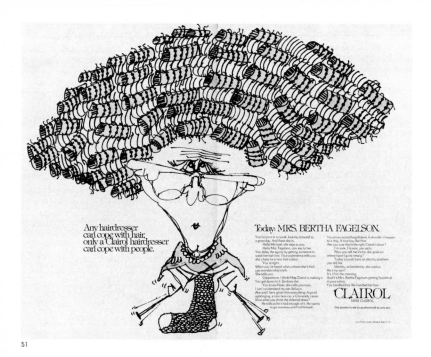

51

52

53

54

55

ARTIST / KÜNSTLER / ARTISTE:

51, 52 Barry Chemel
53–55 Costa Bello
56, 57 Leon Tadrick

DESIGNER / GESTALTER / MAQUETTISTE:

51, 52 Barry Chemel
53–55 Geri Garcia
56, 57 Tom Haynes

**51, 52** Double-spread trade magazine advertisements from a series for *Clairol* hair care products. Addressed to hairdressers, they illustrate awkward customers, whose idiosyncrasies are described in the copy. (USA)
**53–55** Full-colour illustrations and one complete double-spread advertisement from a series about men's clothing made of *Diolen*. The copy refers to the qualities of the personnel in the various departments of *Polyenka*. (BRA)
**56, 57** Detail of the illustration and complete double spread of an advertisement placed in medical magazines about a new drug for the relief of pain and inflammation in rheumatoid arthritis, made by McNeil Laboratories, Inc. (USA)

**51, 52** «Jeder Coiffeur kommt mit den Haaren zurecht, aber nur *Clairol*-Coiffeure kommen auch mit den Kundinnen zurecht.» Doppelseitige Zeitschriftenanzeigen aus einer Serie für *Clairol*-Haarpflegemittel, in der die bei der Behandlung von schwierigen Kundinnen auftretenden Probleme graphisch dargestellt werden. (USA)
**53–55** Mehrfarbige Illustrationen und doppelseitige Anzeige aus einer Werbekampagne für Herrenanzüge aus *Diolen*. Der Text weist auf das qualifizierte Personal hin, das in den verschiedenen Abteilungen von *Polyenka* arbeitet. (BRA)
**56, 57** Detail der Illustration und vollständiges, doppelseitiges Inserat für *Tolectin*, ein neues pharmazeutisches Präparat zur Behandlung und Linderung der Schmerzen bei rheumatischen Gelenkentzündungen. (USA)

**51, 52** Exemples figurant dans une série d'annonces professionnelles pour les produits *Clairol*. Publicité destinée aux coiffeurs qui – d'après le texte – réussissent mieux à se débrouiller avec les idiosyncrasies de leur clientèle grâce à *Clairol*. (USA)
**53–55** Illustrations polychromes et annonce double page complète extraite d'une série publicitaire pour les vêtements d'homme en *Diolen*. Le texte fait l'éloge du personnel employé dans les divers départements de la compagnie *Polyenka*. (BRA)
**56, 57** Détail de l'illustration et annonce double page complète publiée dans des périodiques médicaux. Pour le lancement d'un nouveau produit pharmaceutique utilisé ou pour le traitement des inflammations ou pour le soulagement des douleurs causées par l'arthrite rhumatismale. Les deux pages sont en couleurs. (USA)

**Advertisements / Inserate / Annonces**

ART DIRECTOR / DIRECTEUR ARTISTIQUE:

51, 52 Barry Chemel
53–55 Rainer Yablonka
56, 57 Tom Haynes

AGENCY / AGENTUR / AGENCE – STUDIO:

51, 52 Grey-Philips, Bunton, Mundel & Blake
53–55 CBB + A
56, 57 Sudler & Henessy, Inc.

57

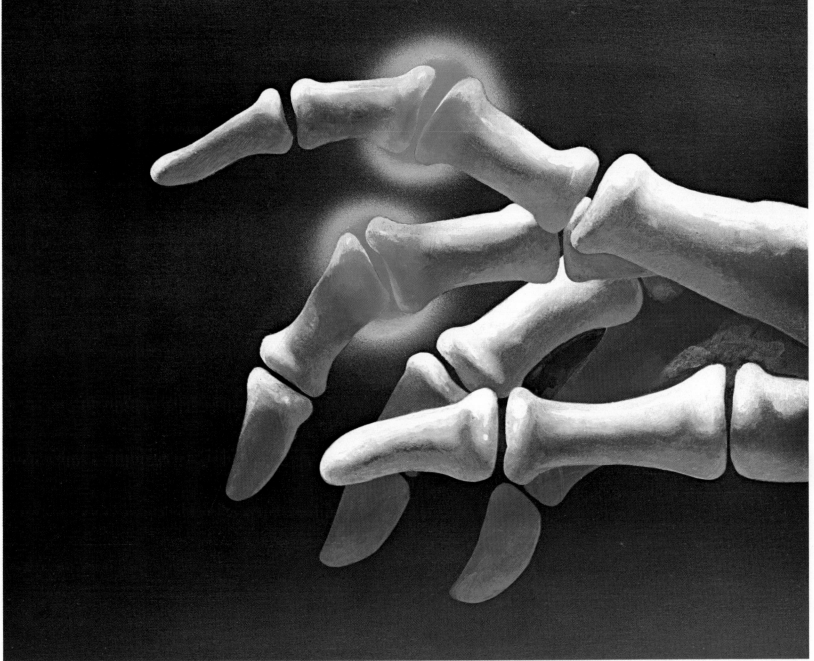

56

**58, 59, 63** Double spreads and detail of an illustration from a full-colour insert in medical journals advertising an essential drug nutrient made by McGaw Laboratories. (USA)
**60** Magazine advertisement for Frames Unlimited, Inc., custom framing specialists. (USA)
**61** Advertisement underlining the wide production range of the Grumman Corporation. (USA)
**62** From a series of ads about the new frosted shades of *Cutex* nail varnishes. (USA)
**64** Trade ad for serum reference control substances made by Clinton Laboratories. (USA)
**65** Magazine ad for an *English Leather* cologne containing ginseng. Black and red. (USA)

**58, 59, 63** Medizinischen Fachzeitschriften beigeheftete mehrseitige Anzeige für ein neues pharmazeutisches Produkt zur künstlichen Ernährung schwerkranker Patienten. (USA)
**60** Fachzeitschriftenanzeige für einen Hersteller von Rahmen aller Art. (USA)
**61** Anzeige eines diversifizierten Industriekonzerns. Mehrfarbige Illustration. (USA)
**62** Aus einer Anzeigenserie für *Cutex*-Nagellacke in neuen Modefarben. Mehrfarbig. (USA)
**64** Fachzeitschriftenanzeige für ein lyophilisiertes Mittel für Seren-Kontrollen. (USA)
**65** Zeitschriftenanzeige für ein Kölnisch-Wasser mit Ginseng-Extrakt. (USA)

**58, 59, 63** Pages doubles et illustration d'un encart inséré dans des périodiques médicaux en faveur d'un produit pharmaceutique pour l'alimentation artificielle. (USA)
**60** Annonce de magazine pour un fabricant d'encadrements. (USA)
**61** Annonce mettant en évidence la gamme des produits d'une entreprise diversifiée. (USA)
**62** D'une série d'annonces pour le lancement d'une nouvelle gamme de vernis à ongles. (USA)
**64** Annonce professionnelle pour un produit lyophilisé pour le contrôle des sérums. (USA)
**65** Annonce de magazine pour une eau de Cologne contenant du ginseng. Rouge et noir. (USA)

58

59

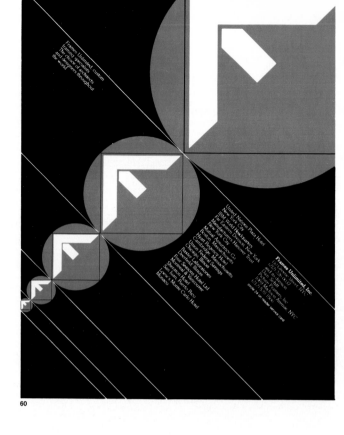

60

63

61

62

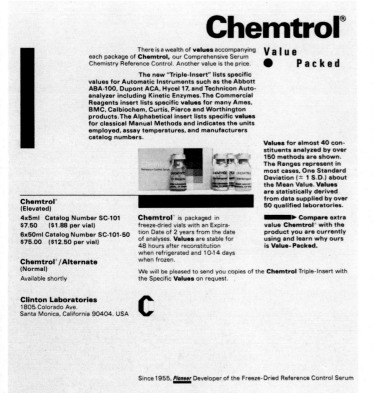

64

65

ARTIST / KÜNSTLER / ARTISTE:

58, 59, 63  Robert Hickson
61  Richard Hess
62  Heather Cooper
65  Eugen Karlin

DESIGNER / GESTALTER / MAQUETTISTE:

58, 59, 63  Douglas Boyd/Gordon Tani
60  Elliot Schneider
61  Art Christy/Frank Perry
64  Gregory Thomas
65  Eugen Karlin

ART DIRECTOR / DIRECTEUR ARTISTIQUE:

58, 59, 63  Douglas Boyd/Bruce Kaump
61  Frank Perry/Art Christy
62  Terry Isles
65  Joel Nissen

AGENCY / AGENTUR / AGENCE – STUDIO:

58, 59, 63  Maher, Kaump & Clark
60  Schneider Graphics, Inc.
61  Fuller & Smith & Ross
62  McCann-Erikson
65  Chalk, Nissen & Hanft

**Advertisements**
**Inserate**
**Annonces**

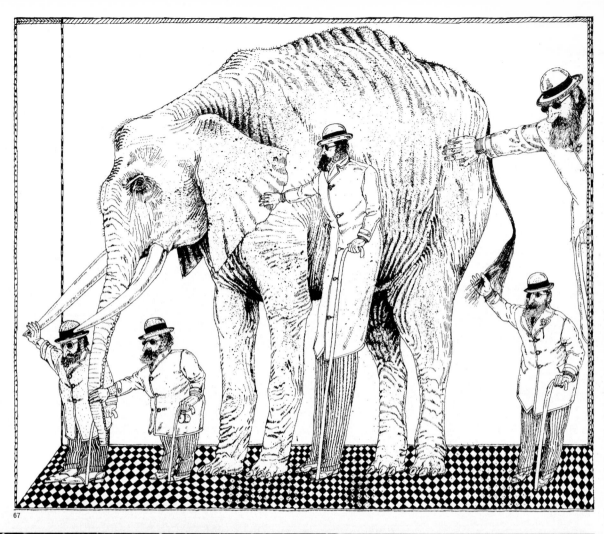

ARTIST / KÜNSTLER / ARTISTE:

66, 67  Jack Unruh
68  Jerome Snyder
69  Pierre Peyrolles
70  Louis Hart
71  Dick Drayton

DESIGNER / GESTALTER / MAQUETTISTE:

66, 67  Bob Lawton
68  Erwin Glusker
70  Duncan Mackintosh

ART DIRECTOR / DIRECTEUR ARTISTIQUE:

66, 67  Bob Lawton
68  Gordon Bowman
69  Olivier Bensimon
70  Duncan Mackintosh
71  Lee Clow

66

67

68

69

71

AGENCY / AGENTUR / AGENCE – STUDIO:

66, 67 Crume & Assoc.
69 Dupuy Compton
70 KVH/CDP
71 Chiat/Day Inc.

**66, 67** Complete magazine ad and black-and-white drawing in which the story of the five blind men and the elephant is applied to the production range of Gifford-Hill & Company, Inc. (USA)
**68** One of a series of reconstructions, for Mobil Oil Corporation, of scenes from famous football games under the title "The Way It Was". Full-colour ads and posters. (USA)
**69** Trade advertisement for a manufacturer of synthetic fabrics. Full colour. (FRA)
**70** Newspaper advertisement suggesting that house builders can learn something from shipbuilders. For *Bruynzeel* laminated boards. (NLD)
**71** Double-spread newspaper ad for a 1900-style amusement park in St. Louis. (USA)

**66, 67** Vollständige Zeitschriftenanzeige und dazugehörige Illustration für ein diversifiziertes Industrieunternehmen. Schwarzweiss. (USA)
**68** Beispiel aus einer von der *Mobil Oil* herausgegebenen Serie von mehrfarbigen Anzeigen und Plakaten. Als Motive für die ganze Serie wurden rekonstruierte Szenen aus berühmten Fussballspielen gewählt. (USA)
**69** Fachzeitschriftenanzeige für einen Hersteller von Kunstfasern. Mehrfarbig. (FRA)
**70** «Vielleicht können die Herren Häuserbauer von einem einfachen Schiffbauer noch etwas lernen.» Aus einer Serie von Anzeigen für einen Hersteller von geleimten Holzplatten. (NLD)
**71** Doppelseitige Zeitungsanzeige für einen Vergnügungspark in St. Louis, dessen Attraktionen an die Jahrhundertwende erinnern. (USA)

**66, 67** Annonce de magazine complète et dessin en noir et blanc. L'histoire de l'éléphant et des cinq aveugles devrait illustrer la grande variété des produits d'une entreprise industrielle largement diversifiée. (USA)
**68** Exemple d'une série de reconstructions de scènes de célèbres jeux de football, intitulée «Comment ça s'est passé». Annonces et affiches en couleurs publiées par la Mobil Oil Corp. (USA)
**69** Annonce de revue professionnelle pour un fabricant de tissus synthétiques. Polychrome. (FRA)
**70** Annonce de presse. Le texte dit que les constructeurs de maisons peuvent encore apprendre des choses des ingénieurs en construction navale. Publicité pour des planches laminées. (NLD)
**71** «Au cas où vous n'auriez pas été là en 1900.» Annonce de journaux sur page double pour un parc d'attraction style 1900 à Saint Louis. (USA)

70

**Advertisements / Inserate / Annonces**

73

72

74

## Nixdorf Computer
### tre piccoli grandi geni da assumere subito.

(facciamo pure dei confronti)

**Hardware Nixdorf:**
Modularità, elasticità, potenza; pluralità di apparecchiature periferiche; elaboratori a dischi; minicomputer a schede magnetiche, terminali; sistemi multitastiera intelligenti. **Solo alcuni vi danno tutto questo.**

**Software Nixdorf:**
Programmi parametrici e modulari, generalizzati o specifici di settore. **Solo pochi vi danno tutto questo.**

**Prontimpiego Nixdorf:**
Pressoché esclusiva rapidità di installazione del sistema più utile per voi (già funzionante in 30 giorni). **Solo Nixdorf oggi vi dà questo.**

Nixdorf: 35.000 installazioni. Nel mondo.

**Traetene le conclusioni, ora.**
I nostri telefoni sono:
Milano: 02/632110-632119-661387- 661346
Torino: 011/587746-587764
Roma Eur: 06/5911712.

**NIXDORF COMPUTER**
la grande azienda tedesca di sistemi elettronici.

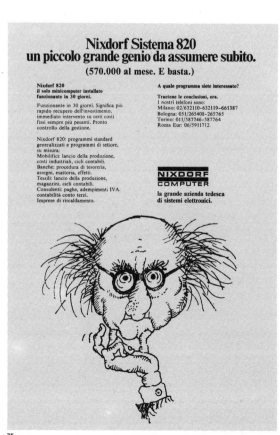

### Nixdorf Sistema 820
## un piccolo grande genio da assumere subito.

(570.000 al mese. E basta.)

**Nixdorf 820**
**il solo minicomputer installato funzionante in 30 giorni.**

Funzionante in 30 giorni. Significa più rapido recupero dell'investimento, immediato intervento su certi costi fissi sempre più pesanti. Pronto controllo della gestione.

Nixdorf 820: programmi standard generalizzati e programmi di settore, su misura:
Mobilifici: lancio della produzione, costi industriali, cicli contabili.
Banche: procedura di tesoreria, assegni, esattoria, effetti.
Tessili: lancio della produzione, magazzini, cicli contabili.
Consulenti: paghe, adempimenti IVA, contabilità conto terzi.
Imprese di riscaldamento.

A quale programma siete interessato?

**Traetene le conclusioni, ora.**
I nostri telefoni sono:
Milano: 02/632110-632119-661387
Bologna: 051/265408-265765
Torino: 011/587746-587764
Roma Eur: 06/5911712.

**NIXDORF COMPUTER**

la grande azienda tedesca di sistemi elettronici.

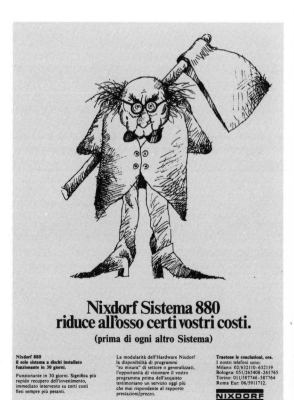

### Nixdorf Sistema 880
## riduce all'osso certi vostri costi.

(prima di ogni altro Sistema)

**Nixdorf 880**
**il solo sistema a dischi installato funzionante in 30 giorni.**

Funzionante in 30 giorni. Significa più rapido recupero dell'investimento, immediato intervento su certi costi fissi sempre più pesanti.

**Nixdorf 880**
**la strada scientifica del risparmio di gestione.**

La modularità dell'Hardware Nixdorf la disponibilità di programmi "su misura" di settore o generalizzati, l'opportunità di visionare il vostro programma prima dell'acquisto testimoniano un servizio oggi più che mai rispondente al rapporto prestazioni/prezzo.

**Traetene le conclusioni, ora.**
I nostri telefoni sono:
Milano: 02/632110-632119
Bologna: 051/265408-265765
Torino: 011/587746-587764
Roma Eur: 06/5911712.

**NIXDORF COMPUTER**
la grande azienda tedesca di sistemi elettronici.

44

75

76

77

78

79

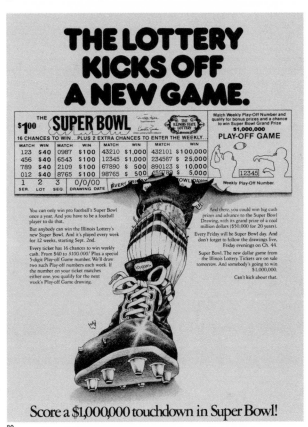

80

81

82

83

## Advertisements / Inserate / Annonces

81—84 Illustrations and complete advertisement from a series for the winter and summer resort of Flaine in Savoy. (FRA)
85, 86 Illustration and complete black-and-white advertisement to attract industry to country Victoria, where staff turnover is very low compared with metropolitan areas. (AUS)
87 Newspaper ad for a social security deposit service offered by The Citizens and Southern Banks of Georgia. (USA)
88 Newspaper advertisement for *Guillamet* data processing equipment. The illustration shows how companies grow up. (SPA)

81—84 Illustrationen und vollständige Zeitungsanzeige für einen Winter- und Sommersportort in den Savoyer Alpen. (FRA)
85, 86 Illustration und doppelseitiges Zeitungsinserat des Amtes für industrielle Entwicklung des Staates Victoria. Der Text weist darauf hin, dass Wechsel in der Belegschaft in dezentralisierten Industrien weniger häufig vorkommen und deshalb goldene Uhren als Treueprämien bereits heute gekauft werden können. (AUS)
87 Zeitungsanzeige für den neuen Kundendienst einer Bank – automatische Bezahlung regelmässig anfallender Beträge, hier z. B. für Sozialversicherungsleistungen. (USA)
88 Zeitungsanzeige für elektronische Anlagen. (SPA)

81—84 D'une campagne pour la promotion touristique de Flaine, station de sports d'hiver et d'été de la Haute-Savoie. (FRA)
85, 86 Illustration et annonce complète publiée par l'état de Victoria en faveur de l'industrialisation de cette région. D'après le texte le chiffre des mutations est inférieur dans les industries décentralisées comparé à celui des industries situées dans les régions urbaines. (AUS)
87 Pour le lancement d'un nouveau service d'une banque, ici pour le paiement des prestations de la sécurité sociale. (USA)
88 Annonce en faveur d'installations pour le traitement de l'information, se référant au développement de l'entreprise. (SPA)

84

85

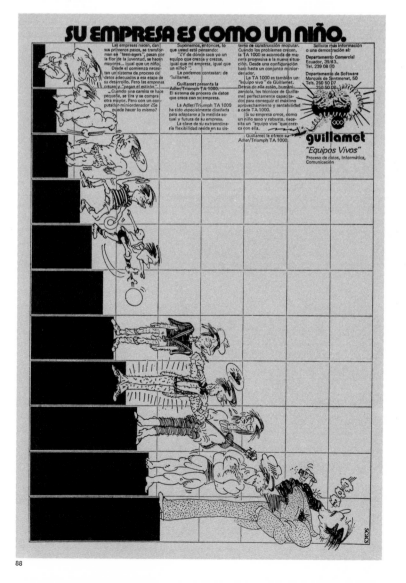

# Der Solvay-Service hat Hand und Fuß.

Bei der Verarbeitung von Kunststoffen entscheidet das „Gewußt-wie" über Erfolg oder Mißerfolg. Denn auch der beste Kunststoff ist nur so gut wie die Qualität seiner Verarbeitung. Deshalb legen wir bei Solvay großen Wert auf gründliche und zuverlässige anwendungstechnische Information unserer Kunden. Z. B. für die Verarbeitung von ELTEX,‚das zu denmeist-verwendeten Niederdruckpolyäthylenen der Welt zählt.

Unsere Anwendungstechniker beraten bei der Wahl des für den je-weiligen Verwendungszweck geeigneten Materials. Für Sonderaufgaben entwickeln sie spezielle, maßgeschneiderte Rezepturen. Sie stellen im Laborversuch fest, welche Rezeptur auf welchen Maschinen die besten Ergebnisse liefert. Sie beraten den Kunden in seinem eigenen Betrieb über optimale Verarbeitungsbedingungen. Sie erarbeiten rationelle Prüf-methoden zur laufenden Qualitätskontrolle der Fertigprodukte. Und vieles mehr. Denn wir wollen, daß auch die Kunden unserer Kunden zufrieden sind.

Das Zeichen für
Kunststoffe mit Service.

**SOLVAY**

89

# Der Solvay-Service hat den Bogen raus.

Solvay liefert nicht nur Kunststoffe!
Der Anwendungstechnische Beratungsdienst trägt auch dazu bei, daß unsere Kunden aus guten Kunststoffen gute Fertigerzeugnisse zu wirtschaftlichen Bedingungen herstellen. Z. B. aus dem Polyvinylchlorid SOLVIC°und SOLVIC-PREMIX°, dem meistverwendeten PVC auf der Welt.

Unsere Anwendungstechniker beraten bei der Wahl des für den je-weiligen Verwendungszweck geeigneten Materials. Für Sonderaufgaben entwickeln sie spezielle, maßgeschneiderte Rezepturen. Sie stellen im Laborversuch fest, welche Rezeptur auf welchen Maschinen die besten Ergebnisse liefert. Sie beraten den Kunden in seinem eigenen Betrieb über optimale Verarbeitungsbedingungen. Sie erarbeiten rationelle Prüf-methoden zur laufenden Qualitätskontrolle der Fertigprodukte. Und vieles mehr. Denn wir wollen, daß auch die Kunden unserer Kunden zufrieden sind.

Das Zeichen für
Kunststoffe mit Service.

**SOLVAY**

90

**89–91** Large black-and-white advertisement from a campaign underlining the advisory services offered to users of *Solvay* plastic materials. The illustrations incorporate the trade mark in playing upon points made in the headlines. (GER)
**92** Black-and-white advertisement placed in the medical press for a *Geigy* drug for the treatment of depression. (USA)
**93** Full-page newspaper advertisement, with animals in colour, for two covered shopping malls in Dallas. The point made is that, just as Noah took two of each species of animal, Dallas has chosen to have two shopping malls, one situated at either end of town. (USA)

**89–91** Aus einer umfangreichen Anzeigenkampagne, in welcher auf den gut ausgebauten Kunden-beratungsdienst der Kunststoffwerke *Solvay* hingewiesen wird. Das Firmenzeichen wird als Grund-motiv der Illustrationen verwendet. (GER)
**92** «Ich bin nur ein Schatten meines früheren Ichs.» Schwarzweiss-Anzeige für ein Antidepressi-vum von *Geigy*. (USA)
**93** «Noah hatte gar nicht so unrecht.» Mehrfarbige Zeitungsanzeige für zwei Einkaufs-Zentren, die in zwei verschiedenen Gegenden der Stadt Dallas errichtet wurden, damit sie von überall her leicht erreichbar sind und die Leute in Ruhe alle Einkäufe erledigen können, auch wenn es «vierzig Tage und Nächte regnet». (USA)

**89–91** Exemples figurant dans une campagne d'annonces grand format en faveur du service de consultation offert aux clients de *Solvay*, fabrique de matières plastiques. La marque sert de motif central pour illustrer chaque slogan de façon humoristique. (GER)
**92** «Je ne suis que l'ombre de mon moi d'autrefois.» Annonce de presse noir-blanc pour le lance-ment d'un antidépresseur *Geigy*. Publicité dans les périodiques médicaux. (USA)
**93** Annonce de presse pleine page, avec animaux en couleurs, pour deux centres d'achat couverts à Dallas. Profitant des bonnes expériences qu'a fait Noé en choisissant des couples de tous les animaux, on a construit deux centres de chaque côté de la ville. (USA)

# Der Solvay-Service ist ständig auf Trab.

Wer sich am Kunststoffmarkt behaupten will, muß der Konkurrenz um Nasenlänge voraus sein. Das gilt auch für den Verarbeiter. Der hat es besonders schwer, unter dem vielfältigen Angebot von Kunststoffen und Verarbeitungsmaschinen die richtige Wahl zu treffen. Deshalb legen wir bei Solvay so großen Wert auf gründliche und zuverlässige anwendungs-technische Beratung. Z. B. für die Verarbeitung von ELTEX°P, dem Poly-propylen mit den ausgezeichneten mechanischen und thermischen Eigen-schaften.

Unsere Anwendungstechniker beraten bei der Wahl des für den je-weiligen Verwendungszweck geeigneten Materials. Für Sonderaufgaben entwickeln sie spezielle, maßgeschneiderte Rezepturen. Sie stellen im Laborversuch fest, welche Rezeptur auf welchen Maschinen die besten Ergebnisse liefert. Sie beraten den Kunden in seinem eigenen Betrieb über optimale Verarbeitungsbedingungen. Sie erarbeiten rationelle Prüfme-thoden zur laufenden Qualitätskontrolle der Fertigprodukte. Und vieles mehr. Denn wir wollen, daß auch die Kunden unserer Kunden zufrieden sind.

Das Zeichen für
Kunststoffe mit Service.

**SOLVAY**

91

ARTIST / KÜNSTLER / ARTISTE:

89–91 Tomi Ungerer
92 Eugene Mihaesco
93 Larry Sons

DESIGNER / GESTALTER / MAQUETTISTE:

92 John DeCesare
93 Larry Sons

ART DIRECTOR:

89–91 Robert Pütz
92 John DeCesare
93 Larry Sons

AGENCY / AGENTUR / AGENCE – STUDIO:

89–91 Robert Pütz GmbH
92 Geigy Pharmaceuticals
93 The Richards Group

**Advertisements / Inserate / Annonces**

92

# Noah had the right idea.

Pairs.

Sometimes two is better. And that is why we have two shopping malls. Almeda and Northwest. One at each end of town. So we're sure to be close to you.

Both malls are identically beautiful. Identically charming. With nooks, crannies and corners that reveal a new surprise each time you pass by. Like a sparkling fountain. Or bright fresh flowers. Or a place to just sit and watch.

And it is all inside under a beautiful glass dome. So, you can shop comfortably. Even if it rains for forty days and forty nights.

## Almeda & Northwest Malls

We love you twice as much.

93

49

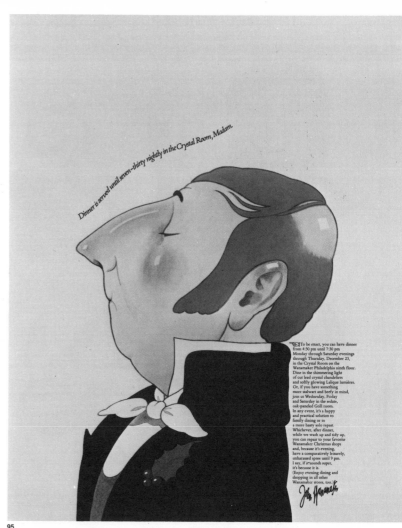

94

95

**94–97** From a long and continuing series of full-page newspaper advertisements in colour for the *John Wanamaker* department stores in Philadelphia. Here for canvas handbags with or without monograms (Fig. 94), for dinners in the Crystal Room and Grill (Fig. 95), for a historical film retrospective in the Auditorium (Fig. 96, showing Yankee Doodle) and for school clothes permitting combinations (Fig. 97). (USA)

**94–97** Aus einer langjährigen Serie von mehrfarbigen Zeitungsanzeigen des Warenhauses *John Wanamaker* in Philadelphia. Abb. 94: für Handtaschen aus Segeltuch, rostrot und grau, gelbe Lederriemen; Abb. 95: «Das Nachtessen wird bis halb acht Uhr im Cristal Room serviert, Madame.» Für das zum Warenhaus gehörende Restaurant. Abb. 96: für eine Retrospektive historischer Filme im Auditorium. Abb. 97: für praktische Schulkleidung. (USA)

**94–97** Exemples d'une longue série d'annonces de presse pleines pages pour les grands magasins *John Wanamaker* à Philadelphie. Les illustrations se réfèrent aux sacs à main en canevas avec ou sans monogrammes (fig. 94), aux dîners au restaurant Crystal Room (fig. 95), à une rétrospective historique présentée à l'Auditorium (fig. 96 avec Yankee Doodle) et aux vêtements pour enfants pouvant être combinés à volonté (fig. 97). (USA)

ARTIST / KÜNSTLER / ARTISTE:

94 Henry Heitman
95, 96 Arnold Varga
97 John + Linda Gist

DESIGNER / GESTALTER / MAQUETTISTE:

94, 97 Louise Reeves
95 Jean Seibert/Arnold Varga
96 Louise Reeves/Arnold Varga

ART DIRECTOR:

94–97 Albin Smagala

AGENCY / AGENTUR / AGENCE – STUDIO:

94–97 John Wanamaker

**Advertisements / Inserate / Annonces**

96

FARAH® school clothes
unlock lots of combinations.
That means more school clothes
for the money at John Wanamaker

It's elementary school logic!
Dress slacks, vests, jackets — important
parts key into your youngster's present
wardrobe for a new look everyday
at school, and handsome coordinated outfits when he really wants to wow 'em.
Every carefully tailored piece made for easy machine care and
long lasting good looks so your boys can finish the semester looking great too.
The look of gray flannel in hard-finished polyester/cotton/rayon: gray, green, blue or taupe.
Sportcoat in junior sizes 8-10-12, 18.00; prep sizes 14-16-18-20, 23.00.
Matching vest in junior sizes 8-10-12, 11.00; prep sizes 14-16-18-20, 13.50. Matching slacks in
junior sizes 8-10-12 regular or slim, 12.00; prep sizes 25-26-27-28-29-30 waist, 14.00.
J-pocket slacks in texturized polyester. Sizes 4-7 regular or slim; navy or green, 8.00.
Sizes 8-12 regular or slim; navy, brown, green, tan, 11.50. Prep sizes 25-26-27-28-29-30 waist; m-l-x inseam;
navy, brown, green, tan, 13.00. Husky sizes 28-29-30-31-32-34-36 waist; navy, brown or tan, 13.00.
Boyswear, fourth floor, central, Philadelphia; all JW stores.
Crisp cotton Bedford cord coordinates — rust or tan for
little boys 4-5-6-7. Dress slacks, regular or slim, 9.50.
Sportcoat, 18.00. Matching vest, 'brass' buttoned, 10.00.
Young John, fourth floor, Market, Philadelphia; all JW stores.

*John Wanamaker*

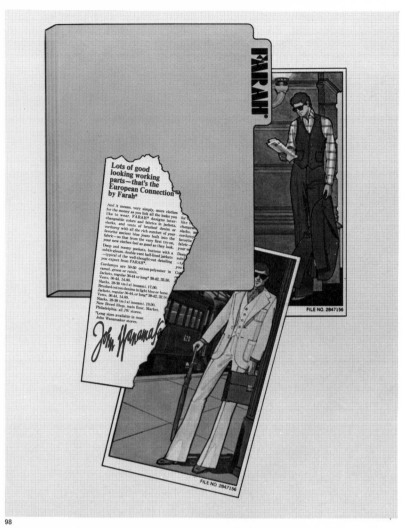

98

**98, 99** Two further full-page newspaper advertisements for the *John Wanamaker* stores in Philadelphia (see Fig. 94–97), here for co-ordinated clothing for men and for the Christmas shopping assortment. (USA)
**100** Full-page black-and-white newspaper advertisement announcing a new series of articles in the business magazine *Fortune* on major issues of American politics, to mark the opening of the new administration after the Presidential elections. (USA)
**101** Full-page newspaper advertisement inviting the people of Arnhem to the opening of a new *Bijenkorf* department store. (NLD)
**102** Full-page black-and-white newspaper advertisement from a long series for soy sauce made by Kikkoman Shoyu Co. Ltd. (JPN)
**103** Full-page newspaper advertisement in brown and blue to announce the reopening of Faneuil Hall Marketplace in Boston. (USA)

**98, 99** Zwei weitere Beispiele aus der mehrfarbigen Anzeigenserie des Warenhauses *John Wanamaker* in Philadelphia (siehe auch Abb. 94–97). Abb. 98: für gutsitzende Herrenanzüge. Abb. 99 weist auf die Riesenauswahl an Artikeln hin, die dieses Warenhaus führt. (USA)
**100** Ganzseitige Zeitungsanzeige des Wirtschaftsmagazins *Fortune,* das eine Artikelfolge über die von der neuen Administration auf verschiedenen Gebieten gestellten Forderungen und Lösungsvorschläge ankündigt. (USA)
**101** Ganzseitige Zeitungsanzeige, die zur Neueröffnung eines Warenhauses in Arnhem erschien. (NLD)
**102** Ganzseitige Zeitungsanzeige aus einer langjährigen, einheitlich gestalteten Serie für Soja-Sauce. (JPN)
**103** Zeitungsanzeige zur Neueröffnung eines Einkaufs-Zentrums, das in alten Markthallen eingerichtet wurde. Druck in Braun und Blau. (USA)

**98, 99** Deux annonces de presse pleine page pour les grands magasins *John Wanamaker* à Philadelphie (voir aussi les figs. 94–97), ici pour le lancement de complets pour messieurs et la gamme des produits pour Noël. (USA)
**100** Annonce de presse du magazine économique *Fortune* pour une nouvelle série d'articles sur les questions principales de la politique américaine, publiée à l'occasion de l'instauration de la nouvelle administration après les élections présidentielles. Pleine page en noir et blanc. (USA)
**101** Annonce de presse pleine page faisant part d'une invitation aux habitants d'Arnhem de participer à l'ouverture d'un grand magasin. (NLD)
**102** Annonce de presse pleine page figurant dans une longue série pour une marque de sauce soja. Noir et blanc. (JPN)
**103** Annonce de presse pleine page en brun et bleu annonçant la réouverture d'un marché couvert à Boston. (USA)

ARTIST / KÜNSTLER / ARTISTE:

98 Ray Yeldham
99 Arnold Varga
100 Geoffrey Moss
102 Tadashi Ohashi
103 Don Grimes/Jim Hradecky/Steve Miller/Woody Pirtle/
    Ron Sullivan/Mike Washlesky

DESIGNER / GESTALTER / MAQUETTISTE:

98 Louise Reeves
99 Susan Lesse/Arnold Varga
100 Glenn L. Scheuer
101 Nico van Rossum
102 Tadashi Ohashi
103 Bob Dennard

ART DIRECTOR:

98, 99 Albin Smagala
100 Glenn L. Scheuer
101 Louis van Beek/Rico van Rossum
102 Tadashi Ohashi
103 Bob Dennard

AGENCY / AGENTUR / AGENCE – STUDIO:

98, 99 John Wanamaker
100 Young & Rubicam
101 Young & Rubicam-Koster BV
103 The Richards Group

99

# Our campaign issues.

Next month, Fortune will begin a new series called "An Agenda for the New Administration." As Fortune sees it, the inauguration of a President next January—whoever wins the election—will open a new era in American public life.

It will be a time for fresh assessment of the major problems facing the country...and for fresh strategies to deal with them.

Fortune's series will begin in September with inflation. Why has it fallen no lower than to about six percent? Can we drive it lower—and keep it there?

Then, month by month, we will examine unemployment, the environment, the Federal budget, the troubles of the cities, the financing of health care, defense, tax reform, and other issues. What are the dimensions of each, the possible solutions, the new opportunities?

The series begins in the midst of the campaign debates. But it will continue into the first months of the new administration, when the debate moves into the houses of Congress and the offices of the policymakers.

Fortune's purpose: to provide these all-important national debates with a broad background of fact and analysis.

It is a task that only Fortune, among all business publications, could take on. Fortune, after all, has always been the magazine that clarifies the big issues for leaders of business, of government, of national opinion.

And our first concern is business...well, is there any campaign issue that business isn't affected by or that businessmen won't want to affect?

The people who read Fortune are experts at managing. They're specialists at making things work. And how to make government work for everybody's good is what an election is supposed to be about.

When the important decisions are made...in business and government...you can be sure that Fortune will be there.

**FORTUNE**

100

---

土の香りが帰って来る日

102

---

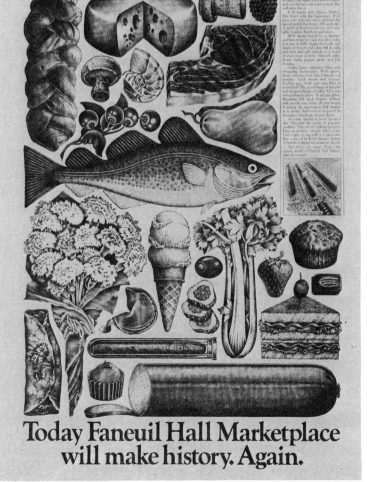

# Morgen, vanaf 11 uur, zijn alle Arnhemmers van harte welkom in de nieuwste Bijenkorf.

Op de eerste dag is er alleen toegang op vertoon van een blij gezicht.

**de Bijenkorf**

101

---

# Today Faneuil Hall Marketplace will make history. Again.

103

No two feet are exactly the same. Be they yours and mine or yours and yours. That's why space shoes were invented. To make sure each foot is treated as an individual.

Travers Space Shoes offer a new design and principle into a proper foot care. The shape of the shoe is determined by a technique of plaster casting that translates your specific foot shape into a shoe with comfort and function found in no other shoe.

This process is unique. A plaster cast is taken of each foot. Then, these casts are used to hand mold a Space shoe to fit each foot perfectly. This hand molding process creates a shoe that fits every contour of your foot, so there are no uncomfortable pressure points.

This is particularly important to people who walk or stand a lot.

Granted, it's not an easy or inexpensive process. It takes an hour to properly cast your feet. Then two months for our skilled craftsman to handmake your shoes with the finest leather and materials. The cost is $120, and it's worthwhile because Travers Space Shoes will last two or three times longer than conventional shoes as well as provide comfort you've never found before.

At David Travers Space Shoes we only have shoes in your size. So, come in, see our styles and discuss your foot care needs. Then step into a new world of comfort. Custom made, hand molded shoes.

David Travers Space Shoes, since 1959. 1228 Sutter St. (At Polk), S.F., Ca. 94109. (415) 885-1926.

## We never make the same shoe twice.

### David Travers Space Shoes
1228 Sutter St. (At Polk), San Francisco, Ca. 94109
In San Francisco since 1959.

104

"Mera Malmö åt Malmöborna!"

Kvällspostens Malmö-Extra, måndagar till fredagar!

105

106

107

108

110

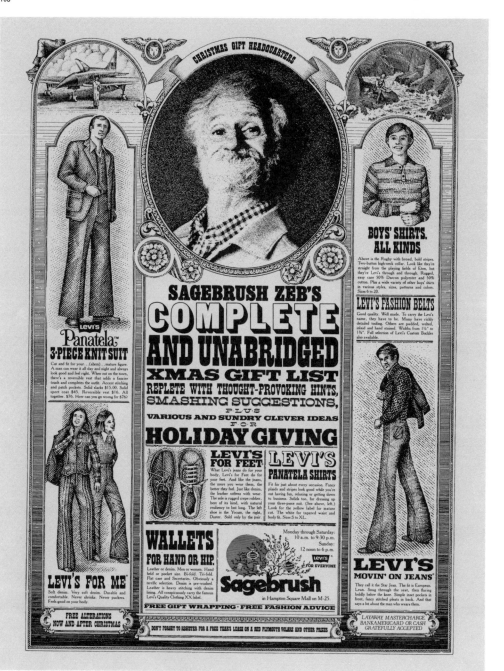

109

**2**

Booklets

Folders

Catalogues

Invitations

Programmes


Broschüren

Faltprospekte

Kataloge

Einladungen

Programme


Brochures

Dépliants

Catalogues

Invitations

Programmes

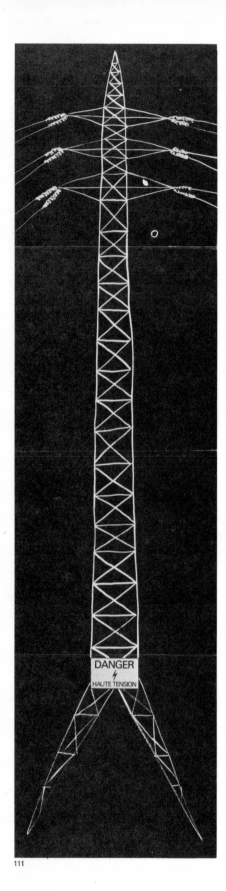

111

ARTIST / KÜNSTLER / ARTISTE:

111–118 May Néama
119 May Néama/Von der Stockt (Photo)

DESIGNER / GESTALTER / MAQUETTISTE:

111–119 May Néama

**Booklets / Prospekte / Brochures**

**111** One side of a folder about a *Roche* medicine against hypertension. Red danger sign. (BEL)
**112** Cover of a folder about a *Roche* polyvitamin product recommended for children starting back to school in autumn. Autumn is suggested by a collage in brown shades on yellow. (BEL)
**113** Cover of a folder about a *Roche* tranquillizer to combat various bladder control disorders. A piece of sandpaper is attached to represent the irritable bladder. (BEL)
**114, 115** Complete cover of a folder, and detail of the drawing, for the pharmaceutical *Librium*, which is said to ensure quiet nights and alert days. (BEL)
**116** "Gather laurels and keep your red cheeks." Card for a *Roche* polyvitamin product recommended for young people. Oak twigs in full colour, pink cheeks. (BEL)
**117** "Full of resilience." Folder for a *Roche* polyvitamin product. The real rubber bands are stretched when the folder is opened. (BEL)
**118** Cover of a folder about a *Roche* product used in ophthalmology. Flowers in colour. (BEL)
**119** Cover of a folder for a *Roche* tranquillizer. Tablets in two greens and black. (BEL)

**111** Ganze Seite eines Faltprospektes für ein *Roche*-Medikament gegen erhöhten Blutdruck. (BEL)
**112** Vorderseite eines Faltprospektes über ein Polyvitaminpräparat von *Roche*, das besonders Kindern zum Schulbeginn im Herbst empfohlen wird. Figur des Herbstes in Brauntönen auf Gelb. (BEL)
**113** Vorderseite eines Prospektes für ein *Roche*-Beruhigungsmittel gegen Störungen in der Blasenfunktion. Das Stück Schmirgelpapier weist auf die Reizbarkeit der Blase hin. (BEL)
**114, 115** Ganze Vorderseite und Ausschnitt aus der Zeichnung für einen Prospekt über *Librium*, das nachts beruhigend und tagsüber belebend wirken soll. (BEL)
**116** «Lorbeeren pflücken und die roten Wangen behalten.» Für ein Polyvitaminpräparat von *Roche*, das besonders für Heranwachsende empfohlen wird. Eichenzweige naturfarbig, Wangen rosa. (BEL)
**117** «Voller Spannkraft.» Faltprospekt für ein Polyvitaminpräparat von *Roche*. Beim Öffnen werden die echten roten Gummibänder gedehnt. (BEL)
**118** Vorderseite eines Prospektes für ein Augenmedikament. Strohblumen mehrfarbig. (BEL)
**119** Prospektvorderseite in Grüntönen und Schwarz, für ein *Roche*-Beruhigungsmittel. (BEL)

**111** Panneau d'un dépliant consacré à un médicament *Roche* contre l'hypertension. Panneau de danger rouge. (BEL)
**112** Couverture d'un dépliant pour une préparation vitaminée *Roche* recommandée pour les enfants, en particulier à la rentrée en automne; feuilles brunes sur fond jaune évoquant cette saison. (BEL)
**113** Couverture d'un dépliant consacré à un calmant *Roche* administré en cas de troubles fonctionnels de la vessie. Un bout de papier de verre symbolise la sensibilité de cet organe. (BEL)
**114, 115** Couverture complète et détail du dessin qui l'illustre. Dépliant consacré à *Librium*, médicament qui vous procurerait la «quiétude la nuit» et la «vivacité le jour». (BEL)
**116** Carte publicitaire pour un polyvitamine *Roche* pour adolescents. En couleurs. (BEL)
**117** «Plein de ressort...» Dépliant en faveur d'un polyvitamine *Roche*; si on l'ouvre, les (vrais) élastiques rouges s'étendent. (BEL)
**118** D'un dépliant présentant un produit ophtalmologique *Roche*. Fleurs sèches en couleurs. (BEL)
**119** Couverture d'un dépliant en faveur d'un calmant *Roche*. Pilules en tons verts et noir. (BEL)

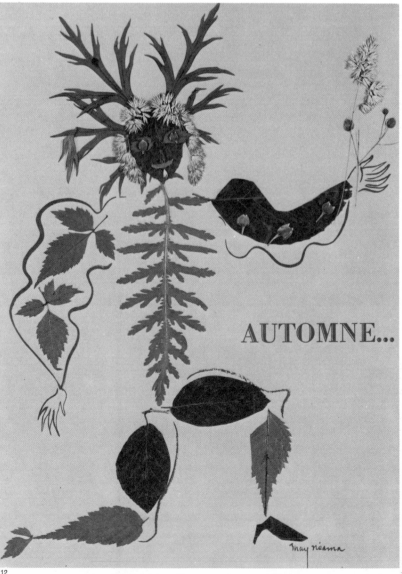

112

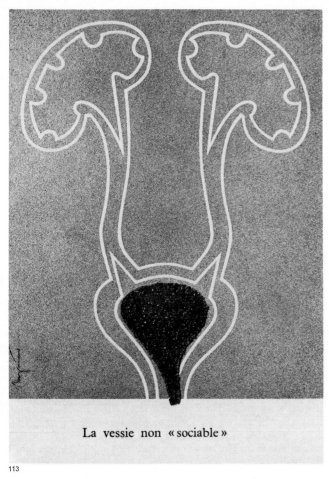

La vessie non « sociable »

113

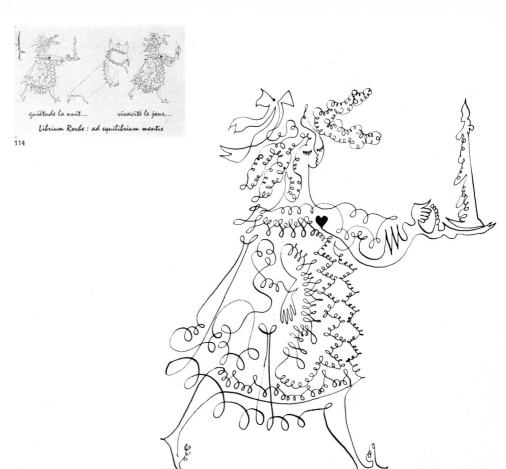

114

quiétude la nuit... vivacité le jour...
Librium Roche : ad equilibrium mentis

115

Cueillir des lauriers et garder des joues roses :
SUPRADYN ROCHE

116

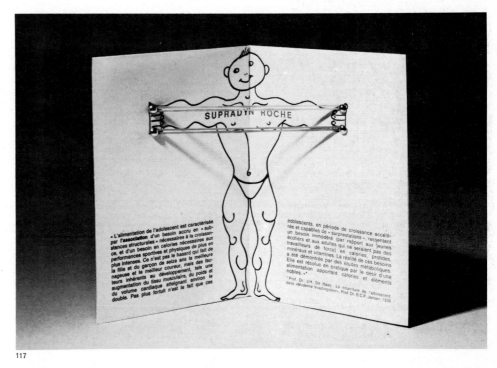

117

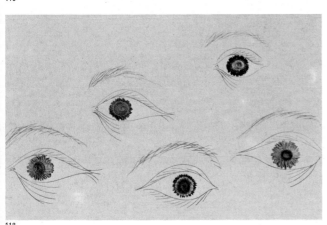

118

119

**Creative Psychiatry**

**3** Creativity:
The Process and Its Stimulation.
Morris I. Stein, Ph.D.

120

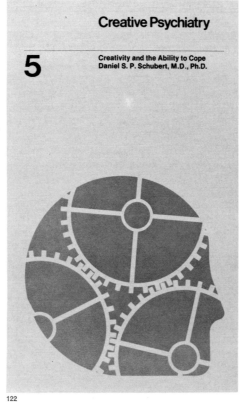

**Creative Psychiatry**

**5** Creativity and the Ability to Cope
Daniel S. P. Schubert, M.D., Ph.D.

122

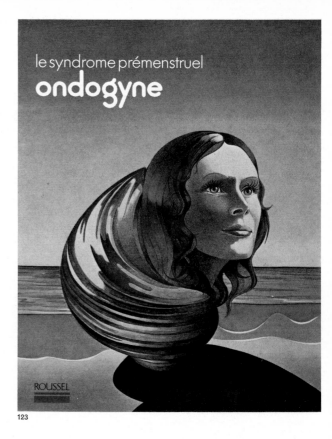

le syndrome prémenstruel
**ondogyne**

ROUSSEL

123

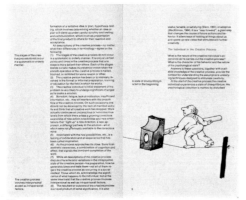

121

120–122 Two covers (artwork in colour) and double page from a *Geigy* publication on psychiatry sent out regularly to physicians. (USA)
123 Full-colour card about a *Roussel* pharmaceutical against premenstrual disturbances. (FRA)
124 Cover of a brochure about a *Ciba-Geigy* product against cardiac disorders. Yellow, black and red. (URU)
125, 126 Double page (with colour illustrations in pastel shades) and cover artwork for *Respiratory World*, a *Geigy* publication about a bronchodilator. The booklet contains abstracts from the medical press and is sent regularly to physicians. (USA)

120–122 Zwei Titelseiten (Illustrationen in Farbe) und eine Doppelseite aus einer *Geigy*-Publikation, die regelmässig an Ärzte verschickt wird. (USA)
123 Mehrfarbige Karte (vor allem Blau- und Brauntöne) für ein Medikament gegen prämenstruelle Beschwerden. (FRA)
124 Vorderseite einer Broschüre über ein *Ciba-Geigy*-Medikament, das gegen Herzbeschwerden verschrieben wird. Gelb, rot und schwarz. (URU)
125, 126 Doppelseite (Illustrationen in Pastelltönen) und Vorderseite von *Respiratory World,* einer *Geigy*-Publikation, die regelmässig an Ärzte versandt wird. Die Broschüre enthält Auszüge aus der medizinischen Fachpresse über Bronchien- und Lungenkrankheiten. (USA)

120–122 Deux couvertures (illustrations en couleurs) et page double d'une publication *Geigy* traitant de problèmes psychiatriques; élément destiné au corps médical. (USA)
123 Carte publicitaire en faveur d'un médicament *Roussel* pour combattre les troubles prémenstruels. Illustration en couleurs vives (tons bleus et brun clair). (FRA)
124 Couverture d'une brochure présentant un produit *Geigy* contre les troubles cardiaques. Jaune, rouge et noir. (URU)
125, 126 Page double (avec illustrations en couleurs atténuées) et illustration de couverture pour *Respiratory World,* une brochure *Geigy* déstinée aux médecins. Elle contient des extraits de périodiques médicaux au sujet de troubles respiratoires. (USA)

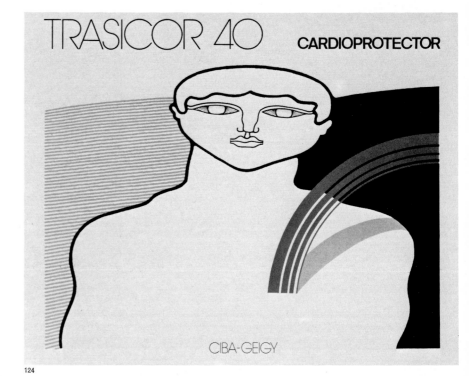

TRASICOR 40    CARDIOPROTECTOR

CIBA-GEIGY

124

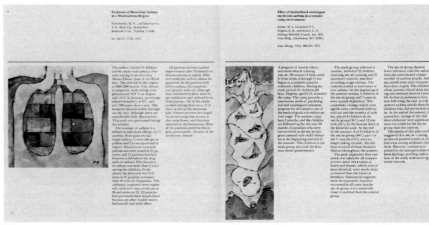

125

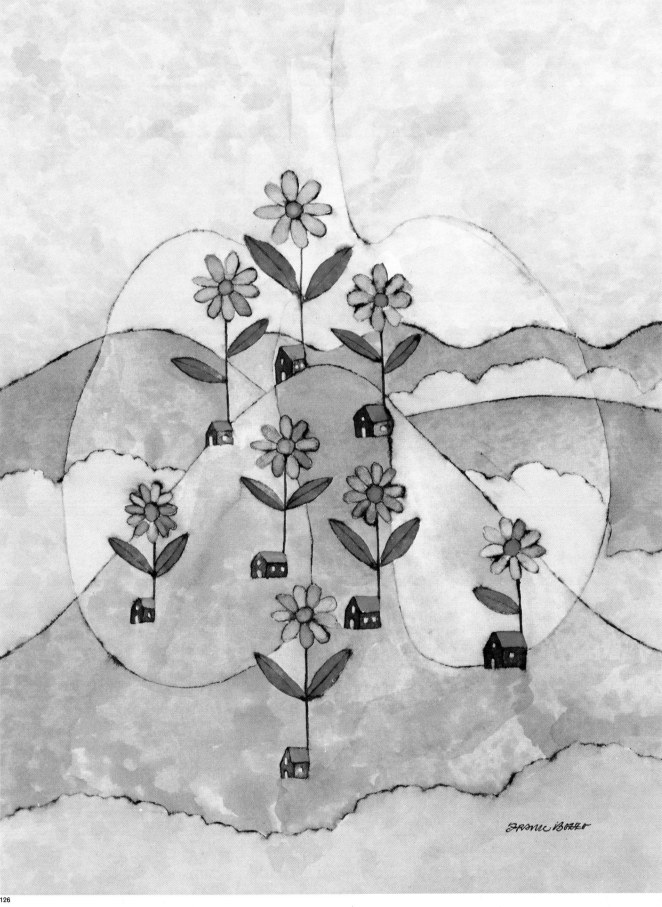

126

**Booklets**
**Prospekte**
**Brochures**

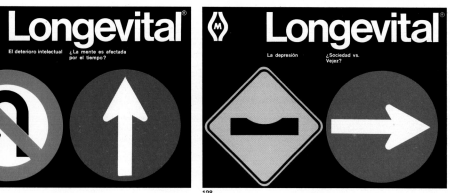

127

128

130

**Booklets
Prospekte
Brochures**

129

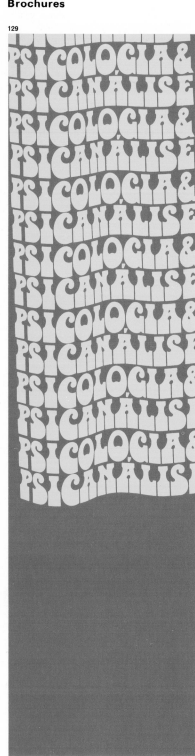

131

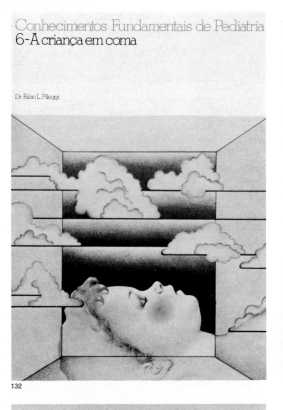

Conhecimentos Fundamentais de Pediatria
6-A criança em coma

Dr. Fábio L. Pileggi

132

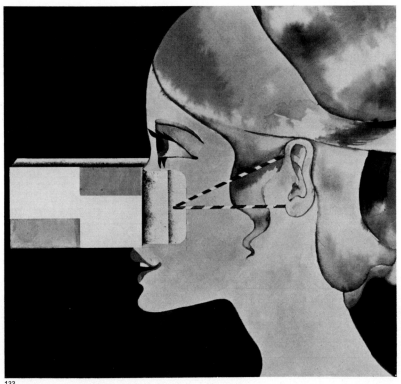

133

ARTIST / KÜNSTLER:

127, 128 Eduardo Cánovas
129 João Lauro
133 Adolf Kapeller
134 Olle Roos
135 Juichi Matsusaki

DESIGNER / GESTALTER:

127, 128 Eduardo Cánovas
130–132 Licínio De
Almeida/Fabio Boer/
Alfonso Gordano
133 Adolf Kapeller
134 Christer Holmqvist

ART DIRECTOR:

127, 128 Eduardo Cánovas
129 João Lauro
130–132 Fabio Boer
133 Dr. Zischka
134 Olle Roos
135 José Paulo Krauniski

AGENCY / AGENTUR:

127, 128 Estudio Cánovas
130–132 Gang S.A.
133 Ado Kapeller
134 MK/Ideinformation AB
135 Darta Propaganda

# Frihet åt förtryckta

det är temat för kyrkornas gemensamma u-vecka.

**Vad tänker du på när du hör ordet förtryck?**
Politisk förföljelse, tortyr, fattigdom, svält. Det är en del av verkligheten bakom förtryck i världen.

**På samma sätt kan du pröva frihet.**
Vad är det för? Mat, hälsa, hopp inför framtiden, möjlighet att uttrycka sin vilja och sin åsikt. Men så kan också se frihet som används fel. Friheten att hävda sin vilja leder till förtryck av andra. Frihet och valfrihet för en grupp människor bör ofta samman med ofrihet och fattigdom hos andra.

När Jesus talade om frihet gällde det alla. Han kom för att "predika frihet för de fångna och syn för de blinda, ja, till att giva förtryckta frihet". Skall vi förstå vad frihet är måste vi undersöka förtrycket i världen. Vi måste låta oss mer om sambandet mellan människor och länder, mellan rikedom och fattigdom, mellan frihet och förtryck.
I den här utställningen skall vi låta känna huvudarbetaren Pedro Moreno från Colombia och en svensk industriarbetare, Tage Larsson från Arvika.

134

135

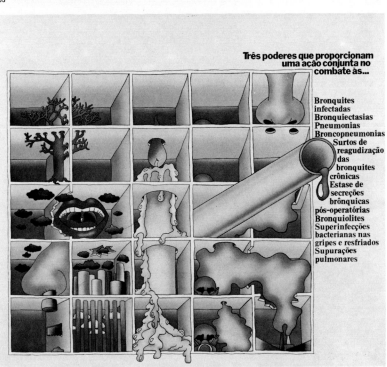

Três poderes que proporcionam uma ação conjunta no combate às...

**Bronquites infectadas
Bronquiectasias
Pneumonias
Broncopneumonias
Surtos de reagudização das bronquites crônicas
Estase de secreções brônquicas pós-operatórias
Bronquiolites
Superinfecções bacterianas nas gripes e resfriados
Supurações pulmonares**

---

**127, 128** Covers of booklets about a product of the *Bagó* laboratories to prevent mental deterioration and depression in old age. (ARG)
**129** Cover of a small folder listing works on psychology and psychoanalysis published by *Editora Vozes*. (BRA)
**130–132** Covers of booklets, and illustration from one in actual size, from a series of seven on pediatrics issued by the *Rhodia* pharmaceutical company. (BRA)
**133** From a colour folder for a medicament against colds. (GER)
**134** "Freedom for the oppressed." Page from a booklet about the Third World issued by the churches. (SWE)
**135** Page of a large folder about *Pravacilin,* a pharmaceutical for the treatment of affections of the respiratory tract. In full colour. (BRA)

**127, 128** Zwei Umschläge von Broschüren über ein Produkt der *Bagó*-Laboratorien, das gegen die Abnahme der geistigen Kräfte und gegen Depressionen im Alter verordnet wird. (ARG)
**129** Umschlag für eine Liste der bei *Editora Vozes* erschienenen psychologischen und psychoanalytischen Werke. (BRA)
**130–132** Prospektumschläge und originalgrosse Illustration aus einem davon, aus einer siebenteiligen Serie über Pädiatrie, die von der Pharma-Gesellschaft *Rhodia* publiziert wurde. (BRA)
**133** Aus einem Prospekt für ein Schnupfenmittel. In Farbe. (GER)
**134** «Freiheit für die Unterdrückten.» Seite aus einer von den Kirchen herausgegebenen Broschüre über die Dritte Welt. (SWE)
**135** Seite aus einem grossformatigen Prospekt für *Pravacilin,* ein Medikament, das bei Erkrankungen der Atemwege verordnet wird. Illustration mehrfarbig. (BRA)

**127, 128** Couvertures de deux brochures présentant des produits des laboratoires *Bagó,* qui sont prescrits aux personnes âgées en cas de détérioration mentale et de dépressions. (ARG)
**129** Couverture d'un petit dépliant présentant les publications de psychologie et de psychanalyse de *Editora Vozes*. (BRA)
**130–132** Couvertures complètes et l'une des illustrations en grandeur nature, d'une série de sept brochures pédiatriques de la société pharmaceutique *Rhodia*. (BRA)
**133** Illustration de couverture d'un dépliant en faveur d'un produit anti-rhume. En couleurs. (GER)
**134** «Liberté pour les opprimés.» Page tirée d'une brochure sur le Tiers Monde publiée par les Eglises. (SWE)
**135** Page tirée d'un dépliant grand format pour le *Pravaciline,* remède contre les affections respiratoires. En couleurs. (BRA)

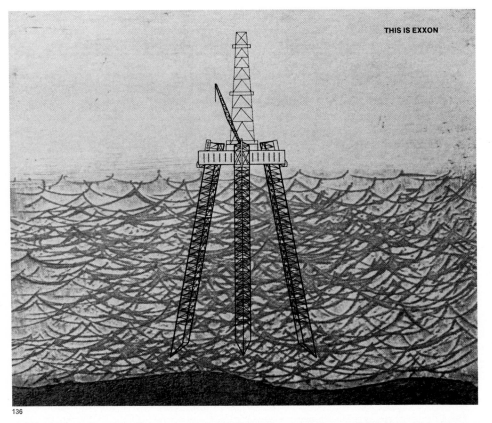

THIS IS EXXON

136

5. La fleur du bien et du mal

Depuis les h simples jusqu'aux hypnotiques

138

137

139

**136, 137** Front and back covers of a booklet about the activities of Exxon Corporation. Fig. 136 shows a black drilling platform in green waves, brown ocean bed; Fig. 137 illustrates drilling techniques, with black wells sunk into brown rock strata. (USA)
**138** Booklet from a *Roche* series, here on sleep-inducing drugs. (CAN)
**139** Linocut illustrating a booklet about a fertilizer for improving the quality of barley used for brewing (as opposed to feed barley). (GER)
**140, 141** Covers from a series of *Ciba-Geigy* guides to the use of various products—here textile whitening agents and dyeing auxiliaries. (USA)
**142** Cover of a catalogue of BASF industrial films. The red of the lamps appears through die-cut holes. (GER)
**143, 144** Double spread and detail of the black-and-white illustration (symbolizing "breakthroughs to new lives") from a large AT&T report on the subject of stress. (USA)

**136, 137** Erste und letzte Umschlagseite einer Broschüre über die Tätigkeit der Exxon Corporation. Abb. 136 zeigt eine schwarze Bohrinsel in grünen Wellen, über braunem Meeresboden; Abb. 137 erläutert Bohrtechniken, mit blauschwarzen Vorkommen zwischen braunen Erdschichten. (USA)
**138** *Roche*-Broschüre aus einer Serie, hier für Schlafmittel. (CAN)
**139** Linolschnitt aus einem Prospekt über ein Düngemittel, mit dem bessere Braugerste (im Gegensatz zur Futtergerste) erzielt werde. (GER)
**140, 141** Umschläge aus einer Serie von Gebrauchsanweisungen der *Ciba-Geigy*, hier für einen «Weissmacher» und für verschiedene Färbemittel. (GER)
**142** Umschlag eines Katalogs der BASF-Werksfilme. Das Rot der Lampen erscheint durch ausgestanzte runde Löcher. (GER)
**143, 144** Doppelseite und schwarzweisse Illustration (Titel: Durchbruch zu neuem Leben) aus einem grossformatigen Bericht der amerikanischen Telephon- und Telegraphengesellschaft AT&T über den Stress. (USA)

**Booklets**
**Prospekte**
**Brochures**

**CIBA–GEIGY**

A guide to the use of Uvitex® fluorescent whitening agents for textiles

FWA-6

140

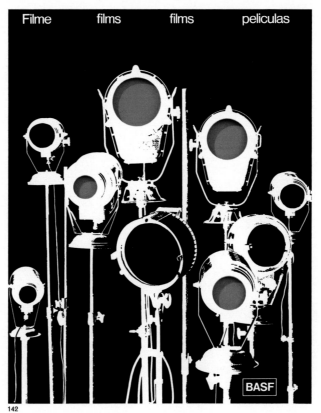

Filme    films    films    peliculas

BASF

142

ARTIST / KÜNSTLER / ARTISTE:

136, 137 Anatole Pastenak
139 Eduard Prüssen
143, 144 Colleen Quinn

DESIGNER / GESTALTER / MAQUETTISTE:

136, 137 Harry O. Diamond
138 Rolf Harder
139 Eduard Prüssen
140, 141 Markus Löw
142 Grafisches Büro, Abt. Öffentlichkeitsarbeit BASF
143, 144 Michael Manwaring

ART DIRECTOR:

136, 137 Harry O. Diamond
138 Rolf Harder/Monique Simond
140, 141 Markus Löw
143, 144 Michael Manwaring

AGENCY / AGENTUR / AGENCE – STUDIO:

138 Design Collaborative
140, 141 Ciba-Geigy, Corporate Art Service Department
143, 144 The Office of Michael Manwaring

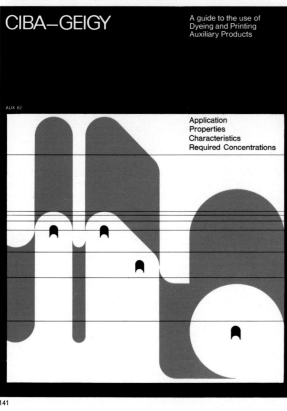

**CIBA–GEIGY**

A guide to the use of Dyeing and Printing Auxiliary Products

AUX 62

Application
Properties
Characteristics
Required Concentrations

141

143

144

**136, 137** Recto et verso d'une brochure au sujet des activités de la Exxon Corporation. Fig. 136 montre une plate-forme de forage noir, vagues vertes, fond marin brun; fig. 137 illustre divers techniques de forage, avec des gisements noirs dans des strates de rocher bruns. (USA)
**138** Brochure tirée d'une série publiée par *Roche*, consacrée aux somnifères. (CAN)
**139** Gravure sur linoléum illustrant une brochure pour introduire un engrais nouveau qui améliore la qualité de l'orge utilisé pour le brassage (comparée à celle de l'orge fourragère). (GER)
**140, 141** Couvertures d'une série de guides donnant des renseignements sur l'utilisation de divers produits chimiques – ici des produits pour le blanchissage de tissus et des colorants. (USA)
**142** Couverture d'un catalogue énumérant les films industriels produits par BASF. Le rouge des lampes apparaît à travers de découpes rondes. (GER)
**143, 144** Page double et détail de l'illustration noir et blanc (intitulée «la percée vers une vie nouvelle») tirés d'un rapport grand format au sujet du stress. Elément publicitaire de AT&T (compagnie américaine de télécommunication). (USA)

145

ARTIST / KÜNSTLER:

145, 146 Zelio Alves Pinto
148 Errol Mitchell
149 Tudor Mironesco
150, 151 Katrin Lindley

DESIGNER / GESTALTER:

147 Tor Pettersen
148 Errol Mitchell
149 Tudor Mironesco

ART DIRECTOR:

147 Tor Pettersen
148 Brian Stones
149 Tudor Mironesco
150, 151 Hans Peter Weiss

AGENCY / AGENTUR:

147 Lock/Pettersen Ltd.
148 Ciba-Geigy Ltd.,
Design Studio
150, 151 GGK

146

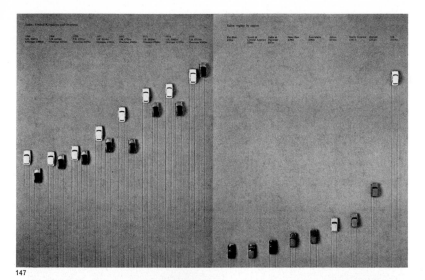

147

148

**MOBILIER PROFESSIONNEL MODERNE**

149

150

151

**145,146** Complete spirally bound notebook issued by the *Melhoramentos* (improvements) company, with detail of the cover illustration. (BRA)
**147** Double spread from a booklet about *British Leyland*, here showing sales by year and by region. Coloured cars on a sand background. (GBR)
**148** Cover of a *Ciba-Geigy* export bulletin about plasticizers for polyvinyl chloride. Title blind embossed, printed in red. (GBR)
**149** Cover of a folder about furniture and appointments used in cosmetology. (FRA)
**150** Colour spread from a small *Volkswagen* booklet containing a test to help readers decide whether they are driving the right car. Here the dynamic and the critical driver. (GER)
**151** Opening of a large colour folder on a *Volkswagen* model upholstered with jeans cloth: "The car for you." (GER)

**145,146** Spiralgebundenes Notizbuch und Titelbildillustration ungefähr in Originalgrösse, herausgegeben von der Industriegesellschaft *Melhoramentos* (Verbesserungen). (BRA)
**147** Doppelseite aus einer Broschüre der *British Leyland*; buntfarbene Autos auf sandigem Grund bilden Tabellen der Verkäufe pro Jahr und pro Region. (GBR)
**148** Titelseite eines Bulletins der *Ciba-Geigy* über ihren Export an Produkten, die für die PVC-Herstellung benötigt werden. Titel einmal blind geprägt, einmal rot gedruckt. (GBR)
**149** Umschlag eines Faltprospektes über Mobiliar für kosmetische Institute. (FRA)
**150** Doppelseite aus einer schmalen Broschüre von VW mit einem Test, bei dem man feststellen kann, ob man «noch das richtige Auto fährt». Hier zwei Fahrertypen. (GER)
**151** Innenansicht eines grossformatigen, mehrfarbigen Faltprospektes über den *Jeans Polo*, einen VW mit Sitzüberzügen und Türverkleidungen aus blauem Jeans-Stoff. (GER)

**145,146** Carnet à reliure spirale publié par la compagnie *Melhoramentos* (améliorations), et détail de l'illustration de couverture. (BRA)
**147** Page double tirée d'une brochure consacrée à *British Leyland*; on montre ici les chiffres de vente par année et par région. Voitures polychromes sur fond beige sable. (GBR)
**148** Couverture d'un bulletin publié par *Ciba-Geigy*, sur les exportations de plastifiants utilisés dans la fabrication du PVC. Titre: gaufrage à sec et impression en rouge. (GBR)
**149** Couverture d'un dépliant présentant du mobilier de cosmétologie. En couleurs. (FRA)
**150** Page double en couleurs tirée d'une petite brochure publiée par *Volkswagen* et contenant un test pour voir si on a la voiture appropriée. Ici pour le chauffeur dynamique et critique. (GER)
**151** Intérieur d'un dépliant grand format présentant un modèle de *Volkswagen* dont les sièges et les portes sont recouverts de tissu jean bleu. «La voiture pour vous». (GER)

154

**152, 153** Booklet in the form of a label (blue, red, black and white) and a double page from it. It advertises an IBM merchandise processing system for the garment industry. (USA)
**154–157** Double spreads and colour pages from a hard-cover booklet issued by IBM Belgium SA. In the form of a private journal kept by an office employee, it seeks to analyse and overcome prejudices against electronic data processing. It was printed in French and Dutch versions. (BEL)
**158** Complete cover and gatefold of a guide issued by IBM for the evaluation of suggestions made by employees, the best of which are rewarded with money prizes. (USA)

**152, 153** Prospekt in der Form eines Etiketts und Doppelseite daraus; er wirbt für ein IBM-System zur Kennzeichnung von Verkaufsgütern, hier von Kleidern. Rot und blau, Photographien in Schwarzweiss. (USA)
**154–157** Doppelseiten und Farbseiten aus einer grossen, gebundenen Broschüre der IBM Belgium SA. In der Form eines persönlichen Tagebuches, geführt von einem Angestellten, werden Vorurteile gegen elektronische Datenverarbeitung untersucht und abgebaut. Gedruckt in holländischer und französischer Fassung. (BEL)
**158** Ganzer Umschlag mit Ausleger eines IBM-Führers zur Behandlung von Vorschlägen der Angestellten. Die besten Vorschläge werden honoriert. (USA)

**152, 153** Prospectus sous forme d'étiquette et page double (en bleu, rouge et noir-blanc), en faveur d'un système IBM pour l'étiquettage de marchandises, ici de vêtements. (USA)
**154–157** Pages doubles et pages en couleurs tirées d'une brochure reliée publiée par l'IBM belge. Ce journal intime d'un employé cherche à analyser et à réduire les préjudices contre le traitement électronique des informations. Imprimée en versions française et hollandaise. (BEL)
**158** Couverture complète avec feuille tripartite d'une publication IBM renseignant sur l'évaluation des propositions faites par les employés, propositions dont les meilleures sont rétribuées. (USA)

152

153

155

157

156

ARTIST / KÜNSTLER / ARTISTE:

152, 153  Bill Farrel (Photo)
154–157  Heinz Edelmann
158  Bob Paganucci

DESIGNER / GESTALTER / MAQUETTISTE:

152, 153, 158  Bob Paganucci
154–157  Luk Mestdagh/Antoon de Vylder

ART DIRECTOR / DIRECTEUR ARTISTIQUE:

152, 153, 158  Bob Paganucci
154–157  Heinz Edelmann/Luk Mestdagh/Antoon de Vylder

AGENCY / AGENTUR / AGENCE – STUDIO:

152, 153, 158  Bob Paganucci

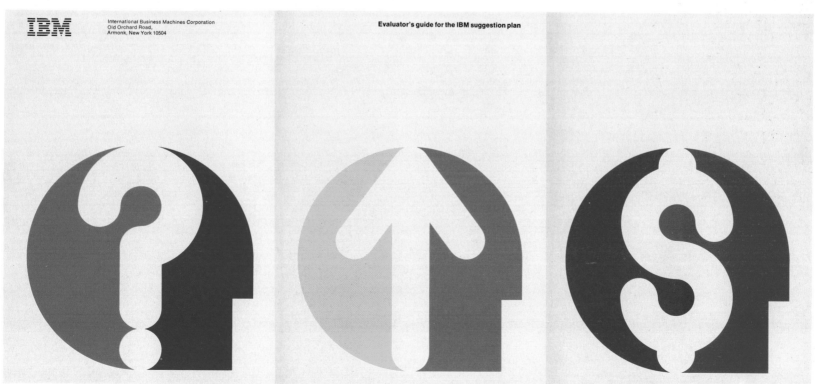

158

159

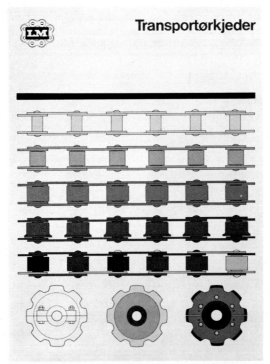

160

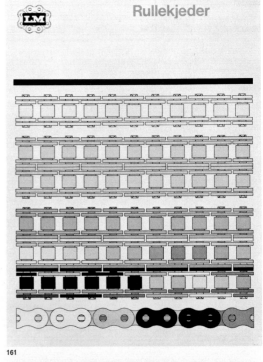

161

162

163

ARTIST / KÜNSTLER / ARTISTE:

160, 161 Italo Moro
162, 163 Sally Springer
164 Mike Wade
165–167 Olle Eksell

DESIGNER / GESTALTER / MAQUETTISTE:

159 Jeremy Knight
160, 161 Italo Moro
162, 163 Lew Ford
164 Glenn Tutssel
165–167 Olle Eksell

165

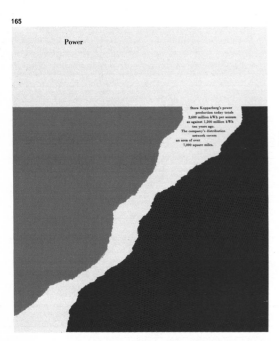

166

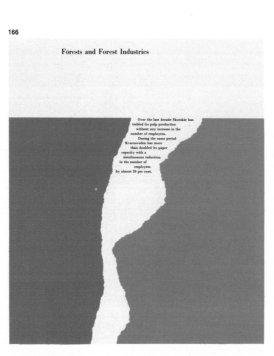

167

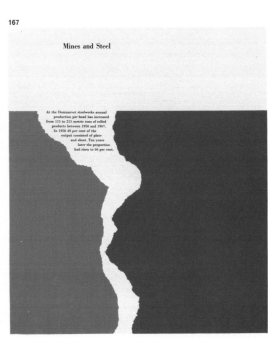

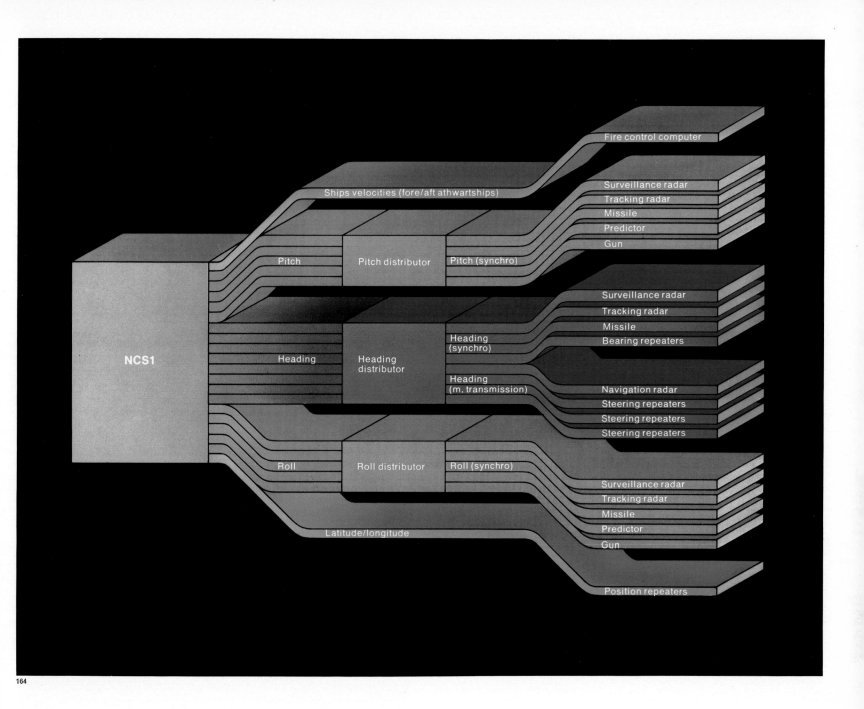

164

159 Cover of a folder about pure nickel for cast alloys supplied by *Inco*. (GBR)
160, 161 Covers of two folders about conveyor and roller chains made by AS Løwener, Mohn, Oslo. Fig. 160 mainly orange, Fig. 161 mainly green shades. (NOR)
162, 163 Covers of two folders about *Countrycut* fibre-glass shingle for the roofing of houses. Ochre and olive brown on black, Fig. 162 with die-cut holes. (USA)
164 Diagram explaining the operation of a stabilized gyrocompass for naval vessels, from a booklet issued by Marconi-Elliott Avionic Systems Ltd. (GBR)
165–167 Pages introducing the sections in a brochure about a large diversified industrial company, Stora Kopparberg. (SWE)

159 Umschlag eines Faltprospektes über reines Nickel für wertvolle Legierungen. (GBR)
160, 161 Titelseiten von zwei Prospekten über Förderketten, die von der Firma Løwener, Mohn in Oslo hergestellt werden. Abb. 160 in Orange-, Abb. 161 in Grüntönen, je mit Blau. (NOR)
162, 163 Umschläge von zwei Faltprospekten über die neuen Fiberglasziegel für Dächer von *Countrycut*. In Ocker und Oliv auf Schwarz, Abb. 162 mit ausgestanzten «Schusslöchern», Abb. 163 mit geprägtem «Brandzeichen» auf dem Fell der Kuh. (USA)
164 Diagramm zur Erläuterung eines stabilisierten Gyrokompasses für Kriegsschiffe und seiner Funktionen, aus einer Broschüre der Marconi-Elliott Avionic Systems Ltd. (GBR)
165–167 Drei Titelseiten zu je einem Kapitel aus einer Broschüre über Stora Kopparberg, eine grosse und weitverzweigte Industriegesellschaft. (SWE)

159 Couverture d'un dépliant recommandant du nickel pur pour les alliages de haute qualité. (GBR)
160, 161 Couvertures de dépliants présentant des transporteurs et des tapis roulants fabriqués par la Løwener, Mohn SA, Oslo. Fig. 160 en teintes orangé, fig. 161 en teintes vertes. (NOR)
162, 163 Couvertures de dépliants introduisant les tuiles *Countrycut* en fibre de verre destinées à la couverture de bâtiments. En ocre, olive et noir; fig. 162 avec découpes à l'emporte-pièce. (USA)
164 Diagramme expliquant les fonctions d'un compas gyroscopique installé dans un navire de guerre. D'une brochure publiée par la Marconi-Elliott Avionic Systems Ltd. (GBR)
165–167 Pages initiales de trois chapitres d'une brochure présentant Stora Kopparberg, une compagnie industrielle importante et largement diversifiée. (SWE)

ART DIRECTOR / DIRECTEUR ARTISTIQUE:

159 Jeremy Knight
160, 161 Italo Moro
162, 163 Ford, Byrne & Associates
164 Glenn Tutssel
165–167 Olle Eksell

AGENCY / AGENTUR / AGENCE – STUDIO:

159 Stuart & Knight
160, 161 Otto Falch
162, 163 Ford, Byrne & Associates
164 Lock/Pettersen Ltd.
165–167 Gullers Studio

**Booklets / Prospekte / Brochures**

168

168–170 Endpapers and two pages from a gift edition of Voltaire's *Candide* published in Italian translation by *Olivetti*, with illustrations by R.O. Blechman. Fig. 169 black and pale pink, Fig. 170 yellow and brown with pink sheep. (ITA)
171 Full-page illustration, chiefly in dark blue shades with an orange moon, from a gift edition of Thoreau's *Walden* published by *Olivetti*, with paintings by Paul Davis. (ITA)
172 Cover of a book about baseball published by *Xerox* as a gift to customers during the baseball championship games. (USA)
173 Cover of a catalogue for a Bicentennial exhibition organized by the Fairtree Fine Crafts Institute. The exhibition was sponsored by *Xerox*. Blue and red design. (USA)

168–170 Vorsatzpapier und zwei Seiten aus einer Geschenkausgabe von Voltaires *Candide* in italienischer Sprache, herausgegeben von *Olivetti*, mit Illustrationen von R.O. Blechman. Abb. 169 (Cunégonde) schwarz und hellstes Rosa; Abb. 170 gelbbraun, rötliche Schafe. (ITA)
171 Ganzseitige Illustration in dunklen Blautönen mit orangegelbem Mond aus einer Geschenkausgabe von Thoreaus *Walden*, mit Bildern von Paul Davis, herausgegeben von *Olivetti*. (ITA)
172 Titelseite (in Farbe) einer Broschüre über Baseball, die von *Xerox* während der Baseball-Meisterschaftsspiele an Kunden verschenkt wurde. (USA)
173 Umschlag des Katalogs für eine Ausstellung, die das Fairtree Fine Crafts Institute, von *Xerox* finanziell unterstützt, zur 200-Jahrfeier der USA veranstaltete. Blau und rot auf Weiss. (USA)

168–170 Pages de garde et deux pages de *Candide* de Voltaire, livre-cadeau publié en version italienne par *Olivetti*, avec des illustrations de R.O. Blechman. Fig. 169, Cunégonde, en noir et rose très clair; Fig. 170 en tons jaune-brun, moutons rouge clair. (ITA)
171 Illustration sur pleine page en teintes bleu foncé, avec la lune orange, tirée d'une publication-cadeau de *Walden*, de Thoreau, avec des peintures par Paul Davis, publiée par *Olivetti*. (ITA)
172 Couverture d'une brochure au sujet du baseball dont *Xerox* faisait cadeau à ses clients pendant les matchs du championnat de baseball. (USA)
173 Couverture du catalogue d'une exposition patronnée par *Xerox* et organisée par le Fairtree Fine Crafts Institute à l'occasion du Bicentenaire des E.-U. Bleu et rouge sur fond blanc. (USA)

ARTIST / KÜNSTLER / ARTISTE:

168–170 R. O. Blechman
171 Paul Davis
172, 173 Richard Wehrman

DESIGNER / GESTALTER / MAQUETTISTE:

172, 173 Kenneth Mackay

ART DIRECTOR / DIRECTEUR ARTISTIQUE:

168–171 Giorgio Soavi
172, 173 Kenneth Mackay

AGENCY / AGENTUR / AGENCE – STUDIO:

172, 173 Xerox Communications

171

169

170

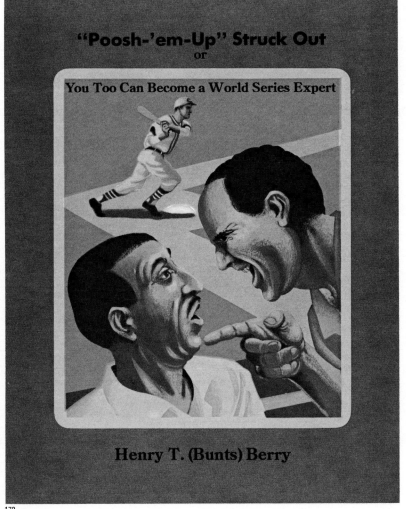

172

173

174

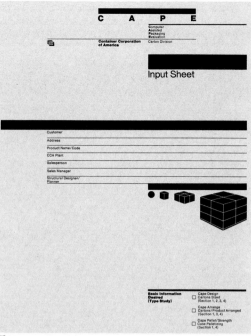

175

178

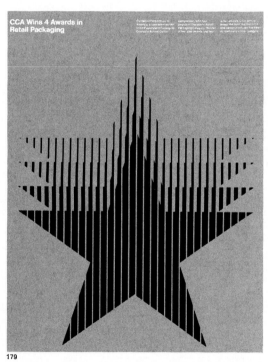

179

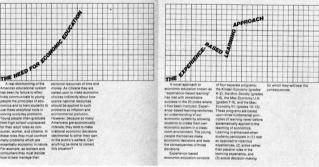

181

**174** Page (in full colour) from a Bicentennial booklet issued by *Warren*, papermakers, with a map of historical Boston. (USA)
**175** Input sheet for computer-assisted packaging for the Container Corporation of America. (USA)
**176** Cover of a capabilities brochure for Mobil Corp. (USA)
**177** One side of a mailer announcing a television special on a new *Celanese* fibre. Full colour. (USA)
**178** Cover of a direct mailer on garden pests and helpers to advertise a *Warren* paper. Green shades. (USA)
**179** Announcement of packaging awards won by CCA. (USA)
**180** Mailer about a multi-media presentation of a *Westinghouse* nuclear steam supply system. Yellow, red, brown on silver. (USA)
**181** Opening of a CCA-sponsored booklet on education. (USA)
**182, 183** Complete cover and detail of the artwork for a brochure about the capabilities of *Case-Hoyt*, colour printers. (USA)

**174** Farbseite (Lageplan des historischen Boston) aus einer Broschüre der *Warren*-Papierfabrik zur 200-Jahrfeier der USA. (USA)
**175** Informationsblatt für computergeplante Verpackungen, herausgegeben von der Container Corporation of America. (USA)
**176** Umschlag einer Broschüre über die Mobil Corp. (USA)
**177** Farbseite aus einem Versandprospekt, der eine TV-Sendung über eine neue synthetische Faser ankündigt. (USA)
**178** Titelseite eines doppelt gefalteten Prospektes für *Warren*-Papier: «Freund und Feind im Garten». In Grüntönen. (USA)
**179** Bekanntgabe der Preise der CCA für Packungen. (USA)
**180** Prospekt für eine Dia-Schau über ein *Westinghouse*-System der atomaren Energieerzeugung. (USA)
**181** Aus einer CCA-Broschüre zum Thema Bildung. (USA)
**182, 183** Titelseite und Ausschnitt aus der Illustration, für eine Broschüre über die Farbdruckerei *Case-Hoyt*. (USA)

**Booklets / Prospekte / Brochures**

176

177

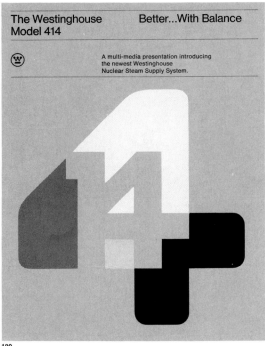

The Westinghouse
Model 414

Better...With Balance

A multi-media presentation introducing
the newest Westinghouse
Nuclear Steam Supply System.

180

**174** Page en couleurs (plan de l'ancien Boston) d'une brochure
publiée par *Warren,* fabricant de papiers. (USA)
**175** Feuillet en faveur d'un système de conditionnement par ordi-
nateur, publié par CCA. (USA)
**176** Couverture d'une brochure présentant la Mobil Corp. (USA)
**177** Panneau d'un dépliant annonçant une émission TV spéciale
au sujet d'une nouvelle fibre synthétique de *Celanese.* (USA)
**178** Couverture d'un dépliant consacré aux «amis et ennemis du
jardin», pour la promotion des papiers *Warren.* Tons verts. (USA)
**179** Liste des emballages-lauréats de CCA. (USA)
**180** Dépliant annonçant un nouveau système *Westinghouse* pour
la production d'énergie nucléaire. Fond argent. (USA)
**181** D'une brochure patronnée par CCA sur l'éducation. (USA)
**182, 183** Couverture complète et détail du dessin pour une brochure présentant *Case-Hoyt,* imprimerie. (USA)

182

183

184

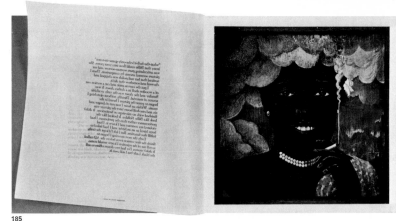

185

186

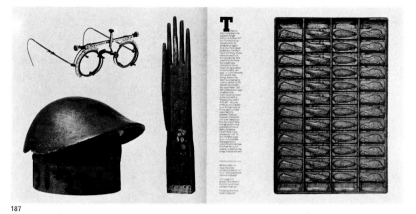

187

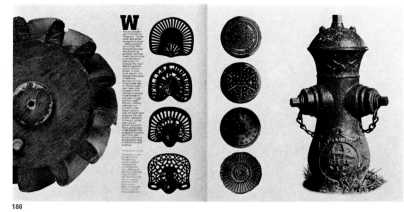

188

189

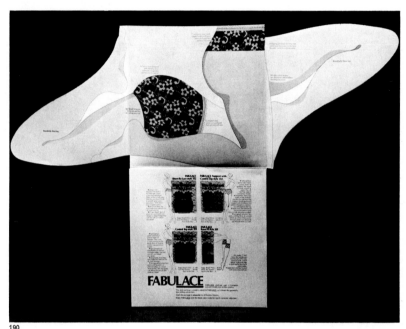

190

**184–186** Cover (red raspberries, green sepals), sample double page with transparent overlay, and one illustration from a booklet issued by Neenah Paper. It shows ten pieces of rejected art done by reputed designers and illustrators, and gives the stories behind them. Fig. 186 is a portrait of Billie Holiday. (USA)
**187, 188** Two openings of a booklet entitled "Artless Art" and presenting designs and objects once unnoticed in everyday use that we now appreciate as art—here such things as a glove form, a chocolate mould, tractor seats and a hydrant. The booklet demonstrates the quality of *Westvaco* papers. Production notes are given on each spread. (USA)
**189, 190** Cut-out wings, here shown folded and unfolded, forming the cover of a booklet addressed to retailers and describing the advantages of *Fabulace* hosiery fashions. (USA)

**184–186** Umschlag (rote Himbeeren, grüne Kelchblättchen), Doppelseite mit transparentem Zwischenblatt und eine der zehn Illustrationen; es handelt sich um Werke bekannter Designer und Illustratoren, die bestellt aber dann nicht akzeptiert wurden. Auf den Seiten links steht jeweils die Geschichte dieser Ablehnung. Abb. 186: Portrait der Jazz-Sängerin Billie Holiday. (USA)
**187, 188** Zwei Doppelseiten aus «Kunstlose Kunst», einer Broschüre über Gegenstände, einst unbeachtet und täglich in Gebrauch, die aber heute als Kunstwerke betrachtet werden, wie hier die Handschuhform, die Gussform für Schokolade, Traktorsitze oder der rote Hydrant. Auf jeder Doppelseite stehen Angaben über die Druckverfahren. Das ganze wirbt für *Westvaco*-Papier. (USA)
**189, 190** Ausklappbare «Flügel» (geschlossen und offen gezeigt), als Vorderseite einer an Detaillisten versandten Broschüre, die für *Fabulace*-Strumpfwaren wirbt. (USA)

**184–186** Couverture (framboises rouges, sépales verts), page double avec feuille transparente intercalée et l'une des illustrations d'une brochure publiée par Neenah Paper. On y montre dix œuvres créées par des illustrateurs de renom que les clients ont refusées; les pages à gauche donnent les raisons secrètes de ces refus. Fig. 186: Billie Holiday, chanteuse de jazz. (USA)
**187, 188** Deux pages doubles tirées de «L'art sans art», brochure présentant des objets utilisés jadis sans y faire attention, mais qui sont appréciés aujourd'hui comme objets d'art: ici une forme de gant en bois, une moule à chocolat, des sièges de tracteur et une bouche d'incendie rouge. Le tout est censé démontrer la qualité des papiers *Westvaco*. (USA)
**189, 190** Ces «ailes» découpées (montrées pliées et dépliées) forment la couverture d'un prospectus envoyé aux détaillants et décrivant les avantages de la bonneterie *Fabulace*. (USA)

ARTIST / KÜNSTLER / ARTISTE:

184–186 Richard Hess
187, 188 Arthur Maillet/Simpson Kalisher/Richard Hess (Photographers)
189, 190 Peter Mariotti

DESIGNER / GESTALTER / MAQUETTISTE:

187, 188 Richard Hess
189, 190 Peter Mariotti

ART DIRECTOR / DIRECTEUR ARTISTIQUE:

184–186 Glen Smith
187, 188 Richard Hess
189, 190 Peter Mariotti

AGENCY / AGENTUR / AGENCE – STUDIO:

187, 188 Richard Hess, Inc.
189, 190 DeKrig Advertising

**Booklets**
**Prospekte**
**Brochures**

191

193–196

197

ARTIST / KÜNSTLER:

191 Marlow Goodson/
Kit Hinrichs/Gerald
Huerta/Tim Lewis/
George Masi/
Emanuel Schongut/
Nancy Stahl
193–196 Heather Cooper/
Leigh Warren (Photo)
197 Bob Pepper
198 Joseph Essex
199 Susan Jackson Keig/
James L. Ballard
(Photo)

DESIGNER / GESTALTER:

191 Kit Hinrichs
192 Gad Ullman
193–196 Jim Donoahue
197 Carl Anderson
198 Joseph Essex
199 Susan Jackson Keig

192

198

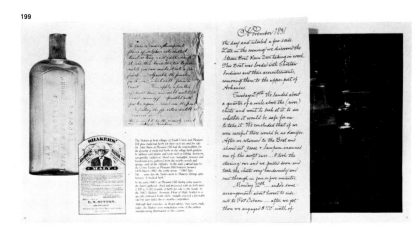

THE ASIAN WALL STREET JOURNAL.

199

**191** Inside of a colour folder from *Letraset* in which typefaces and graphic techniques are presented in the form of a menu. (USA)
**192** Cover of a folder about the Samuel Rubin Israeli Academy of Music in Tel Aviv. (USA)
**193–196** Large sheets printed on coated papers (named after famous printers and presses) from the range of Abitibi Provincial Paper Co. They were contained in a promotion folder. (CAN)
**197** Inside spread of a supplement to a textile trade paper, for *Cranston* printed fabrics, with a history dating back to 1824. Polychrome painting. (USA)
**198** Folder containing information on advertising in *The Asian Wall Street Journal*. (HKG)
**199** Opening of an album issued by The Beckett Paper Company about the Shakers as traders. The narrow interleaved pages show a facsimile trade report dating from 1831. (USA)

**191** Innenseite eines mehrfarbigen Faltprospektes, der in der Art einer Menükarte alle Schrifttypen und graphischen Techniken aufführt, die von *Letraset* angeboten werden. (USA)
**192** Vorderseite eines Faltprospektes über eine Musikakademie in Tel Aviv. (USA)
**193–196** Vier grossformatige Blätter aus beschichteten Papiersorten (alle nach berühmten Druckern benannt) der Abitibi Provincial Paper Co. Sie stecken zusammengefaltet in einer Mappe. (CAN)
**197** Innenseite einer Beilage zu einer Textil- und Modezeitung für *Cranston*; die Firma befasst sich seit 1824 mit Stoffdruck und -finish. Bild in bunten Farben gemalt. (USA)
**198** Faltprospekt mit Insertionsanweisungen für das *Asian Wall Street Journal*. (HKG)
**199** Innenansicht eines Albums der Beckett Paper Company über die Sekte Shaker, Handeltreibende seit Generationen. Zwischenseiten mit Faksimile-Rapport einer Handelsreise anno 1831. (USA)

**191** Intérieur d'un dépliant polychrome publié par *Letraset* et présentant, sous forme d'une carte de menus, tous les caractères et les techniques graphiques offerts par cette maison. (USA)
**192** Couverture d'un dépliant consacré à une académie de musique à Tel-Aviv. (USA)
**193–196** Larges feuilles en divers papiers couchés (portant chacun le nom d'un imprimeur célèbre) toutes contenues dans un dépliant promotionnel pour la Abitibi Provincial Paper Co. (CAN)
**197** Intérieur d'un supplément inséré dans un journal de modes, en faveur des tissus imprimés *Cranston*, maison fondée en 1824. Peinture polychrome. (USA)
**198** Dépliant avec renseignements sur l'insertion dans le *Asian Wall Street Journal*. (HKG)
**199** Page double d'un album publié par la Beckett Paper Company; thème: la secte des Shakers, commerçants. Les pages intercalées montrent un fac-similé d'un rapport de voyage de 1831. (USA)

ART DIRECTOR / DIRECTEUR ARTISTIQUE:

191 Kit Hinrichs
193–196 Robert Burns
197 Carl Anderson
198 Joseph Essex

AGENCY / AGENTUR / AGENCE – STUDIO:

191 Jonson Pedersen Hinrichs
193–196 Burns, Cooper, Donoahue, Fleming & Co. Ltd.
197 Essie Pinsker Associates
198 Jim Johnston Inc.

**Booklets / Prospekte / Brochures**

**200** Promotional piece for the Rose & Stone Advertising Agency. (USA)
**201, 202** Pages in full colour from a promotional piece issued by WPT European Advertising Partnership. It describes in an allegory how accounts in Europe can be rescued from the big American advertising agencies—here featured as wolves. (ITA)
**203** Cover of a folder in which Pacific Eye & Ear Co. Inc. offers creative help to the harassed advertiser. Grey shades, brown filters. (USA)
**204** Cover of a small folder about the accountants MacGillivray & Co. Orange on brown. (CAN)

**200** Eigenwerbung der Werbeagentur *Rose & Stone*. (USA)
**201, 202** Zwei Farbseiten aus einer Eigenwerbungsbroschüre der WPT European Advertising Partnership. In einem Gleichnis wird erzählt, wie trotz der Konkurrenz der grossen amerikanischen Werbeagenturen (hier in Wolfsgestalt) in Europa noch Gewinne zu machen sind. (ITA)
**203** Vorderseite eines Faltprospektes, mit dem die Pacific Eye & Ear Co. Inc. den geplagten Inserenten ihre kreative Hilfe anbietet. Grautöne, mit hellbraunen Filterstücken. (USA)
**204** Titelseite eines schmalen Prospektes für eine Treuhandfirma. Orange auf Braun. (CAN)

**200** Carte autopromotionnelle de l'agence de publicité *Rose & Stone*. (USA)
**201, 202** Pages en couleurs tirées d'une brochure autopromotionnelle de WPT European Advertising Partnership. On présente ici de façon allégorique les possibilités de «sauver» les budgets européens de la prise des grandes agences de publicité des E.-U. représentées comme loups. (ITA)
**203** Couverture d'un dépliant par lequel la Pacific Eye & Ear Co. Inc. offre ses services «créatifs» aux annonceurs désespérés. Teintes grises, bouts de filtre bruns. (USA)
**204** Couverture d'un petit dépliant présentant une société fiduciaire. Orange sur fond brun. (CAN)

201

202

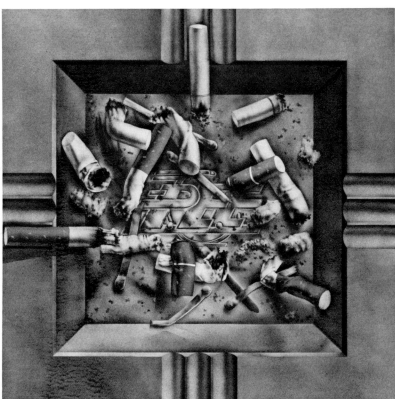

203

204

ARTIST / KÜNSTLER / ARTISTE:

200 James Endicott
201, 202 Juan Ballesta
203 Carl Ramsey
204 Eric Morrell

DESIGNER / GESTALTER / MAQUETTISTE:

200 James Endicott/Doug Stone
203 Pacific Eye & Ear
204 Eric Morrell

ART DIRECTOR / DIRECTEUR ARTISTIQUE:

200 Doug Stone
201, 202 Mario Barbi
204 Gottschalk & Ash Ltd.

AGENCY / AGENTUR / AGENCE – STUDIO:

200 Rose & Stone Advertising
201, 202 Publinter
203 Pacific Eye & Ear Co. Inc
204 Gottschalk & Ash Ltd.

206

207

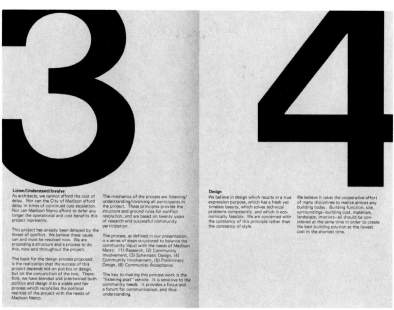

205

**205** Double page from a small brochure in which Flad & Associates, Inc., architects and engineers, give six reasons why they are well qualified to design a bus maintenance and administration facility for Madison Metro. (USA)
**206–209** Three double spreads and one illustration from a newsletter of the Dallas Society of Visual Communications presented as a show of freaks. Black and white on beige stock. (USA)
**210** Outside of a small promotional folder about the flautist Jorge Caryevschi. Silver handwriting on black. (ARG)
**211, 212** Cover and double spread from a brochure about the services of the freelance typist Margriet Staal, with specimens of almost illegible texts neatly typed in various typefaces. (NLD)

**205** Doppelseiten aus einer kleinen Broschüre, in der die Architekten und Ingenieure der Flad & Associates, Inc., sechs Gründe angeben, warum sie für den Entwurf einer Busgarage mit Verwaltungsgebäuden der Madison Metro die nötige Befähigung besitzen. (USA)
**206–209** Drei Doppelseiten und eine der Illustrationen in Originalgrösse aus einer Broschüre, die regelmässig an die Mitglieder der Dallas Society of Visual Communications versandt wird. Hier zum Thema: Monstren und Missgeburten, Absonderliches und Unglaubliches. Grautöne auf Beige. (USA)
**210** Ganze Aussenseite eines kleinen Faltprospektes über den Flötisten Jorge Caryevschi. Bläulichsilberne Handschrift auf schwarzem Grund. (ARG)
**211, 212** Umschlag und Doppelseite aus einer Broschüre für die freischaffende Sekretärin Margriet Staal, die auch fast unleserliche Handschriften fein säuberlich abtippt. (NLD)

**205** Page double d'une petite brochure énumérant les six raisons pourquoi l'équipe d'architectes et d'ingénieurs de Flad & Associates, Inc. est bien qualifié pour la construction d'une station d'entretien des bus et du bâtiment administratif de la Madison Métro. (USA)
**206–209** Trois pages doubles et l'une des illustrations tirées d'une brochure distribuée aux membres de la Dallas Society of Visual Communication; ce numéro est consacré aux monstres. Dessins en noir et blanc sur papier teint. (USA)
**210** Recto et verso d'un petit prospectus publicitaire sur le flûtiste Jorge Caryevschi. (ARG)
**211, 212** Couverture et page double d'une brochure par laquelle Margriet Staal, dactylo indépendante, offre ses services: elle est capable de taper avec soin des textes presqu'illisibles. (NLD)

209

208

ARTIST / KÜNSTLER / ARTISTE:

206–209  Larry Sons
211, 212  Tineke Wieringa (Photo)

DESIGNER / GESTALTER / MAQUETTISTE:

205  Stan Reed/Neil Bernstein
206–209  Larry Sons
210  Eduardo López/Gustavo G. Pedroza/Hector
Romero
211, 212  Koos Staal

ART DIRECTOR / DIRECTEUR ARTISTIQUE:

205  Stan Reed
206–209  Larry Sons
211, 212  Koos Staal

AGENCY / AGENTUR / AGENCE – STUDIO:

205  Flad & Associates, Inc.
206–209  The Richards Group
211, 212  Koos Staal

**Booklets**
**Prospekte**
**Brochures**

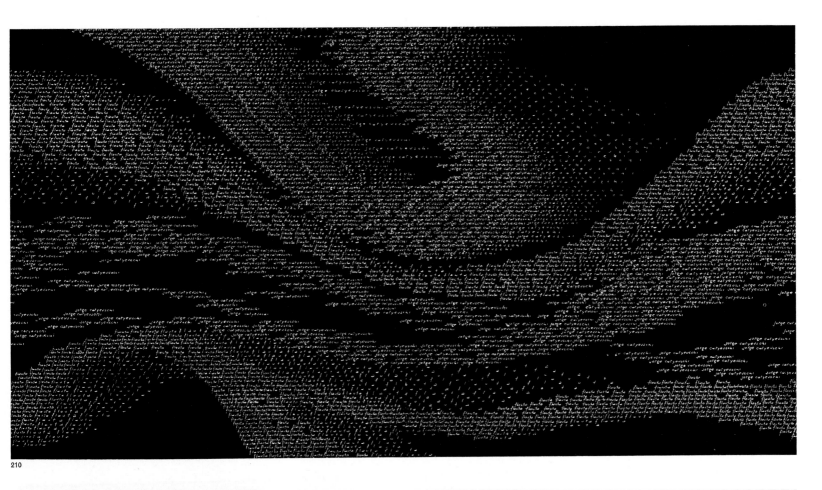

210

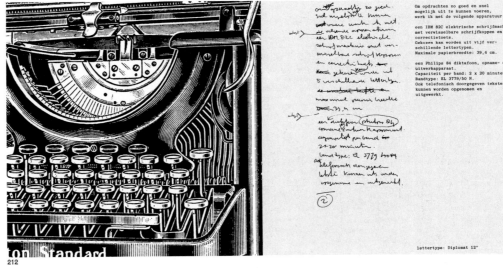

211

212

213

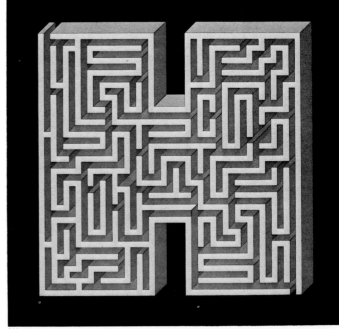

214

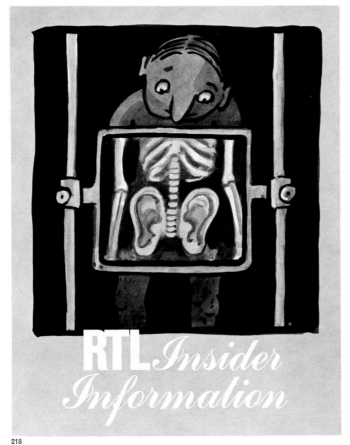

218

219

ARTIST / KÜNSTLER / ARTISTE:

213, 214  Skip Davis
216  W. Kosterman/P. Turner/O. Cabanban
217  Walter Sparks/Roger Takiguchi
218  Tomi Ungerer
220, 221  Heather Cooper

DESIGNER / GESTALTER / MAQUETTISTE:

213, 214  Skip Davis
215  April Greiman
217  Walter Sparks
218  Tomi Ungerer
219  Sheldon Seidler/Naomi Burstein
220, 221  Dawn Cooper Tennant

ART DIRECTOR / DIRECTEUR ARTISTIQUE:

213, 214  Skip Davis
215  April Greiman
216  Wayne Kosterman
217  Walter Sparks
218  Robert Pütz
219  Sheldon Seidler
220, 221  Robert Burns

AGENCY / AGENTUR / AGENCE – STUDIO:

213, 214  George N. Sepetys & Associates, Inc./
    Anthony M. Franco, Inc.
215  Frank Delano & Associates, Inc.
216  The Shipley Associates
217  Gauger Sparks Silva
218  IPA-RTL
219  Sheldon Seidler Inc.
220, 221  Burns, Cooper, Donoahue, Fleming
    & Co. Ltd.

215

216

217

220

213, 214 Cover (black and white, red type matter) and page (yellow, red, blue, green, purple) of a booklet about Helm, Inc., marketing and distribution specialists. (USA)
215 Cover of a folder addressed to potential clients by Frank Delano & Associates, marketing communications. Grey and white on red. (USA)
216 Cover of a brochure for the Frank Klein Co. (USA)
217 Set of sheets describing homes in a development of Dividend Industries, Inc. The cut tops of the sheets build up to form the hilly landscape in beige and brown. (USA)
218 Cover of a brochure for Radio Tele Luxemburg. (GER)
219 Cover of a *Merrill Lynch* review of stocks in 1976. Red and blue, white figures. (USA)
220, 221 Page and corresponding spread from a recruitment brochure for the accountants Delvitte, Haskins & Sells. (CAN)

213, 214 Umschlag (schwarzweiss, rote Schrift) und Seite (gelb, grün, violett, rot und türkis) aus einer Broschüre über die Marketing- und Verteilungsspezialisten Helm, Inc. (USA)
215 Titelseite eines Faltprospektes für Frank Delano & Associates, Imagewerbung, der sich an potentielle Kunden richtet. Helles Grau und weiss auf Rot. (USA)
216 Umschlag einer Broschüre über die Frank Klein Co. (USA)
217 Lose, verschieden grosse Blätter mit der Beschreibung diverser Häusertypen einer neuen Siedlung. Die welligen Ränder formen eine Hügellandschaft in Beige- und Brauntönen. (USA)
218 Titelseite einer Broschüre über Radio Tele Luxemburg. (GER)
219 Titelseite eines Lagerrapportes für 1976 der *Merrill Lynch*. Weisse Zahlen auf Rot und Blau. (USA)
220, 221 Farbseite und entsprechende Doppelseite aus einer Personalwerbebroschüre einer Treuhandfirma. (CAN)

213, 214 Couverture (noir et blanc, lettres rouges) et l'une des pages (jaune, vert, rouge, bleu et mauve) d'une brochure consacrée à Helm, Inc., spécialiste en publicité et distribution. (USA)
215 Couverture d'un dépliant destiné aux clients éventuels de Frank Delano & Associates, agence de publicité. En gris clair et blanc sur fond rouge. (USA)
216 D'une brochure en faveur de la Frank Klein Co. (USA)
217 Feuilles volantes décrivant divers logements à vendre. Les bords ondulés des feuilles évoquent un paysage vallonné. En tons beiges, ciel bleu foncé. (USA)
218 Couverture d'une brochure consacré à RTL. (GER)
219 Couverture du rapport 1976 des stocks, publié par *Merrill Lynch*. En bleu et rouge, avec chiffres blancs. (USA)
220, 221 Page et page double correspondante d'une brochure de recrutement d'une société fiduciaire. (CAN)

221

222

ARTIST / KÜNSTLER / ARTISTE:

222–224 Helmut Kraft
225 Tom Houtz
226 Cathy Hull
227 Jörg Hermle
229 Allen Welkis
230, 231 Walt Spitzmiller

DESIGNER / GESTALTER / MAQUETTISTE:

222–224 Helmut Kraft
225 Tom Houtz
226 Sue Skoorka
227 Jörg Hermle
228 Mervyn Kurlansky
229 Arnold Kushner
230, 231 Nicholas M. Stano

ART DIRECTOR / DIRECTEUR ARTISTIQUE:

222–224 Helmut Kraft
225 Bert Greene
226 Sue Skoorka
227 Jörg Hermle
228 Mervyn Kurlansky
229 Arnold Kushner/Andrew Kner
230, 231 Nicholas M. Stano

AGENCY / AGENTUR / AGENCE – STUDIO:

222–224 Kraft Design
227 Industrie Service
228 Pentagram
230, 231 NBC-TV

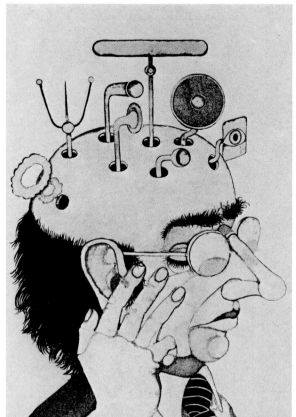

223

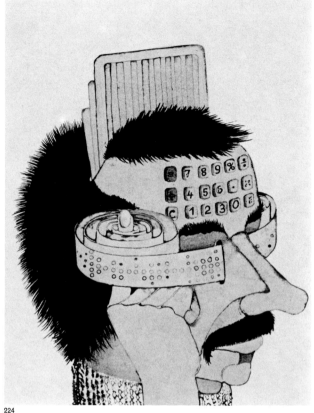

224

225

**The Prevalence of Polls**

226

227

Monitor X c'est une équipe de spécialistes à votre service.

**222–224** Opening and two full-page illustrations from a composite folder about the capabilities of *Marplan* marketing research. Black and white. (GER)
**225** Cover of a brochure addressed to advertisers in which well-known writers give their opinion of the magazine *Esquire*. Black, cerise title. (USA)
**226** Cover for the education programme of Time, Inc. Figure in brown shades, red cross in black box. (USA)
**227** Page of a small guide to advertising in the trade magazine *Le Moniteur*. It shows a "team of specialists" in full colour. (FRA)
**228** Family tree from a booklet issued by *Reuters* to commemorate the unveiling of a statue of Paul Julius Reuter. (GBR)
**229** Cover of a large education and camp directory published by *The New York Times*. Landscape mostly in green and blue shades. (USA)
**230, 231** Complete cover of an NBC calendar of sporting events, and detail of the black-and-white drawing. (USA)

230

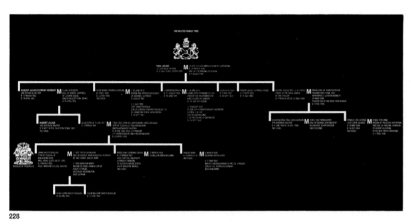

228

THE NEW YORK TIMES 1975
EDUCATION & CAMP DIRECTORY

229

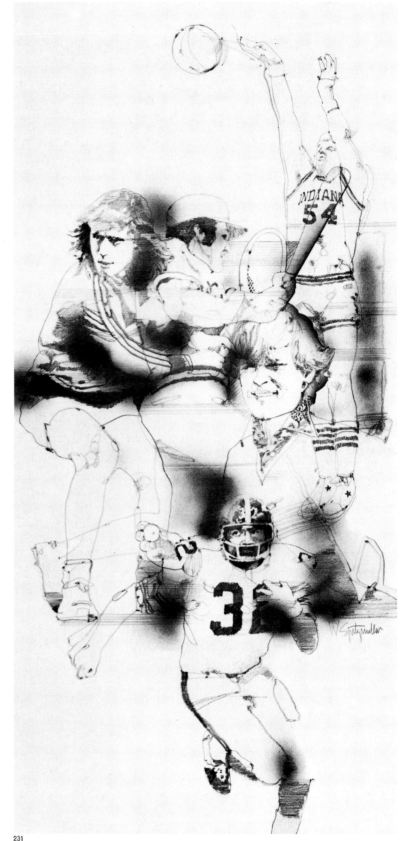

231

222–224 Doppelseite und zwei ganzseitige Illustrationen aus einem lose zusammengesetzten Faltprospekt über das Marplan Marktforschungsinstitut. Schwarzweiss. (GER)
225 Umschlag einer Broschüre mit den Kommentaren bekannter amerikanischer Schriftsteller über die Zeitschrift *Esquire*. Schwarz auf Weiss mit rosa Titel; Versand an Inserenten. (USA)
226 «Die häufige Anwendung von Umfragen.» Umschlag eines Prospektes über das Bildungsprogramm des Verlags Time, Inc. Figur in Sepiatönen, rot durchkreuztes schwarzes Kästchen. (USA)
227 Seite aus einem kleinen Werbeführer der Handelszeitschrift *Le Moniteur*, hier mit einem «Team von Spezialisten» in voller Aktion. Mehrfarbig, in Blau-, Grün- und Gelbtönen. (FRA)
228 Stammbaum der Familie Reuter aus einer Broschüre, die zur Feier der Enthüllung einer Büste von Paul Julius Reuter, Gründer der Nachrichtenagentur, herausgegeben wurde. (GBR)
229 Titelseite eines grossen Ferienführers (Kurse und Lager), der von der *New York Times* veröffentlicht wird. Landschaft in Grüntönen, mit wenig Rot und Blau. (USA)
230, 231 Vollständige Vorderseite und Ausschnitt aus der Zeichnung, für einen Kalender der wichtigsten sportlichen Ereignisse, herausgegeben von einer amerikanischen Fernsehgesellschaft. (USA)

222–224 Page double et deux des illustrations sur pleines pages tirées d'un dépliant à feuilles volantes sur *Marplan,* société d'études des marchés. En noir et blanc. (GER)
225 Couverture d'une brochure promotionnelle du magazine *Esquire*; des auteurs renommés y expriment leurs avis sur le magazine. Noir sur blanc, titre rose. (USA)
226 Couverture du programme d'éducation des editions Time, Inc. Figure en teintes sépia, croix rouge dans une caisse noire. (USA)
227 Page d'un petit guide publicitaire du périodique commercial *Le Moniteur*; on montre ici «une équipe de spécialistes» en activité. En couleurs. (FRA)
228 Arbre généalogique sur une page double de la brochure publiée par *Reuters*, célébrant le dévoilement d'un buste de Paul Julius Reuter, fondateur de la grande agence de presse. (GBR)
229 Couverture d'un guide de vacances (cours et camps) publié par le *New York Times*. Paysage en teintes vertes et bleues. (USA)
230, 231 Couverture complète d'un calendrier des événements sportifs, publié par la National Broadcasting Corporation, et détail de l'illustration en noir et blanc. (USA)

232

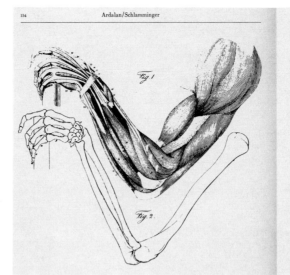

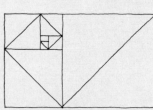

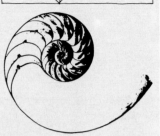

*Mathematics, Nature and Man*

Man shares with nature a commonality of structure and proportion that is most appropriately quantifiable through mathematics. All of his creations and that of nature can be viewed as forms observable through mathematical laws of similitude, symmetry and geometry. The beauty observed in a snow crystal, a DNA molecule, a plant, a man or a star system depends as much on their geometrical order as on their ability to reflect a higher and more profound order in all creation.

The sphere is the most evident symbol of Unity and its division by inscribed regular polygons constitutes the basis of all traditional laws of proportion. One of the most profound man/nature proportional systems is that of the golden mean which develops in a proportional series of whole integers, and gives the harmonic progression (known as the Fibonacci scale) of 1, 1, 2, 3, 5, 8, 13, 21, which exhibits the characteristic that any two successive integers is equal to the following integer.

Man exhibits such a Fibonacci series of proportional relationships in his anatomical structure while his capacity to fill, perceive, transverse and define space is a direct extension of it. Thus numerical correspondences within the body, taken individually or corporately in accordance with an anatomical unity (such as the inch), allow man to create in resonance with nature and to perpetuate the harmonic beauty that he archetypically manifests.

233

ARTIST / KÜNSTLER / ARTISTE:

234 Celestino Piatti
236 Paul Brühwiler
237 Michele Spera

DESIGNER / GESTALTER / MAQUETTISTE:

232, 233 George Lorenz/David Runtz
235 René Gauch
237 Ter Roma
238 Stuart Ash/Peter Adam
239, 240 Claudia Ronzi

ART DIRECTOR / DIRECTEUR ARTISTIQUE:

232, 233 George Lorenz
237 Michele Spera
238 Gottschalk & Ash Ltd.

AGENCY / AGENTUR / AGENCE – STUDIO:

232, 233 George Nelson & Co.
238 Gottschalk & Ash Ltd.
239, 240 Studio Lupi

Zürcher Klassenlese-Serien
der Schweizerischen
Volksbibliothek    1975/76

234

Museum
Bellerive
Transparente
Formen
4 Glasmacher
aus Prag

Zur Eröffnung der Ausstellung am Mittwoch, dem 1. Dezember, um 20 Uhr, sind Sie und Ihre Freunde herzlich eingeladen. Der Glaskünstler František Vizner wird anwesend sein.

Begrüssung durch Herrn Stadtrat Jakob Baur.

Aus dem Museumsbestand zeigen wir weiterhin Musikinstrumente der ehemaligen Sammlung Hug.

Ausstellungsdauer:
2. Dezember 1976 bis 13. Februar 1977
Öffnungszeiten:
Dienstag–Sonntag 10–12 und 14–17 Uhr
Montag geschlossen

235

**232, 233** Back cover (in red and yellow on black) and double page (black and white) from the catalogue of a design exhibition marking the opening of the Cooper-Hewitt Museum. (USA)
**234** Cover of a catalogue of readers for Swiss schools. Red and black on pink ground. (SWI)
**235** Wrapper of green transparent paper for the catalogue of an exhibition of Czech glass in Zurich. (SWI)
**236** Catalogue of a Calder exhibition in Zurich. Name in blue and green on red. (SWI)
**237** Announcement of a conference on Umbria's future. (ITA)
**238** Catalogue cover in greys and black for a national visual arts exhibition in Montreal. (CAN)
**239, 240** Both sides of a folder about a Naval Museum in Milan, with the envelope in which it was despatched. (ITA)

**232, 233** Umschlagrückseite (rot und gelb auf Schwarz) und Doppelseite (schwarz und weiss) aus dem Katalog einer Design-Ausstellung zur Eröffnung des Cooper-Hewitt-Museums. (USA)
**234** Titelblatt des SVB-Verzeichnisses der Zürcher Klassenlese-Serien. Rot und schwarz auf Weiss. (SWI)
**235** Grünes, durchscheinendes Einschlagpapier für den Katalog einer Ausstellung tschechischer Glaskünstler in Zürich. (SWI)
**236** Katalog einer Calder-Ausstellung. Name des Künstlers in Blau und Grün auf Rot. (SWI)
**237** «Das Umbrien von heute für das Umbrien von morgen.» Ankündigung einer Konferenz über die Zukunft Umbriens. (ITA)
**238** Ausstellungskatalog «Spektrum». Grau und schwarz. (CAN)
**239, 240** Umschlag und beide Seiten eines Faltprospektes über das Marine-Museum in Mailand. (ITA)

**232, 233** Verso (jaune et rouge sur noir) et page double (noir et blanc) du catalogue d'une exposition organisée à l'occasion de l'inauguration du musée Cooper-Hewitt. (USA)
**234** Couverture d'un catalogue présentant la série SVB pour la lecture en classe. Rouge et noir sur rose. (SWI)
**235** Feuille en papier vert transparent pour le catalogue d'une exposition d'objets en verre tchèques à Zurich. (SWI)
**236** Catalogue de l'exposition de Calder à Zurich. Le nom de l'artiste est imprimé en bleu et vert sur fond rouge. (SWI)
**237** Annonce d'une conférence sur l'avenir de l'Ombrie. (ITA)
**238** Couverture du catalogue (en noir et teintes grises) pour une exposition nationale des arts visuels à Montréal. (CAN)
**239, 240** Les deux côtés d'un dépliant consacré au musée de la marine à Milan ainsi que l'enveloppe qui le contenait. (ITA)

Kunsthaus Zürich
23. August bis 2. November 1975
Öffnungszeiten: Montag 14–17 Uhr, Dienstag–Sonntag 10–17 Uhr
und Dienstag–Freitag auch 20–22 Uhr
Sonntag, 21. September (Bettag) geschlossen

CALDER

236

"UMBRIA D'OGGI"
PER
L'UMBRIA DI DOMANI

A CURA DI UMBRIA D'OGGI PERIODICO DI INFORMAZIONE REPUBBLICANA

REDAZIONE ANN ME PERUGIA VIA DEGLI UFFICI, 4 CCP 19/2482 TELEFONO 62392 DIRETTORE RESPONSABILE MASSIMO ARCAMONE

CONVEGNO SULLE PROPOSTE DI ASSETTO TERRITORIALE DELLA REGIONE

ACQUASPARTA 9/10 NOVEMBRE 1973 PALAZZO CESI

237

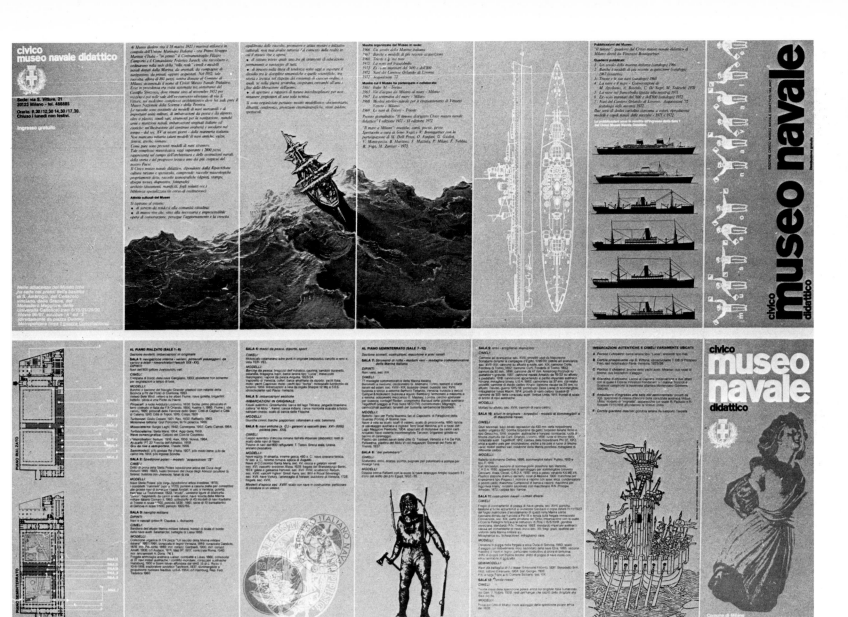

239

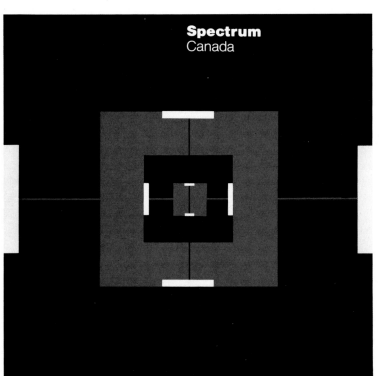

238

**Spectrum**
Canada

240

241

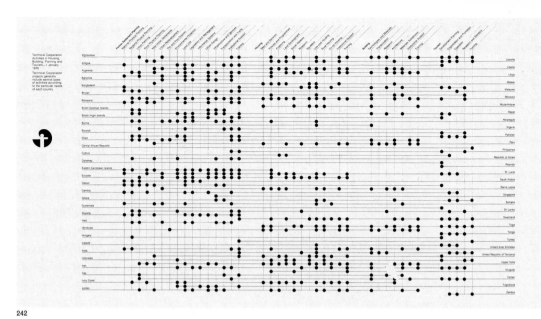

242

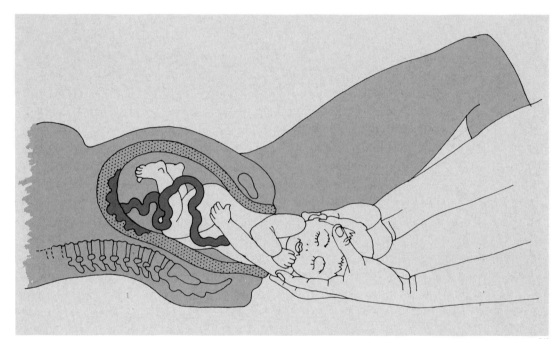

243

ARTIST / KÜNSTLER / ARTISTE:

243, 244  Benoit de Pierpont
246, 247  Dave Epstein

DESIGNER / GESTALTER / MAQUETTISTE:

241, 242  Roger Cook/Don Shanosky
243, 244  Benoit de Pierpont
245  Ulrich Höfs
246, 247  Dave Epstein
248  Richard Danne

ART DIRECTOR / DIRECTEUR ARTISTIQUE:

241, 242  Roger Cook/Don Shanosky
243, 244  Benoit de Pierpont
246, 247  Dave Epstein
248  Richard Danne

AGENCY / AGENTUR / AGENCE – STUDIO:

241, 242  Cook and Shanosky Assoc., Inc.
246, 247  Dave Epstein, Inc.
248  Danne & Blackburn, Inc.

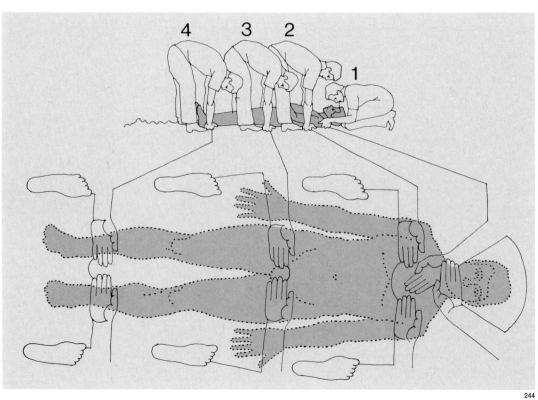

244

245

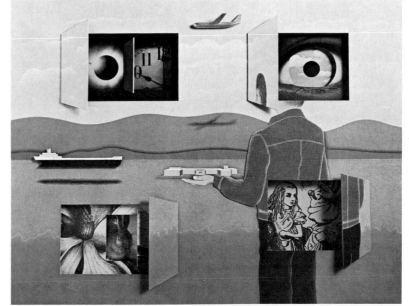

246

247

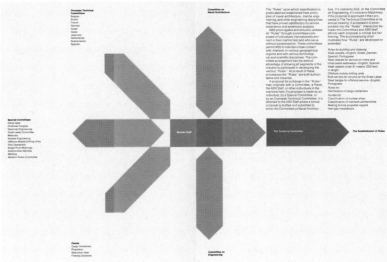

248

**241, 242** Cover and fold-out chart (technical co-operation projects) from a book-let on the UN Centre for Housing, Building and Planning. Blue symbol. (USA)
**243, 244** Drawings from a first-aid manual issued by the Belgian Red Cross: instructions for assistance at childbirth and for lifting a person with spinal injuries on to a stretcher. (BEL)
**245** Folder announcing a performance of The Cleveland Orchestra as part of the cultural programme of the BASF in Ludwigshafen. (GER)
**246, 247** Cover and page (both in full colour) from a large folder forming part of a promotion campaign for Mercy College, Dobbs Ferry, N.Y. (USA)
**248** Double spread with an organization diagram from a large brochure about the activities of the American Bureau of Shipping. (USA)

**241, 242** Umschlag und ausklappbare Tabelle (über technische Zusammenarbeit auf den Gebieten Wohnbau und -planung und Tourismus) aus einer Broschüre der Vereinten Nationen. Symbol und senkrechte Tabellenstriche blau. (USA)
**243, 244** Zeichnungen aus einem Erste-Hilfe-Handbuch des Belgischen Roten Kreuzes: Anweisungen für Geburtshilfe und das Heben eines an der Wirbelsäule Verletzten auf eine Tragbahre. In Brauntönen. (BEL)
**245** Vorderseite eines Faltprospektes für ein Konzert des Cleveland-Orchesters im Rahmen der kulturellen Veranstaltungen der BASF in Ludwigshafen. (GER)
**246, 247** Umschlag und eine Seite (beide mehrfarbig) aus einem grossformatigen Prospekt zur Eigenwerbung des Mercy College in Dobbs Ferry, New York. (USA)
**248** Doppelseite aus einem Organigramm, aus einer Broschüre über die Tätigkeit des American Bureau of Shipping. (USA)

**241, 242** Couverture et tableau à déplier (montrant des projets de coopération technique) d'une brochure consacrée au Centre de logement, de construction et de planification des Nations Unies. Symbole bleu. (USA)
**243, 244** Dessins d'un nouveau manuel du secouriste publié par la Croix-Rouge Belge, illustrant ici les instructions pour l'assistance à un accouchement et pour le chargement d'un blessé atteint d'une fracture de la colonne sur un brancard. (BEL)
**245** Dépliant annonçant un concert du Cleveland Orchestra organisé par la BASF dans le cadre de son programme culturel à Ludwigshafen. (GER)
**246, 247** Couverture et page (les deux en couleurs) d'un dépliant grand format pour la promotion du Mercy College à Dobbs Ferry, New York. (USA)
**248** Page double, montrant un organigramme, tirée d'une brochure grand format sur les activités du American Bureau of Shipping. (USA)

**Booklets / Prospekte / Brochures**

ARTIST / KÜNSTLER:

249 Fred Otnes
250 Adelchi Galloni
251 Brad Golland

DESIGNER / GESTALTER:

250 Adelchi Galloni
251 Brad Holland

ART DIRECTOR:

249 Vince Maiello
250 Bruno Binosi
251 Gordon Draper

250

249

251

**249** Promotional piece on an Agatha Christie novel for a *Doubleday* publication. (USA)
**250** Catalogue of holiday books published by *Mondadori*. Colour illustrations. (ITA)
**251** Half-yearly catalogue for the *T. Y. Crowell* publishing house. Coloured drawing on a pink background. (USA)

**249** Illustration zur Werbung für einen Kriminalroman von Agatha Christie, erschienen in einer von *Doubleday* publizierten Zeitschrift. (USA)
**250** «Reisen mit einem Buch.» Katalog mit den Ferienbüchern des *Mondadori*-Verlages (für Kinder und Erwachsene). Alle Illustrationen mehrfarbig. (ITA)
**251** Halbjährlich erscheinender Katalog des Verlagshauses *T. Y. Crowell,* hier mit einem Titelbild in Ocker, Grau und Rosa auf blassrosa Hintergrund. (USA)

**249** Illustration parue dans une publication promotionnelle de *Doubleday* pour un roman policier de Agatha Christie. (USA)
**250** «Voyagez avec le livre.» Catalogue des livres *Mondadori* recommandés pour les vacances. Toutes les illustrations sont en couleurs. (ITA)
**251** Catalogue semestriel de la maison d'édition *T. Y. Crowell.* La couverture montrée ici est en couleurs (ocre, gris et rose sur fond rose clair). (USA)

**Booklets / Prospekte / Brochures**

252

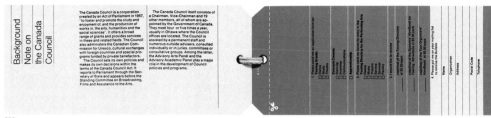

253

254

U.S. Department of Labor        Graphic Communication Standards Manual

255

258

# SCM PRESS
## March-July 1977

*and select list of SCM Press books on*
*Ethics and Social Issues*

259

Housing
Executive

Letter Writing
Staff Handbook

ARTIST / KÜNSTLER / ARTISTE:

254  Mas Nakagawa
255  Gertrud Rössler
256, 257  Vernon Smith/Ira
    Mandelbaum (Photo)
258  Korin Keefe
259  June Lambla

DESIGNER / GESTALTER:

252, 253  Peter Adam
255  Gertrud Rössler
256, 257  Robert P. Gersin/
    Ronald Wong
258  Korin Keefe
259  June Lambla
260  David Ashton
261  Joseph Moore

ART DIRECTOR:

252, 253  Gottschalk & Ash Ltd.
254  Dean R. Lindsay
255  Gertrud Rössler
256, 257  Robert P. Gersin
259  June Lambla
260  David Ashton
261  Stephen Logowitz

AGENCY / AGENTUR:

252, 253  Gottschalk & Ash Ltd.
254  Center for Advanced
    Research in Design
255  Atelier Rössler
256, 257  Robert P. Gersin
    Associates Inc.
260  Ashton-Worthington, Inc.
261  Logowitz & Moore
    Design Associates

**252, 253** Booklet in the form of a travel label and double page from it (with a reply postcard on the right) about the Touring Office of the Canada Council, created to stimulate touring by performing artists and companies. (CAN)
**254** Cover of the Graphic Communication Standards Manual issued by the US Department of Labour. Red and blue. (USA)
**255** One of four cards used by a Swiss skiing association in a campaign to recruit members and raise funds to support racing skiers. (SWI)
**256, 257** Double pages from a brochure calling for support for a burn centre in New York. (USA)
**258** Cover of a catalogue of SCM ethical and social books. Black and blue. (GBR)
**259** Cover of a staff handbook on letter writing for the Northern Ireland Housing Executive. Black and white with red lettering. (IRL)
**260** Catalogue for an exhibition of graphics by six Swiss sculptors that toured the US. Beige shades, pale grey and white. (USA)
**261** Cover of a folder about a Harvard University conference on health care management. Black and white, red type matter. (USA)

**252, 253** Prospekt in Form (und Farbe) einer Anhängeadresse und Doppelseite daraus (mit Bestellkarte auf der rechten Seite). Er wurde herausgegeben vom Reisebüro des Canada Council um Gastspielreisen von Theater- und Musikgruppen zu fördern. (CAN)
**254** Titelseite eines Handbuches für graphische Gestaltung, das vom amerikanischen Arbeitsministerium herausgegeben wurde. In Rot und Blau. (USA)
**255** Eine von vier Karten, die der Schweizerische Skiverband für eine Kampagne zur Mitgliederwerbung und zur Unterstützung der Skirennfahrer drucken liess. (SWI)
**256, 257** Aus einer Broschüre für Mithilfe beim Bau einer Abteilung für Verbrennungskranke. (USA)
**258** Umschlag des Kataloges für Bücher über Ethik und Soziales des SCM-Verlages. (GBR)
**259** Titelseite eines Handbuches über das Schreiben guter Geschäftsbriefe, das die Nordirische Wohnbau-Exekutive für ihre Angestellten herausgab. Schwarzweiss, rote Titel. (IRL)
**260** Katalog für eine Wanderausstellung: Graphiken von sechs bekannten Schweizer Bildhauern in den USA. In Beige, Hellgrau und Weiss. (USA)
**261** Titelseite eines Faltprospektes über eine Konferenz an der Harvard Universität mit dem Thema: finanzielles Management und Politik der Gesundheitspflege. Schwarzweiss, Titel rot. (USA)

256

257

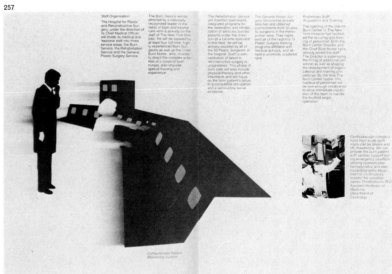

260

Graphics
by        Six
          Swiss        Sculptors

261

Harvard University        Program for Financial        October
                          Management and               24–30, 1976
                          Strategy in Health

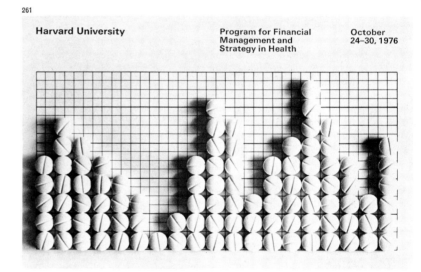

**252, 253** Prospectus sous forme d'étiquette de valise et page double y figurant (avec une carte de commande à droite) publié par l'Office de tourisme du Canada Council pour encourager les tournées des ensembles de théâtre et des orchestres. (CAN)
**254** Couverture d'un manuel consacré à la communication graphique. Elément publié par le Ministère de Travail des Etats-Unis. En rouge et bleu. (USA)
**255** Elément d'une série de quatre cartes destinées à recruter de nouveaux membres et de réunir des fonds pour une association suisse soutenant les skieurs de course. (SWI)
**256, 257** Brochure pour réunir des fonds en faveur d'un hôpital soignant les brûlures. (USA)
**258** Couverture d'un catalogue d'œuvres d'éthique et de sociologie publiés par SCM. (GBR)
**259** Couverture d'un manuel sur l'art d'écrire de bonnes lettres d'affaires, distribué par un service public de l'Irlande du nord à ses employés. Noir et blanc, titres rouges. (IRL)
**260** Catalogue d'une exposition itinérante aux Etats-Unis présentant les travaux graphiques de six sculpteurs suisses de renom. Teintes beiges, gris clair et blanc. (USA)
**261** Couverture d'un dépliant annonçant une conférence à l'Université de Harvard sur la gestion en matière de santé publique. En noir et blanc, caractères rouges. (USA)

**Booklets / Prospekte / Brochures**

ARTIST / KÜNSTLER / ARTISTE:

262, 263 Tony Stewart/
Kate Burness
264, 265 Alexander Kamenz
267 Franklin McMahon
269 René Althaus
270 Jörg Hermle

DESIGNER / GESTALTER:

264, 265 Schumann-Werbung
266 Michele Spera
268 Harry Williams/Tom Morgan
269 René Althaus
270 Jörg Hermle

ART DIRECTOR:

262, 263 Tony Stewart
264, 265 Alexander Kamenz
267 Peter Kiar/Kristie Clemons
268 D. R. Jones
269 Josef Rauchenstein
270 Jörg Hermle

AGENCY / AGENTUR:

262, 263 Grey Advertising Pty. Ltd.
264, 265 Schumann-Werbung
267 Gerhardt & Kiar
270 Industrie Service

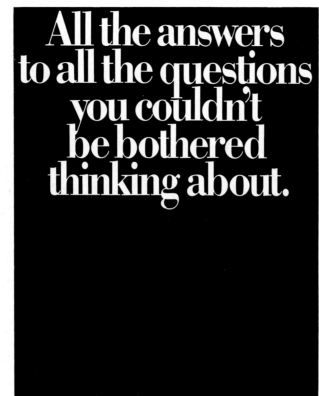

262

## What if you get sea sick like your sister does?

Before we can even attempt to answer this particularly prudent question in the detail it deserves, we really should have some sort of idea of just how seasick the sister in question does get. And obviously, that poses quite a problem, because you're not here to tell us.

So let us begin, by looking at a couple of purely hypothetical situations. For example, suppose the seasickness appears to be the plain, ordinary, not-being-used-to-being-at-sea type seasickness. If this is the case, we will simply give you treatment to relieve the nausea until you're able to find your sea legs naturally; a process which will normally take only a couple of days.

But if what you're suffering from goes beyond the mere nausea, misery and embarrassment which is normally caused by a ship's rolling motion, then the chances are that you're not really seasick at all.

So the first thing we'd have to do, is get one of our doctors to take a good, long look at you.

Although any kind of illness is liable to cause you a certain amount of pain and discomfort, we're pleased to be able to say that it shouldn't cause too much of a problem for the Navy.

For the simple reason that wherever you happen to be, and whenever you happen to be there, you can feel rest assured that at least one Navy doctor will always be somewhere in the immediate vicinity.

Of course, it's all very comforting to know that highly skilled medical assistance will always be nearby, but that doesn't really solve a whole lot of other problems that are liable to arise when you fall ill.

Because with most illnesses, it's not just your body that's being attacked. Even when you're well and truly on the road to recovery, you could still be losing a lot of money in the pay that you don't get while you're off work sick. So while you're no longer sick with illness, you could very easily start to become sick with worry.

At least that's the sort of thing that is able to happen to people in most jobs.

Once again, we're very happy to be able to inform you that in a lot of ways, a job in the Royal Australian Navy is completely different to just about any other type of job, just about anywhere else. So it probably won't come as any great surprise to you when you learn that the Navy just happens to have found a very clever solution to this rather worrying problem.

While our immediate reaction will be to get our doctors onto your case our next reaction will be to keep our pay office well and truly out of it.

That way, you won't be required to pay a single, solitary cent in medical bills, and you won't have to lose a single, solitary cent from your pay packet. So when you do recover, you'll probably find that your bank balance will be just as healthy as you are.

Even in the unlikely event that you come down with the sort of illness that requires a very long, very slow convalescence, you'll still be encouraged to convalesce, and you'll be encouraged on full pay. And the same applies if things become even worse than that.

The way the Navy looks at it, if you're going to be sick, you might as well be sick in relative security, with compensation or a disability pension if you need it.

Although that's probably not the complete solution, it's certainly not a bad beginning.

So by now, it should be perfectly clear that the Navy will do everything possible to look after you completely.

All you have to do is supply the illness. Which could be harder than you think when you remember all that fresh, salt air you'll be getting.

263

MICHELE SPERA
GRAFICA
E COMUNICAZIONE

CON IL PATROCINIO
DEL COMUNE
SIENA/ENTRONE DEL
PALAZZO COMUNALE
19 LUGLIO
9 AGOSTO 1974

266

The Institute of Psychiatry

Northwestern
Memorial Hospital

267

Ferien 76

Bulgarien        Ägypten
Frankreich       Israel
Griechenland     Marokko
Italien          Tunesien
Jugoslawien      Türkei
Portugal
Rumänien
Spanien

Schweizerische Volksbank

269

**262, 263** Black-and-white spreads from a tall, large-format recruitment brochure for the US Navy. (USA)
**264, 265** Cover and page (both in full colour) from an album of stick-in pictures for a zoo in Münster, sponsored by a company operating 20 petrol stations in the neighbourhood. (GER)
**266** Catalogue for an exhibition of graphics by Michele Spera organized by the city of Siena. Red, purple, black and white. (ITA)
**267** Cover of a booklet about the Institute of Psychiatry attached to the Northwestern Memorial Hospital of Chicago. (USA)
**268** Double page from a tourist's guide to mid Wales. Photographs and diagrams in full colour. (GBR)
**269** Cover of a holiday information booklet issued by a Swiss bank. Orange, green, red and black. (SWI)
**270** One side of a folder about the *Mercure* chain of hotels. Information is given on the other side of the folder. (FRA)

Booklets
Prospekte
Brochures

264

15. ›Nancy‹
Eine Seelöwin, die Bälle jongliert, auf einer Flosse "Handstand" macht und auf Kommando wie ein Pfeil durch das Wasser schießt. Zur Belohnung bekommt sie reichlich Fisch, und paßt der Trainer nicht auf, stibitzt sie sich eine Zusatzration aus dem Fischeimer.

16. ›James‹
Ein Delphin von der Gattung Großer Tümmler. Diese höchst intelligenten Tiere sind besonders zahm und gelehrig. Was sie alles können, zeigen sie täglich in einer großartigen artistischen Show und begeistern nicht nur die kleinen Besucher.

17. ›Milly‹
Diese Tümmler-Dame liebt das Blindekuh-Spiel. Delphine können sich auch mit verdeckten Augen im Wasser orientieren. Sie verfügen über eine Sonaranlage: Mit Hilfe einer Echopeilung wird die Beute blitzschnell geortet.

265

**262, 263** Doppelseiten in Schwarzweiss aus einem grossen, hochformatigen Werbeprospekt für die Marine der Vereinigten Staaten, «Ihre erste Karriere». (USA)
**264, 265** Titelseite und eine Doppelseite aus einem Sammelalbum mit Bildchen zum Einkleben: Verbundwerbung für einen neuen Zoo in Münster und für die Sauerstoffwerk Westfalen AG, die in der Umgebung des Zoos zwanzig Tankstellen unterhält. Alle Illustrationen in bunten Farben. (GER)
**266** Katalog für eine Ausstellung der Graphiken von Michele Spera in Siena, unter dem Patronat der Stadt Siena. Rot, lila und weiss auf Schwarz. (ITA)
**267** Umschlag einer Broschüre über ein psychiatrisches Institut in Chicago. (USA)
**268** Doppelseite aus einem Touristenhandbuch und Reiseführer über das mittlere Wales. Photos, topographische Skizzen und geographische Karten mehrfarbig. (GBR)
**269** Titelblatt eines Ferienführers der Schweizerischen Volksbank. In Orange, Kirschrot, Hellgrün, Oliv und Schwarz auf Weiss. (SWI)
**270** Ganze Aussenseite eines Faltprospektes über die Hotelkette *Mercure*, mit Informationen auf der Innenseite. Mehrfarbig, Decke rosa-weiss gestreift, Bus grün und weiss. (FRA)

**262, 263** Pages doubles en noir et blanc, tirées d'une brochure grand format visant à recruter des jeunes gens pour la marine de guerre des Etats-Unis. (USA)
**264, 265** Couverture et page d'un album avec images à coller pour la promotion d'un nouveau zoo à Munster patronné par une compagnie qui tient vingt postes d'essence dans les allentours. Toutes les illustrations sont en couleurs vives. (GER)
**266** Catalogue pour une exposition des travaux graphiques de Michele Spera à Siéna, patronnée par la ville de Siéna. En rouge, mauve et blanc sur fond noir. (ITA)
**267** Couverture d'un prospectus consacré à un institut de psychiatrie à Chicago. (USA)
**268** Page double d'un guide illustré du pays de Galles central. Photos et croquis (géographiques et topographiques) en couleurs. (GBR)
**269** Couverture d'un guide de vacances publié par la Banque Populaire Suisse. En orange, cerise, vert clair, olive et noir sur blanc. (SWI)
**270** Recto d'un dépliant présentant la chaîne d'hôtels *Mercure*; on donne des renseignements supplémentaires au verso. En couleurs; couverture rayée rose-blanc, bus en vert et blanc. (FRA)

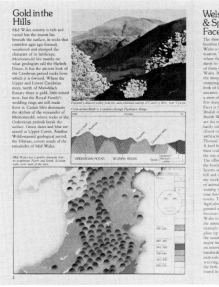

268

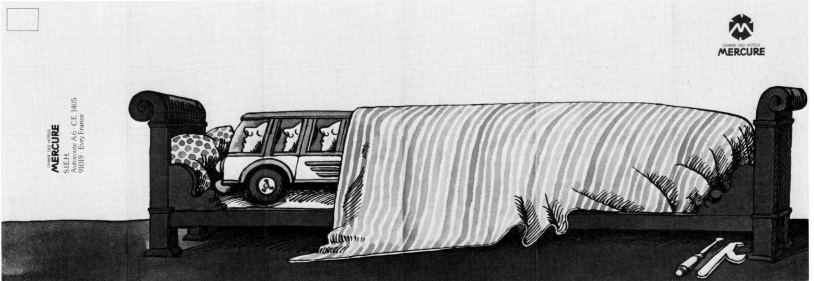

270

**271, 272** Cover and page (showing Nathan Bedford Forrest, black and white) from a booklet about battles in the American Civil War issued by the National Park Service. (USA)
**273** Double spread from a small booklet for Omni International Hotels, Inc. Here illustrating big, dreary hotels. Black and white. (USA)
**274** Bar card for the Atrium Hotel, Brunswick. Bottles in full colour. (GER)
**275, 276, 279** Maps (black and blue on pale beige) and title page from a booklet containing the official maps of the Olympic Games in Montreal, 1976. (CAN)
**277** Leaflet on design quality control at the Montreal Olympic Games. Red ground. (CAN)
**278** Symbol from the signage manual of the Montreal Olympic Games, showing its position in a modular square. (CAN)

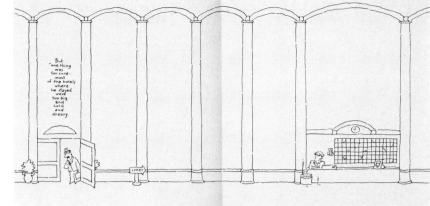

271

Protecting Sherman's Lifeline

272

274

ARTIST / KÜNSTLER / ARTISTE:

271, 272 Michael David Brown
273 Kenny «C. K.» Higdon
274 Günter Bleyl (Photo)
275, 276 Promosit Inc.
277 Pierre Fontaine
278 Georges Huel

DESIGNER / GESTALTER:

271, 272 Michael David Brown
273 Dick Henderson
274 Zisowsky + Oehring
277 Pierre Fontaine
278 Georges Huel
279 Stuart Ash/Peter Adam/
    Marc Soifer

ART DIRECTOR:

271, 272 Michael David Brown
273 Dick Henderson
274 Zisowsky + Oehring
275–277 Pierre-Yves Pelletier/
    Georges Huel
278 Georges Huel
279 Gottschalk & Ash Ltd.

AGENCY / AGENTUR:

271, 272 Michael David Brown
273 Cole Henderson Drake
274 Udo Zisowsky
275–277 Comité organisateur
    des Jeux Olympiques
    de 1976
278 Georges Huel & Associés
279 Gottschalk & Ash Ltd.

Jeux de la
XXIe Olympiade
**Montréal
1976**

Games of the
XXI Olympiad
**Montréal
1976**

Office du contrôle
de la qualité
et du design

Design
Quality Control
Office

277

271, 272 Titelblatt und Seite (Schwarzweissportrait eines berühmten Kavallerie-Hauptmannes) aus einer Broschüre über den Amerikanischen Bürgerkrieg, herausgegeben vom Innenministerium. (USA)
273 Doppelseite aus einem kleinen Prospekt für die Omni International Hotels, Inc., hier mit der Szenerie eines trostlosen riesigen Hotels. Illustrationen alle schwarzweiss. (USA)
274 Barkarte (Flaschen mehrfarbig) für das Atrium Hotel in Braunschweig. (GER)
275, 276, 279 Karten (blau und schwarz auf Hellbeige) und Titelseite aus einem Prospekt mit dem offiziellen Lageplan des Olympischen Geländes 1976 und einem Stadtplan von Montreal. (CAN)
277 Merkblatt über Designqualitätskontrolle an den Olympischen Spielen in Montreal 1976. (CAN)
278 Symbol aus dem umfangreichen Signage Manual der Olympischen Spiele 1976, hier in seiner exakten Stellung innerhalb eines Quadrates. (CAN)

271, 272 Couverture et page (portrait d'un capitaine de cavalerie célèbre) d'une brochure consacrée à la Guerre civile américaine publiée par le National Park Service. (USA)
273 Page double d'une petite brochure consacrée à la Omni International Hotels, Inc. On voit ici un vaste hôtel désolant. Noir et blanc. (AUS)
274 Carte des boissons du bar de l'hôtel Atrium à Brunswick. Bouteilles en couleurs. (GER)
275, 276, 279 Cartes (réseau routier, communications souterraines) et couverture d'une publication officielle des Jeux Olympiques 1976 à Montréal. Noir et bleu sur crème. (CAN)
277 Prospectus sur le contrôle de qualité du design des Jeux à Montréal. Fond rouge. (CAN)
278 Illustration extraite du Manuel de signalisation, montrant l'emblème des Jeux sur fond rouge olympique et sa position exacte dans le module carré. (CAN)

**Booklets**
**Prospekte**
**Brochures**

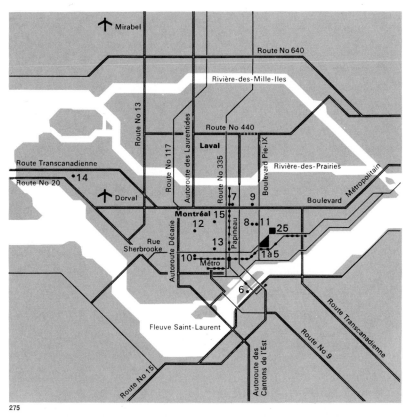

275

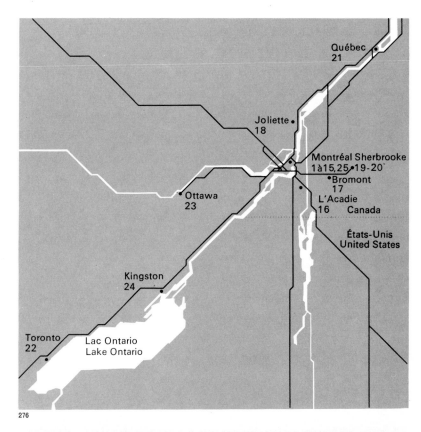

276

278

279

280

281

**280–282** Cover (with gold sun) and two double pages from a retrospective brochure on the Fête des Vignerons in Vevey, published by *Nestlé*. (SWI)
**283, 286** One side of folders about seminars on business planning (Fig. 283 in the food industry), organized in Toronto by Currie, Coopers & Lybrand Ltd. (CAN)
**284** One side of an invitation to an exhibition on the cinema in Zurich. Black and red on brown stock. (SWI)
**285** Invitation to a reading of the works of Sylvia Plath in Adelaide. Black and white. (AUS)
**287** One side of a winegrower's calendar mailed by the Club Français du Vin. Colour illustrations. (FRA)
**288** Fold-over cover (red horse) of a brochure addressed to traders about *Cavallino Rosso* brandy. (ITA)

**280–282** Umschlag (mit goldener Sonne) und zwei Doppelseiten aus einer Broschüre von *Nestlé* über das Winzerfest von Vevey, mit Rückblick auf frühere Winzerfeste (belegt seit 1651). (SWI)
**283, 286** Aussenseite von Faltprospekten für Seminarien über Geschäftsplanung (Abb. 283 in der Lebensmittelbranche). (CAN)
**284** Ganze Aussenseite einer Einladung zur Eröffnung der Ausstellung «Hätte ich das Kino!» im Kunstgewerbemuseum in Zürich. Weiss, schwarz und rot auf braunem Grund, nach einem Motiv aus Ludwig Kainer, «Das Kinobuch», 1914. (SWI)
**285** Illustration auf der Einladung zu einer Lesung aus Sylvia Plaths Werken in Adelaide. Schwarz und weiss. (AUS)
**287** Eine Seite eines Weinbauernkalenders, den der Club Français du Vin versandte. Illustrationen in hellen Farben. (FRA)
**288** Übereinandergefaltete Vorderseite einer Broschüre über den Brandy *Cavallino Rosso* (rotes Pferdchen), für Detaillisten. (ITA)

**280–282** Couverture (soleil doré) et deux pages doubles d'une brochure publiée par *Nestlé* et consacrée à la Fête des Vignerons à Vevey qu'on y célèbre depuis 1651. (SWI)
**283, 286** Couvertures de dépliants annonçant divers séminaires consacrés à la gestion et au planning. (CAN)
**284** Panneau extérieur d'une invitation à une exposition sur le cinéma («Si j'avais le cinéma!») organisée au musée des arts et métiers à Zurich. Rouge et noir sur fond brun. (SWI)
**285** Invitation à une séance de lecture des œuvres de Sylvia Plath à Adelaide. Noir et blanc. (AUS)
**287** Recto du calendrier du vigneron distribué par le Club Français du Vin. Illustrations en couleurs atténuées. (FRA)
**288** Couverture à volet superposé d'un prospectus pour *Cavallino Rosso*, une marque de brandy. Rouge sur crème. (ITA)

ARTIST / KÜNSTLER / ARTISTE:

280–282 Yves Racheter
284 Ludwig Kainer
285 Maire Smith
287 Jean Claverie
288 Aldo Lanfranco

DESIGNER / GESTALTER / MAQUETTISTE:

283 Stuart Ash
284 Heinz Finger
285 Barry Tucker
286 Tiit Telmet
288 Franco Pilutti

**Booklets / Prospekte / Brochures**

283

286

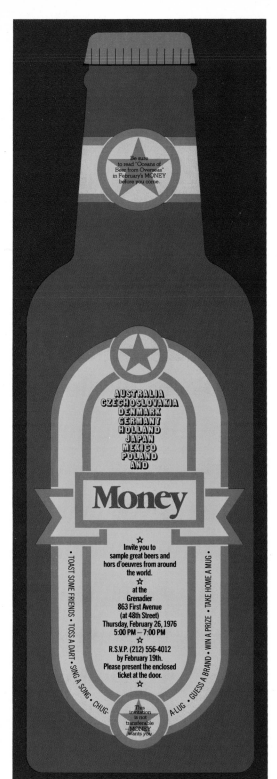

303

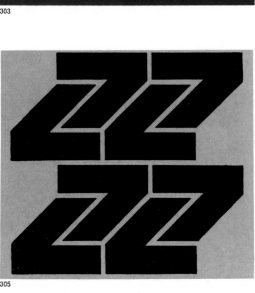

305

ARTIST / KÜNSTLER / ARTISTE:

299 Ramond Savignac
300 Jean Larcher
301 Gisela + Niko Adlesic
302 Iris vom Hof
303 Gilbert Lesser
304 Anton Stankowski
305 Felix Beltran
306 Anne Delahaye/Christian Quennehen
307 Hiromu Hara

DESIGNER / GESTALTER / MAQUETTISTE:

297, 298 Woody Pirtle/Jerry Herring
303 Gilbert Lesser

ART DIRECTOR / DIRECTEUR ARTISTIQUE:

297, 298 Woody Pirtle/Gayle Ware
303 Gilbert Lesser

AGENCY / AGENTUR / AGENCE – STUDIO:

297, 298 Smith, Smith, Baldwin & Carlberg

306

307

**297, 298** Invitation to the opening of the Atascocita Country Club and golf course, with transparent overlay. (USA)
**299** New Year's card from an artist. Man in brown, wife in bright red. (FRA)
**300** Black-and-white New Year's card with graphic treatment of the sevens. (FRA)
**301** New Year's card from an artist couple. Year in purplish blue on lime green. (GER)
**302** An artist's wishes for a new year—or Paradise. Black and white with year in green. (GER)
**303** Large invitation to a beer and hors d'œuvre party organized by the financial magazine *Money*. (USA)
**304** "Change is a sign of the times." New Year's card. Grey figures with a changing colour (green/red/blue). (GER)
**305** New Year's card for 1977. Red on yellow. (CUB)
**306** Artists' New Year's card. Green cats wish the receiver a "purring" year. (FRA)
**307** New Year's card folding to form an envelope, for the Nippon Design Center: star becomes bird. (JPN)

**297, 298** Einladung zur Eröffnung eines Golfklubs, mit durchsichtigem Deckblatt. Grasgrün, gelb, weiss. (USA)
**299** Neujahrskarte eines Künstlers. Mann in Braun, Frau in Kirschrot (Kleid, Stiefel und Haar). (FRA)
**300** Graphische Interpretation der Jahreszahl '77, in Schwarzweiss, für eine Neujahrskarte. (FRA)
**301** Neujahrskarte eines Künstler-Ehepaars: die Zahl '76 in Violett auf gelbgrünem Grund. (GER)
**302** Glückwünsche für ein neues Jahr – oder Paradies? Illustration schwarzweiss, Jahreszahl grün. (GER)
**303** Grossformatige Einladung zu einer Bier- und Hors-d'Oeuvres-Party; Gastgeber ist die Finanzzeitschrift *Money*. (USA)
**304** «Wandlungen sind ein Zeichen der Zeit.» Graue Figuren in wechselnden Farben für eine Neujahrskarte. (GER)
**305** Neujahrskarte mit variierten '77; Rot auf Gelb. (CUB)
**306** Neujahrskarte eines Künstlerpaares: grüne Katzen wünschen ein «schnurrendes» Jahr. (FRA)
**307** Zu einem Umschlag faltbare Neujahrskarte für das Nippon Design Center: aus einem Stern wird ein Vogel. (JPN)

**297, 298** Invitation (avec feuille superposée transparente) à l'ouverture d'un club de golf. Blanc, jaune, vert. (USA)
**299** Carte de Nouvel An réalisée par un artiste. L'homme est en brun, la femme entièrement en rouge cerise. (FRA)
**300** Carte en noir et blanc avec interprétation graphique du chiffre «sept». (FRA)
**301** Carte de Nouvel An réalisée par un couple d'artistes. Chiffres en bleu pourpré sur fond vert citron. (GER)
**302** Meilleurs vœux pour le Nouvel An – ou le paradis? Noir et blanc, chiffres en vert. (GER)
**303** Invitation grand format à une soirée de bière et d'hors d'œuvres offert par le journal *Money*. (USA)
**304** «Changer est un signe des temps.» Motifs gris aux couleurs changeantes (vert/bleu/rouge). Carte de vœux. GER)
**305** Carte de Nouvel An pour 1977. Rouge sur jaune. (CUB)
**306** Carte de Nouvel An réalisée par un couple d'artistes. Chats en vert. (FRA)
**307** Carte de Nouvel An se pliant en enveloppe, l'étoile se muant en oiseau, du Nippon Design Center. (JPN)

308

*(Rum White & Blue booklet)*

309

ARTIST / KÜNSTLER / ARTISTE:

308, 309 Gilbert Lesser
310, 311 Edvard + Marja Mlinar
312 Ivan Chermayeff
313 Atelier Freund
314 Peter Mandzjuk
315, 316 Václav Houf

**308, 309** Cover and one side of a large folder mailed as an invitation to a party hosted by the magazine *People* and Puerto Rican rums. (USA)
**310, 311** New Year's card shown flat and opened to form a standing sphere which also reveals the good wishes from an artist couple. (NLD)
**312** Menu card for "The White Elephant on the River". (USA)
**313** New Year's card despatched by a design studio in Austria. The silver rosette opens to reveal the greetings. (AUT)
**314** Artist's card with a comic strip about a pencil that finally sends New Year's wishes. (SWI)
**315, 316** Two openings of a theatre programme for a drama presented in Brno. The varying page widths permit changes of scene. Drawings black and white. (CSR)

**308, 309** Titelseite und Aussenseite eines grossen Faltprospektes, als Einladung zu einer von der Zeitschrift *People* (Leute) und von Puerto Rican Rum veranstalteten Party versandt. (USA)
**310, 311** Neujahrskarte eines Künstlerehepaars, einmal flach gezeigt, einmal zu einer stehenden Kugel aufgeklappt, wobei die guten Wünsche sichtbar werden. (NLD)
**312** Menükarte für den «Weissen Elefanten am Fluss». (USA)
**313** Neujahrskarte in Silber; beim Öffnen der Rosette werden die guten Wünsche enthüllt. (AUT)
**314** Neujahrskarte eines Künstlers mit einer Bildergeschichte über den Bleistift, der schlussendlich die guten Wünsche schreibt. Schwarz und weiss. (SWI)
**315, 316** Innenansichten eines Theaterprogramms für eine Aufführung in Brünn. Die ungleich grossen Seiten ermöglichen verschiedene «Szenenaufbauten». Illustrationen schwarzweiss. (CSR)

**308, 309** Couverture et l'un des côtés d'un dépliant envoyé comme invitation à une fête organisée par le magazine *People* (gens) et les rums de Puerto Rico. (USA)
**310, 311** Carte de Nouvel An, montré à plat et ouverte, sous forme de globe faisant apparaître les vœux, réalisée par un couple d'artistes. (NLD)
**312** Carte de menus pour «L'éléphant blanc au bord de la rivière». (USA)
**313** Carte de Nouvel An, envoyée par un studio autrichien, en forme de rosette en argent. Les vœux apparaissent à l'ouverture de la carte. (AUT)
**314** Bande dessinée sur le thème du crayon qui enverra les vœux de Nouvel An; noir et blanc. (SWI)
**315, 316** Deux pages doubles figurant dans le programme d'une représentation de théâtre à Brno. Les pages de grandeur différente permettent les changements de scène. (CSR)

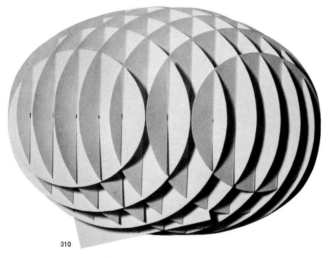

310

311

312

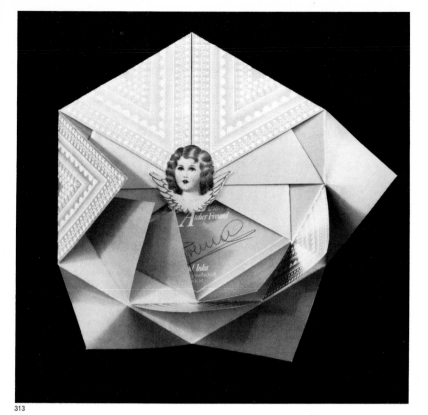

313

314

315

DESIGNER / GESTALTER / MAQUETTISTE:

308, 309  Gilbert Lesser
312  Ivan Chermayeff
315, 316  Václav Houf

ART DIRECTOR / DIRECTEUR ARTISTIQUE:

308, 309  Gilbert Lesser
312  Ivan Chermayeff

AGENCY / AGENTUR / AGENCE – STUDIO:

312  Chermayeff & Geismar Associates

316

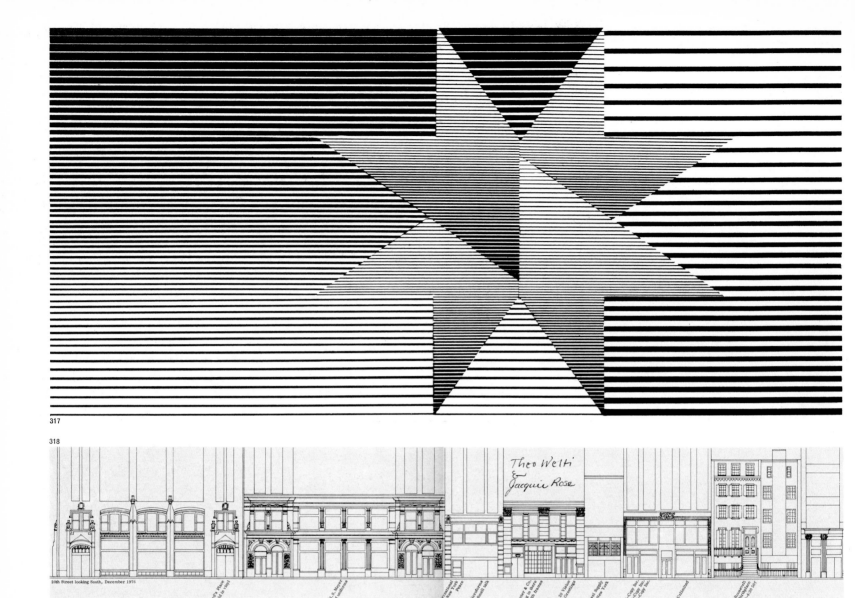

317

318

Theo Welti
Jacquie Rose

20th Street looking South, December 1976

ARTIST / KÜNSTLER / ARTISTE:

318  Theo Welti
319  Hans Hartmann
320, 321  Eduard Prüssen
322, 323  Joseph Boggs
324  Adriano Crivelli
325  Heinz Edelmann

**Booklets / Prospekte / Brochures**

319

320

321

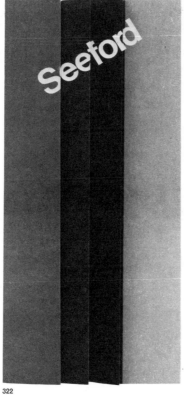

322

323

324

325

**317** One panel of a Christmas card sent out by the printers Industria Gráfica SA with a wish for peace in 1977. Grey and white. (SPA)
**318** Part of a long New Year's card despatched by an artist. The red-brown drawing of a street includes the artist's own headquarters. (USA)
**319** Artist's New Year's card that can be bent over and tucked in to form a standing owl. Grey, white and black with ochre eyes. (SWI)
**320** A fish deity in brown, red and olive green bearing good wishes from an artist for the New Year. Linocut. (GER)
**321** Linocut for a chemical company's New Year's card. (GER)
**322, 323** Christmas card for Seeford Organization, Inc., printers. When the concertina card is opened, the name expands into season's greetings. Red, green, blue and orange. (USA)
**324** Artist's New Year's card in black and red. (ITA)
**325** New Year's card from a publisher. In full colour. (GER)

**317** Mittelteil einer Weihnachtskarte (grau und weiss) der Druckerei Industria Gráfica SA, mit dem Wunsch für Frieden im Jahr 1977. (SPA)
**318** Teil einer langen Neujahrskarte mit einer Zeichnung (rotbraun) der Strasse, in der auch der Künstler selbst lebt. (USA)
**319** Zu einer stehenden Eule zusammensteckbare Karte mit den guten Wünschen eines Künstlers. Grau, schwarz, weiss, mit ockergelben Augen. (SWI)
**320** Eine Fischgottheit (in Braun, Rot und Oliv) bringt die Neujahrswünsche eines Künstlers. Linolschnitt. (GER)
**321** Neujahrskarte der Chem. Fabrik Kalk GmbH, Köln. Linolschnitt. (GER)
**322, 323** Weihnachtskarte einer Druckerei, deren Name sich beim Öffnen des Leporellos zu guten Wünschen erweitert. Weiss auf Rot, Grün, Blau und Orange. (USA)
**324** Eines Künstlers Neujahrskarte in Schwarz und Rostrot. (ITA)
**325** Neujahrskarte des Gertraud Middelhauve Verlages. Mehrfarbig. (GER)

**317** Panneau central d'une carte de Noël envoyée par les imprimeries Industria Gráfica SA qui souhaitent la paix en 1977. En gris et blanc. (SPA)
**318** Partie d'une longue carte de Nouvel An envoyée par un artiste. Le dessin en brun roux comprend aussi le studio de l'artiste. (USA)
**319** Carte qui se plie et se rabat sous forme d'un hibou qui se tient debout. En gris, noir, blanc, aux yeux ochre. (SWI)
**320** Divinité pisciforme (en brun, rouge et olive) apportant les vœux de Nouvel An d'un artiste. Gravure sur linoléum. (GER)
**321** Gravure sur linoléum pour la carte d'une fabrique de produits chimiques. (GER)
**322, 323** Carte d'une imprimerie. Les lettres du nom se retrouvent dans les vœux qui surgissent quand on ouvre le dépliant accordéon. Rouge, vert, bleu, orange. (USA)
**324** Carte de Nouvel An envoyée par un artiste. En noir et brun roux. (ITA)
**325** Carte de Nouvel An (en couleurs) d'une maison d'édition. (GER)

DESIGNER / GESTALTER / MAQUETTISTE:

317 Marcel Pagés
322, 323 Joseph Boggs
324 Adriano Crivelli

ART DIRECTOR / DIRECTEUR ARTISTIQUE:

317 Carlos Catalan

AGENCY / AGENTUR / AGENCE – STUDIO:

317 Printer Industria Gráfica SA
322, 323 Joseph Boggs/Design

# 3

Newspaper Illustrations
Magazine Illustrations
Trade Magazines
Magazine Covers
House Organs
Annual Reports
Book Covers

Zeitungs-Illustrationen
Zeitschriften-Illustrationen
Fachzeitschriften
Zeitschriften-Umschläge
Hauszeitschriften
Jahresberichte
Buchumschläge

Illustrations de journaux
Illustrations de périodiques
Revues professionnelles
Couvertures de périodiques
Journaux d'entreprises
Rapports annuels
Couvertures de livres

326

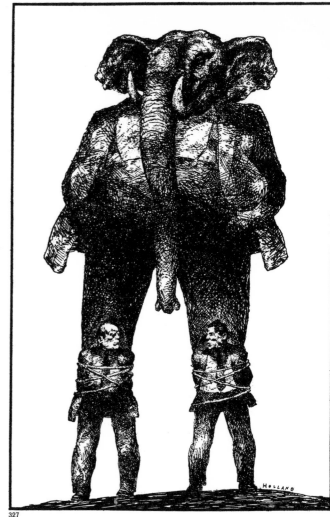

327

**326** Woodcut illustrating an article on the Op-Ed page of *The New York Times.* A professor writes about the reactions of students to his presentation of developments in Nazi Germany. (USA)
**327** Pen-and-ink illustration for an article published in *The New York Times* in which two Republicans discuss the future policy of the Republican Party. (USA)
**328, 329** Complete page of the weekly review section of *The New York Times* and pen-and-ink illustration for an article in which methods of dealing with terrorists are discussed in the light of the Israeli raid in Entebbe. (USA)
**330** Illustration (pen-and-ink drawing) for an article on the Op-Ed page of *The New York Times* discussing the influence of business magnates (known as "fat cats") on politics. (USA)
**331** Illustration for an article in *The New York Times* on "Cruelty in Vegetarianism". (USA)

**326** Holzschnitt zum Artikel eines Professors, der über seine Erfahrungen berichtet, die er in Vorlesungen und Seminaren über Nazi-Deutschland machte. Aus der *New York Times.* (USA)
**327** Illustration zu einem in der *New York Times* erschienenen Artikel, in welchem zwei republikanische Abgeordnete die Politik ihrer Partei diskutieren. (USA)
**328, 329** Vollständige Seite und Illustration aus dem politischen Wochenrückblick der *New York Times.* Die im Zusammenhang mit dem Geiseldrama in Entebbe aufgeworfenen Grundsatzfragen über die gegenüber einzunehmende Haltung werden hier analysiert. (USA)
**330** Illustration der Op-Ed-Seite (gegenüber dem Leitartikel) der *New York Times* zu einem Artikel über die «fat cats», wie die den Präsidentschaftswahlkampf unterstützenden finanzkräftigen Geschäftsleute genannt werden. (USA)
**331** Illustration zu einem Artikel der *New York Times* über «Grausamkeit des Vegetarismus» (USA)

**326** Gravure sur bois pour l'article d'un professeur qui discute les expériences qu'il a faites pendant des cours consacrés à l'Allemagne au temps du nazisme. Du *New York Times.* (USA)
**327** Illustration pour un article du *New York Times* dans lequel deux hommes politiques du parti Républicain discutent les points de vue de leur parti. (USA)
**328, 329** Page entière et illustration d'une rétrospective hebdomadaire du *New York Times.* Article sur la libération des otages à Entebbe et la lutte antiterroriste menée par Israël. (USA)
**330** Illustration de la page Op-Ed (face à l'éditorial) du *New York Times* accompagnant un article sur les «fat cats» (gros chats), nom donné aux magnats de l'industrie et de la finance soutenant la campagne électorale aux Etats-Unis. (USA)
**331** Illustration d'un article sur «la cruauté des végétariens», paru dans le *New York Times.* (USA)

328

329

ARTIST / KÜNSTLER / ARTISTE:

326 Fritz Eichenberg
327 Brad Holland
328, 329 Geoffrey Moss
330 Jean-Claude Suarès
331 Marguerita Bornstein

DESIGNER / GESTALTER:

327, 331 Steve Heller

ART DIRECTOR:

326, 327, 330, 331 Steve Heller
328, 329 Jerelle Kraus

PUBLISHER / VERLEGER / EDITEUR:

326–331 The New York Times

330

331

**Newspaper Illustrations**
**Zeitungs-Illustrationen**
**Illustrations de journaux**

**332** Pen-and-ink drawing illustrating an article in *The New York Times* in which the Swede Gunnar Myrdal argues that the Negro problem is an opportunity for America. (USA)
**333** Illustration on the Op-Ed page of *The New York Times* for an article about the civil war in Lebanon. Pen-and-ink drawing. (USA)
**334, 335** Pen-and-ink drawing illustrating an article in *The New York Times* on the "dangers of exporting design and manufacturing knowledge and skill to other countries", with the complete page. (USA)
**336** Illustration (pen and ink) for an article on the Op-Ed page of *The New York Times* about the problems of power as an instrument of foreign policy. (USA)

**332** Illustration aus der *New York Times* zu einem Auszug aus einem Buch von Gunnar Myrdal, dem schwedischen Soziologen, über das Negerproblem und das Demokratieverständnis der Vereinigten Staaten. (USA)
**333** Illustration zu einem Artikel der Op-Ed-Seite der *New York Times* über den Bürgerkrieg im Libanon und die Gefahr, die den übrigen arabischen Staaten des Nahen Ostens droht, über kurz oder lang mit einer ähnlichen Krise konfrontiert zu werden. (USA)
**334, 335** Illustration und vollständige Seite aus der *New York Times*. Der Artikel diskutiert die Gefahren, die durch den Export des technischen Design und amerikanischen Know-how an befreundete Länder, Warschaupakt-Staaten und Länder der dritten Welt entstehen. (USA)
**336** Illustration zu einem Artikel auf der Op-Ed-Seite der *New York Times* über die Vormachtstellung und die Aussenpolitik der Vereinigten Staaten. (USA)

**332** Dessin à la plume du *New York Times* accompagnant un extrait d'un livre de Gunnar Myrdal, sociologue suédois, sur le problème des noirs et la démocratie moderne pratiquée aux Etats-Unis. (USA)
**333** Illustration de la page Op-Ed du *New York Times* pour un article sur la guerre civile au Liban et le danger imminent menaçant les autres pays du Proche Orient d'être confrontés avec de pareils problèmes. (USA)
**334, 335** Dessin à la plume et page entière du *New York Times* accompagnant un article sur les dangers que renferme l'exportation du design technique et du know-how américains vers les pays amis, les pays du pacte de Varsovie et les pays du Tiers Monde. (USA)
**336** Illustration de la page Op-Ed du *New York Times* pour un article traitant du pouvoir américain et de la politique extérieure de ce pays. (USA)

ARTIST / KÜNSTLER / ARTISTE:

332 Brad Holland
333–336 Eugene Mihaesco

DESIGNER / GESTALTER / MAQUETTISTE:

332 Steve Heller

ART DIRECTOR / DIRECTEUR ARTISTIQUE:

332–336 Steve Heller

PUBLISHER / VERLEGER / EDITEUR:

332–336 The New York Times

332

333

334

335

336

ARTIST / KÜNSTLER / ARTISTE:

337, 338 John Holmes
339, 340 Janet Woolley
341 Jean-Claude Suarès
342 Tim

DESIGNER / GESTALTER / MAQUETTISTE:

337–340 John Pym
342 Maurice Leroux

ART DIRECTOR:

337–340 Jeanette Collins
341 Steve Heller
342 Jean-Jacques Hauwy

PUBLISHER / VERLEGER / EDITEUR:

337–340 Times Newspapers Ltd.
341 The New York Times
342 Express-Union

337

339

340

338

341

**337, 338** Page opening a prize-winning ghost story in *The Times* (Saturday Review) and detail of the black-and-white illustration. (GBR)
**339, 340** Layout and illustration of an article on children's books published in *The Times* (Educational Supplement). (GBR)
**341** Illustration for the Op-Ed page of *The New York Times*, accompanying an article entitled "The Candidate's Self-image". (USA)
**342** Illustration for a Club of Rome report in *L'Express*, symbolizing the unequal growth of the industrial and developing nations. (FRA)

**337, 338** Erste Seite einer preisgekrönten Geistergeschichte, die unter dem Titel «Die Puppe namens Silvio» in der *Times* erschien, und Detail der Illustration. (GBR)
**339, 340** Vollständige Seite und Illustration zu einem Artikel über Kinderbücher, der in der Beilage über Erziehung der *Times* veröffentlicht wurde. (GBR)
**341** Illustration zu einem auf der Op-Ed-Seite der *New York Times* erschienenen Artikel: das Image, das sich der Kandidat selbst gibt. (USA)
**342** Illustration aus dem Wochenmagazin *L'Express* zu einem Bericht des Club of Rome über das ungleiche Wachstum der Industrienationen und der Entwicklungsländer. (FRA)

**337, 338** Page initiale d'une histoire de fantômes primée, publiée dans le Saturday Review du *Times*, et détail de l'illustration en noir et blanc. (GBR)
**339, 340** Maquette et illustration d'un article sur les livres d'enfants publié dans le supplément éducatif du *Times*. (GBR)
**341** Illustration d'un article paru à la page Op-Ed du *New York Times*, au sujet du «self-image» du candidat. (USA)
**342** Illustration du rapport du «Club of Rome» publié dans l'hebdomadaire *L'Express* sur l'inégalité de croissance entre les pays industrialisés d'une part et les pays en voie de développement d'autre part. (FRA)

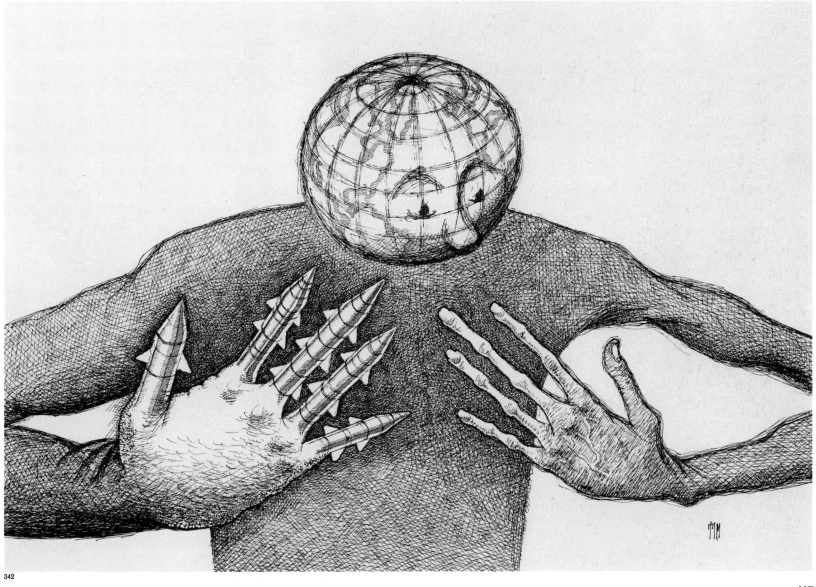

342

343

344

ARTIST / KÜNSTLER / ARTISTE:

343 Alcy Linares
344 Dan Jonsson
345 Michael David Brown
346 Jean-Claude Suarès
347 Tim

DESIGNER / GESTALTER:

345 Ted Weidlen
347 Vieri Andreini

ART DIRECTOR:

343 Juca Martins
345 Ted Weidlen
346 Ellen Roberts
347 Jean-Jacques Hauwy

AGENCY / AGENTUR / AGENCE:

344 Dan Jonsson AB
345 Michael David Brown, Inc.

PUBLISHER / VERLEGER / EDITEUR:

343 Edição S.A.
345 The Chronicle of Higher
    Education
346 Prentice-Hall
347 Express-Union

345

346

343 Illustration for an article in the political paper *Movimento* on "how to talk to peasants". Pen and ink. (BRA)
344 Black-and-white illustration for an article published in the cultural section of a daily newspaper. (SWE)
345 Illustration from *The Chronicle of Higher Education*, accompanying an article on the downfall of the City of New York, written from the point of view of a New York college president. Black and white. (USA)
346 Illustration from a *Prentice-Hall* book entitled *Crash Helmet*. (USA)
347 Illustration for an article published in the weekly *L'Express* on the subject of increasing violence in the urban agglomerations. Black and white. (FRA)

343 Aus einem Artikel in einer politischen Zeitung zum Thema: Wie man mit Bauern redet. (BRA)
344 Illustration aus dem kulturellen Teil einer Zeitung. Schwarzweiss. (SWE)
345 Illustration aus einer Zeitung für Bildungsfragen. Der Artikel beschäftigt sich mit der Stadt New York, sowohl in finanzieller wie auch in sozialer Hinsicht, und mit den fast unlösbaren Problemen, denen sich die Stadt durch die steigende Arbeitslosigkeit gegenüber sieht. Der Autor vergleicht den Fall zweier Städte: Saigon – der endgültige Untergang einer globalen Strategie; New York – die endgültige Auflösung der Ideale einer globalen Macht. (USA)
346 Schwarzweiss-Illustration aus einer Publikation der Push Pin Studios. (USA)
347 Illustration aus dem französischen Wochenmagazin *L'Express* zu einem Artikel über die Gewaltanwendung in städtischen Agglomerationen. (FRA)

343 Illustration du journal politique *Movimento* sur l'art de parler aux paysans. (BRA)
344 Illustration en noir et blanc pour la section culturelle d'un journal. (SWE)
345 Illustration d'un journal éducatif. L'article discute la chute de la ville de New York, déclenchée par une politique financière ratée et par le nombre de chômeurs toujours croissant qui pose des problèmes sociaux quasi insolubles. L'auteur compare la chute de deux villes: Saigon – le débâcle final d'une stratégie globale; New York – l'abandon définitif des idéaux d'une puissance mondiale. (USA)
346 Illustration en noir et blanc figurant dans une publication des Push Pin Studios. (USA)
347 Illustration d'un article paru dans l'hebdomadaire *L'Express* sur la violence dans les concentrations urbaines. (FRA)

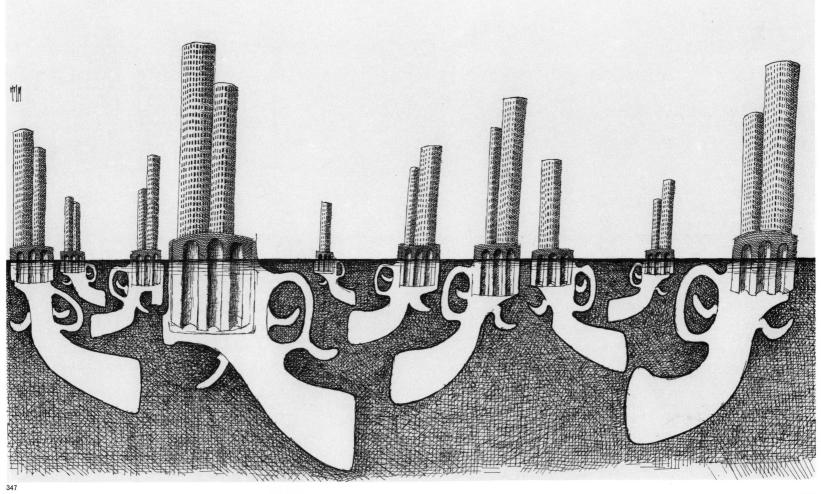

347

348

ARTIST / KÜNSTLER / ARTISTE:

348  José Costa Leite
349, 350  Michael David Brown
351  Sue Coe
352  Eugen Mihaesco
353  Fritz Eichenberg

DESIGNER / GESTALTER / MAQUETTISTE:

349, 350  Ted Weidlen
352  Eric Seidman

ART DIRECTOR / DIRECTEUR ARTISTIQUE:

349, 350  Ted Weidlen
351  Jerelle Kraus
352  Eric Seidman
353  Steve Heller

AGENCY / AGENTUR / AGENCE – STUDIO:

349, 350  Michael David Brown, Inc.

PUBLISHER / VERLEGER / EDITEUR:

348  Neue Zürcher Zeitung
349, 350  The Chronicle of Higher Education
351–353  The New York Times

349

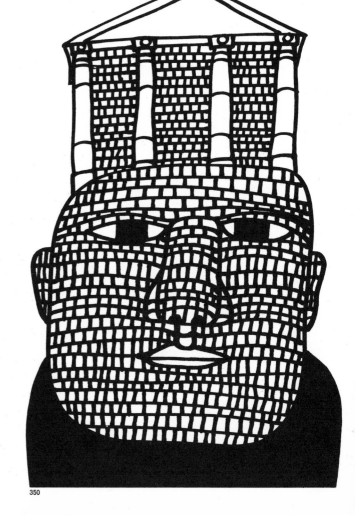

350

120

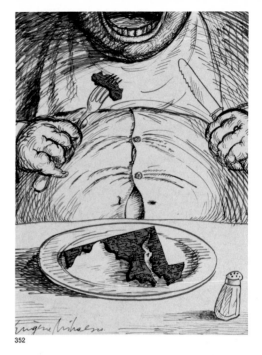

352

351

353

**348** Woodcut from a series about the sugar industry in Brazil, reproduced in the *Neue Zürcher Zeitung.* (SWI)
**349, 350** Complete page and black-and-white illustration from *The Chronicle of Higher Education.* The article deals with the evolution of schools of architecture. (USA)
**351** Illustration from the business section of *The New York Times,* accompanying an article on the rapid withdrawal from mutual funds. (USA)
**352** Pen-and-ink illustration for an article in *The New York Times* on corruption in Maryland. (USA)
**353** Wood engraving illustrating an article in *The New York Times* on the American oil industry and how it should be broken up to make it truly competitive. (USA)

**348** Holzschnitt zu einem Artikel über die Zuckerindustrie, der in der *Neue Zürcher Zeitung* erschien. (SWI)
**349, 350** Seite und Detail der Illustration aus einer Zeitung für Bildungsfragen. Der Artikel beschäftigt sich mit den Problemen der modernen Architektur, die nicht mehr nur intuitive und ästhetische Gesichtspunkte, sondern vor allem soziale Kriterien berücksichtigen sollte. (USA)
**351** Illustration zu einem Artikel im Wirtschaftsteil der *New York Times* über massive Rückzüge von Anlagefonds-Anteilen, die grösste Bewegung dieser Art seit dem grossen Börsenkrach des Jahres 1929. (USA)
**352** Tuschzeichnung zu einem Artikel in der *New York Times* über Korruption in Maryland. (USA)
**353** Holzschnitt aus der *New York Times* zu einem Artikel über die Dezentralisierung der von wenigen Konzernen beherrschten Oelindustrie. (USA)

**348** Gravure sur bois sur l'industrie sucrière, reproduite dans la *Neue Zürcher Zeitung.* (SWI)
**349, 350** Page d'un journal éducatif et illustration qui y figure. L'article traite de l'architecture moderne et des critères sociaux plutôt qu'intuitifs ou esthétiques qui devraient avoir la priorité quant à la conception architecturale. (USA)
**351** Illustration d'un article paru dans la section économique du *New York Times* sur les retraites massives des actionnaires de capitaux d'investissement dont le chiffre égale celui du débâcle boursier de l'année '29. (USA)
**352** Dessin à la plume pour un article du *New York Times* discutant la corruption au Maryland. (USA)
**353** Gravure sur bois du *New York Times* accompagnant un article sur la décentralisation dans l'industrie pétrolière pour réactiver la concurrence. (USA)

**Newspaper Illustrations**
**Zeitungs-Illustrationen**
**Illustrations de journaux**

354 Double spread opening an article in the magazine *Status* on violence in the work of Anthony Burgess. Shades of yellowish brown. (BRA)
355 Double spread opening a "small guide to the pleasures of New York" in *Status* magazine. Full-colour illustration, pale green statue. (BRA)
356–359 Three full-colour illustrations from a series entitled "The Cooking of My Aunt Mélanie" published in *Zeit Magazin* with recipes for such dishes as *Bœuf à la mode* (Fig. 357) or for the use of herbs (Fig. 358). (GER)
360 Illustration in brown shades for a short story published in *Zeit Magazin*. (GER)

354 Erste Doppelseite eines Artikels in *Status* über die Gewalt in den Werken Antony Burgess'. (BRA)
355 Erste Doppelseite eines «kleinen Führers durch New Yorks Vergnügungsstätten» aus der Zeitschrift *Status*. Mehrfarbige Illustration mit blassgrüner Statue. (BRA)
356–359 Seiten und Detail einer Illustration aus der Serie «Die Küche meiner Tante Mélanie», aus dem *Zeit Magazin*. Die illustrierte Rezeptsammlung mit amüsanten Texten und Rezepten des Journalisten und Kunstkritikers Manuel Gasser ist kürzlich in Buchform erschienen. (GER)
360 Illustration zu einer im *Zeit Magazin* erschienenen Kurzgeschichte – «Liebesdienste, Anweisungen zum Töten». Dunkle und hellere Brauntöne. (GER)

354 Page double initiale d'un article du magazine *Status* consacré à la violence dans l'œuvre d'Anthony Burgess. Tons bruns jaunâtres. (BRA)
355 Double page introduisant un «petit guide des plaisirs de New York» publié dans *Status*. Illustration polychrome, statue vert pâle. (BRA)
356–359 Pages et illustration d'une série intitulée «La cuisine de ma tante Mélanie», publiée dans *Zeit Magazin*. Les recettes – ici p. ex. pour *Bœuf à la mode* (fig. 357) ou l'emploi d'épices (fig. 358) – ont été réunies par un journaliste et critique d'art dans le supplément hebdomadaire du *Zeit*. (GER)
360 Illustration et tons bruns pour un récit publié dans le supplément hebdomadaire du *Zeit*. (GER)

## Magazine Illustrations

356

357

354

355

358

360

ARTIST / KÜNSTLER / ARTISTE:

354, 355  Decio Ambroso
356–359  Ute Osterwalder
360  Tomi Ungerer

DESIGNER / GESTALTER / MAQUETTISTE:

356–359  Willy Engeli
360  Karin Gerlach

ART DIRECTOR / DIRECTEUR ARTISTIQUE:

356–360  Günter Halden

PUBLISHER / VERLEGER / EDITEUR:

356–360  Zeitverlag Gerd Bucerius KG

359

**361** Illustration of the "home of a cloud-cuckoo", published in the humorous magazine *Pardon*. The picture is one of a cloud series. (GER)
**362** Double spread opening a Christmas story in *McCall's* magazine. (USA)
**363** Colour illustration of the mammary glands from an article on cancer published in the weekly *Stern*. (GER)
**364** Illustration for a poem. Delicate shades. (FRA)
**365** Pen-and-ink drawing from the *Harvard Business Review*. The artist was invited to illustrate a series of articles with scenes from *Alice in Wonderland* and *Through the Looking Glass*. This one relates to an article on the work of a public executive. (USA)

**361** Illustration aus einer in der Zeitschrift *Pardon* erschienenen Wolkenbilder-Serie von Ernst Schneider, hier mit dem Wolken-Kuckucksheim. (GER)
**362** Titelseiten einer in *McCall's* erschienenen Weihnachtsgeschichte. (USA)
**363** Mehrfarbige Illustration zu einem Artikel über Krebs, der im Wochenmagazin *Stern* veröffentlicht wurde. (GER)
**364** Illustration in matten Farben zu einem Gedicht. (FRA)
**365** Der Künstler wurde beauftragt, eine Artikelserie in der *Harvard Business Review* mit entsprechenden Szenen aus Lewis Carrolls «Alice im Wunderland» und «Alice hinter den Spiegeln» zu illustrieren. Diese Zeichnung begleitet einen Artikel über das Management von öffentlichen Körperschaften. Schwarzweiss. (USA)

**361** Exemple figurant dans une série d'images de nuages de Ernst Schneider parue dans le magazine *Pardon*, ici présentant le *Wolken-Kuckucksheim*, ce que signifie en allemand «planer dans les nuages». (GER)
**362** Premières pages d'un conte de Noël tirée du magazine *McCall's*. (USA)
**363** Illustration polychrome accompagnant un article sur les découvertes les plus récentes dans le domaine de la cancérologie. (GER)
**364** Illustration en couleurs atténuées pour un poème. (FRA)
**365** On a demandé à l'artiste d'illustrer une série d'articles d'un magazine économique de scènes appropriées prises du livre *Alice au pays des merveilles* de Lewis Carroll. Le dessin reproduit accompagne un article sur l'administration d'organisations publiques. En noir et blanc. (USA)

361

## 'TIS THE SEASON TO BE JOLLY

The King hates blackbird pie, the Queen can't seem to get ready for Christmas and the Princess is getting tired of kissing frogs. Can a Simpleton help them live happily ever after?

BY WILL STANTON

Once upon a time there was a King and his wife, the Queen, and their daughter, the Princess. And they had all the things that kings usually have, such as a palace, a kingdom, subjects, a throne, crown, counting house, fiddlers three—in short, everything they could all want to make them as happy as... well, as happy as kings. But they were not.

"Look at me," the King said to a friend one day. "People keep telling me everything is peaches and cream. They don't know what they're talking about. They should cut into a pie sometime and have four-and-twenty blackbirds fly out. Then they'd know what being a King is really like. In the first place it was a blackberry pie I asked for, not blackbird. A dainty dish to set before a King is what they called it. Two dozen live blackbirds in a pie and they've got the nerve to call it dainty. Everything in the Palace tasted like feathers for a week."

"I'll bet they didn't try that again," his friend said.

"Yes, they did. I didn't want to hurt anybody's feelings so I said the pie was delicious. Now any time they want to surprise me with a treat it's always blackbird pie. I can always tell when it's coming. There's all the tippy-toeing around behind the throne, the cooks giggling and the birds squawking. And I always have to pretend to be surprised." He took off his crown and looked at it, frowning. "So if you have any idea that being King is some bed of roses—"

"You should talk," the Queen said. "I gave up a very promising career in yard goods and notions to become Queen. Everyone said there was no telling how far I might have gone if I hadn't married so young."

The Princess was unhappy, too. She was vain and selfish and although she had jewels and clothes of silk and satin she was never satisfied. "Mirror, mirror, on the wall," she would say, "who is the fairest one of all?"

And the mirror would say, "You are the fairest one of all, O Queen."

This would always make the Princess mad. "You stupid mirror," she would say, "can't you even tell a Princess when you see one?"

What the Princess wanted most was for some handsome / turn to page

LINDA GIST

362

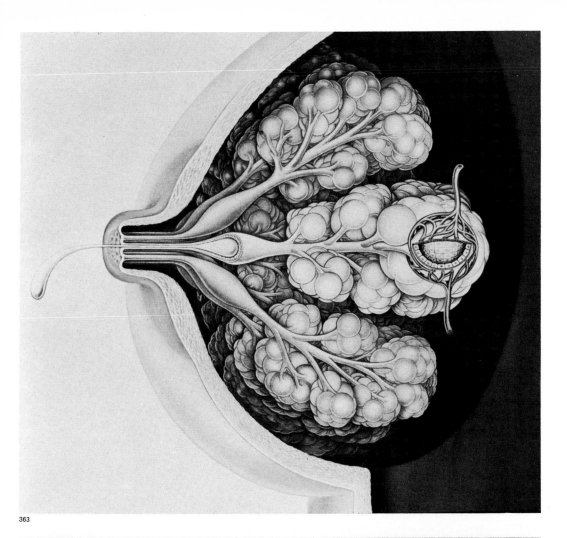

363

ARTIST / KÜNSTLER / ARTISTE:

361 Ernst Schneider
362 Linda E. Gist
363 Ute Osterwalder
364 Tudor Mironesco
365 Ernst Aebi

DESIGNER / GESTALTER / MAQUETTISTE:

362 Linda E. Gist
365 Ernst Aebi

ART DIRECTOR / DIRECTEUR ARTISTIQUE:

362 Modesto Torre
363 Wolfgang Behnken
364 Jean Denis
365 Frank Glickman

AGENCY / AGENTUR / AGENCE – STUDIO:

365 John Locke Studio

PUBLISHER / VERLEGER / EDITEUR:

361 Pardon Verlagsgesellschaft mbH
362 McCall Publishing Co
363 Gruner & Jahr AG & Co
364 Robert Laffont
365 Harvard Business Review

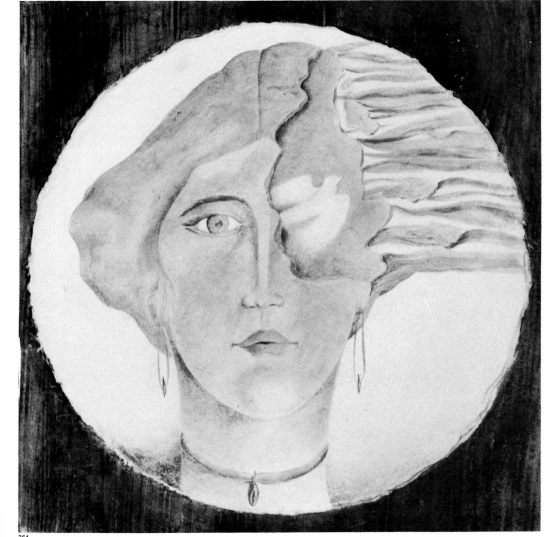

364

365

125

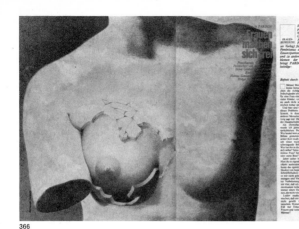

366

## Magazine Illustrations

ARTIST / KÜNSTLER / ARTISTE:

366 Vladimir Borojevic
367 Bob Van Blommestein
368 Theo Kley
369, 370 Charles Santore
371 Seymour Chwast

DESIGNER / GESTALTER / MAQUETTISTE:

366 Jürgen-Horst Frickel
369, 370 Bob Ciano
371 Seymour Chwast

ART DIRECTOR / DIRECTEUR ARTISTIQUE:

367, 368 Dick De Moei
369, 370 Bob Ciano
371 Ruth Ansel

AGENCY / AGENTUR / AGENCE – STUDIO:

371 Push Pin Studios

PUBLISHER / VERLEGER / EDITEUR:

366 Pardon Verlagsgesellschaft mbH
367, 368 De Geillustreerde Pers N.V.
369, 370 Esquire, Inc.
371 The New York Times

367

369

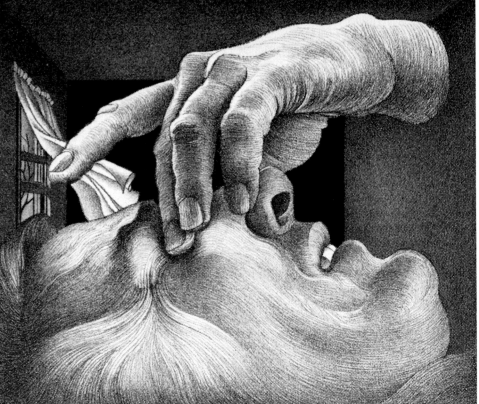

370

126

368

371

**366** Double spread opening an article in the magazine *Pardon* entitled "Women Free Themselves". Pink breast emerging from pale buff plaster, magenta title. (GER)
**367** Full-colour illustration from an article on astrology in the magazine *Avenue:* the Capricorn boss. (NLD)
**368** Illustration with astrological elements for a story published in *Avenue*. Pale brown and pink shades. (NLD)
**369, 370** Black-and-white illustrations for a story of blindness by an American poet published as an excerpt from a novel in the magazine *Esquire*. (USA)
**371** Illustration in grey-green shades for a feature published in *The New York Times Magazine*. (USA)

**366** Erste Doppelseite eines Artikels, der in der Zeitschrift *Pardon* in einer Serie zum Thema Frauenbefreiung erschien. Gipsfarbene Büste, Titel in Magenta. (GER)
**367** Mehrfarbige Illustration zu einer in der Zeitschrift *Avenue* veröffentlichten Artikelserie über Astrologie, hier speziell über den im Steinbock geborenen Boss. (NLD)
**368** Illustration in hellen Braun- und Rosatönen zu einem weiteren Artikel aus *Avenue* über Astrologie. (NLD)
**369, 370** Zwei Schwarzweiss-Illustrationen zu einem in der Zeitschrift *Esquire* veröffentlichten Auszug aus einem Roman von J. Dickey über einen Blinden. (USA)
**371** Illustration zu einem Artikel im Wochenendmagazin der *New York Times*. Vorwiegend in grünlichgrauen Tönen. (USA)

**366** Page initiale d'un article paru dans une série du magazine *Pardon* consacrée à la libération de la femme. Buste en plâtre, titre en magenta. (GER)
**367** Illustration en couleurs accompagnant une série d'articles du magazine *Avenue* sur l'astrologie. (NLD)
**368** Illustration parue dans un autre article de *Avenue* faisant partie de la série sur l'astrologie. Brun et rose. (NLD)
**369, 370** Deux illustrations noir-blanc accompagnant un extrait d'un roman de J. Dickey sur les expériences d'un aveugle. Elément du magazine *Esquire*. (USA)
**371** Illustration pour un article du magazine hebdomadaire du *New York Times*. Prédominance de tons vert-grisâtres. (USA)

372 Double spread in full colour published in *National Lampoon*. Subject: the discovery of America by the Vikings. (USA)
373 From a portfolio of "portraits of the New South" from *National Lampoon*. (USA)
374, 375 Political cartoons in a rather unusual medium—the woodcut. (BRA)
376 Woodcut illustrating an article on dance in America in *The Cultural Post*. (USA)
377 Double spread in colour from *Domus*, showing a plan of the Centre Beaubourg in Paris. (ITA)

372 Illustration sur page double (en tons brunâtres) accompagnant un article sur la découverte de l'Amérique (1000 après J.-C.) paru dans le magazine satirique *National Lampoon*. (USA)
373 «Portraits du nouveau Sud.» D'un portfolio publié dans *National Lampoon*. (USA)
374, 375 Dessins satiriques politiques exécutés sous forme de gravures sur bois. (BRA)
376 Gravure sur bois pour un article sur la danse en Amérique. D'un magazine culturel. (USA)
377 Présentation graphique du Centre Beaubourg à Paris. De *Domus*. En polychromie. (ITA)

372 Vorwiegend in bräunlichen Tönen gehaltene Illustration zu einem Artikel über die Entdeckung Amerikas (1000 n. Chr.), aus der satirischen Zeitschrift *National Lampoon*. (USA)
373 Aus einem Portfolio zum Thema «Portrait des neuen Süden» in *National Lampoon*. (USA)
374, 375 Holzschnitte – eine eher selten gebrauchte Kunstform für politische Karikaturen. (BRA)
376 Holzschnitt zu einem Artikel über den Tanz in Amerika, aus einem Kulturmagazin. (USA)
377 Graphische Darstellung des Centre Beaubourg in Paris. Doppelseite aus *Domus*. (ITA)

372

374

375

373

ARTIST / KÜNSTLER / ARTISTE:

372 Boris Vallejo
373 Don Punchatz
374, 375 Rubem Campos Grilo
376 Michael David Brown
377 H. Cattolica

DESIGNER / GESTALTER:

372, 373 Peter Kleinman
376 David Hausman
377 Giovanni Fraschini

ART DIRECTOR:

372, 373 Peter Kleinman
376 Michael David Brown
377 Gio Ponti

AGENCY / AGENTUR / AGENCE:

376 Michael David Brown, Inc.

PUBLISHER / VERLEGER:

372, 373 National Lampoon/
Twenty-First Century
Communications, Inc.
376 National Endowment for
the Arts
377 Editoriale Domus S.p.A.

376

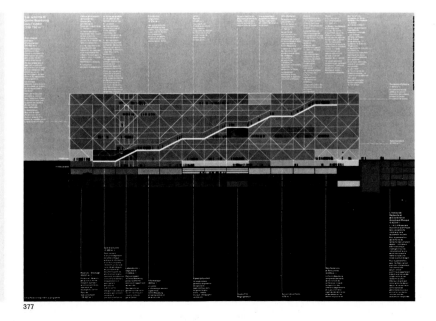

377

**Magazine Illustrations**

129

378

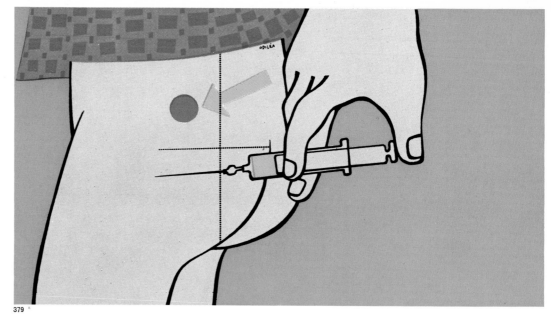

379

381

382

383

384

385

386

**378, 379** Double page and colour detail from an article in the "Emergency" section of the magazine *Nossas Crianças* (Our Children), here referring to injections. (BRA)
**380** Double spread from a Swiss edition of the women's magazine *Elle*, presenting women's lingerie in a full-colour airbrush space fantasy. (SWI)
**381–386** Illustrations for an article planned for *Esquire* magazine, but not published, on the subject of sideburns. The sideburns serve as keys to the professions or the persuasions of their wearers. (USA)
**387** "If I were a monkey, I'd play in the trees from morning till night. And I'd eat bananas and throw the skin on the ground." Illustration from a children's magazine. (FRA)

**378, 379** Doppelseite und Illustration aus einem Artikel, der in der Rubrik «Notfälle» der Zeitschrift *Nossas Crianças* (Unsere Kinder) erschien. (BRA)
**380** Doppelseite aus der deutschsprachigen Ausgabe der Frauenzeitschrift *Elle* zu einem Artikel über modische Damenunterwäsche. Mehrfarbig. (SWI)
**381–386** Illustrationen für einen von der Zeitschrift *Esquire* geplanten Artikel über Backenbärte, der vom Künstler angeregt, bis heute aber noch nicht veröffentlicht wurde. Die Backenbärte sollen Auskunft über den Beruf oder auch über die politische Haltung der Träger geben. (USA)
**387** Illustration in Originalgrösse aus einem Magazin für Kinder, hier zu einer Wenn-und-Aber-Geschichte mit Tieren. (FRA)

**378, 379** Page double et détail d'une illustration d'un article de la section «Cas d'urgence» du magazine *Nossas Crianças* (Nos Enfants); référence est faite aux injections. (BRA)
**380** Page double de l'édition allemande du magazine féminin *Elle*. Elément figurant dans un article présentant la lingerie féminine. En polychromie. (SWI)
**381–386** Illustrations pour un article sur les favoris encore inédit que l'artiste avait proposé au magazine *Esquire*. Les favoris se réfèrent ou à la profession ou aux opinions politiques des hommes présentés. (USA)
**387** Illustration en grandeur nature accompagnant un article paru dans le magazine mensuel pour enfants, *Belles histoires de Pomme d'Api*. (FRA)

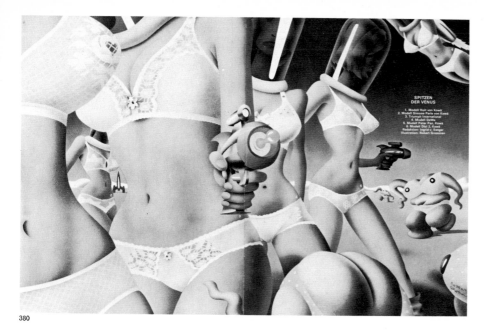

ARTIST / KÜNSTLER / ARTISTE:

378, 379  Odilea Helena Setti
        Toscano
380  Robert Grossman
381–386  Jerome Snyder
387  Etienne Delessert

DESIGNER / GESTALTER:

378, 379  Odilea Helena Setti
        Toscano
387  Michèle Isvy

ART DIRECTOR:

378, 379  João Walter Toscano
380  Monika Frei-Hermann
387  Michèle Isvy/Mijo Beccaria

PUBLISHER / VERLEGER / EDITEUR:

378, 379  Editora Abril Ltda.
380  Elle SA
381–386  Esquire, Inc.
387  Bayard Presse

389

390

388 Page in actual size from a feature on Paris in the German edition of *Playboy*. (GER)
389, 390 Illustration (full colour) and corresponding double page from a feature on country and Western music in the music magazine *Sounds*. "Rope" title. (GER)
391 Double spread with colour illustration from *Skeptic* magazine: money as a drug. (USA)
392 Full-page illustration facing the opening of a feature on Zappa in *Sounds* magazine. Full colour. (GER)

388 Illustration aus der deutschen Ausgabe des *Playboy*. (GER)
389, 390 Illustration und dazugehörige Doppelseite aus *Sounds*, einem Musik-Magazin, hier zu einem Artikel über Country und Western Music. Pastelltöne. (GER)
391 Erste Doppelseite zu einem Artikel über das Geld und wie es Personen verändern und terrorisieren kann. (USA)
392 Ganzseitige Illustration aus dem Musik-Magazin *Sounds*, zu einem Frank Zappa gewidmeten Artikel. Baumkrone, Augenbrauen und Schnauz in Dunkelgrün, hellgrüne Wiese. (GER)

388 Illustration de l'édition allemande de *Playboy*. (GER)
389, 390 Illustration et page double où elle figure. Elément de *Sounds*, un magazine de musique, pour un article sur la Country et Western Music. Tons pastel. (GER)
391 Double page initiale d'un article discutant l'influence de la monnaie qui peut altérer et terroriser les personnes. (USA)
392 Illustration pleine page du magazine de musique *Sounds* accompagnant un article consacré à Frank Zappa. Feuillage, sourcils et moustache en vert, pré en vert clair. (GER)

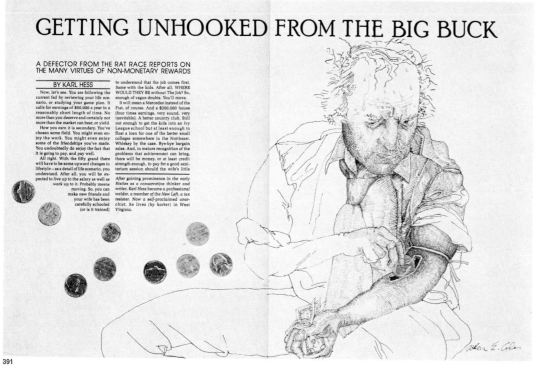

# GETTING UNHOOKED FROM THE BIG BUCK

A DEFECTOR FROM THE RAT RACE REPORTS ON THE MANY VIRTUES OF NON-MONETARY REWARDS

BY KARL HESS

391

392

ARTIST / KÜNSTLER / ARTISTE:

388 Maître Leherb
389, 390 Hans-Ulrich Osterwalder
391 Alan Cober
392 Monika Hahn

DESIGNER / GESTALTER / MAQUETTISTE:

388 George Guther
389, 390, 392 Jürgen Legath
391 Gordon Mortensen

ART DIRECTOR / DIRECTEUR ARTISTIQUE:

388 Rainer Wörtmann
389, 390, 392 Jürgen Legath
391 Gordon Mortensen

PUBLISHER / VERLEGER / EDITEUR:

388 Heinrich Bauer Verlag
389, 390, 392 Sounds Verlag GmbH
391 Skeptic Magazine

**393** Full-page black-and-white drawing opening a strip in the satirical magazine *Satirix*. The rest of the strip shows how the taps are opened and the human being is drained of his potential by his exploiters, finally to be flung on a heap of other empty skins. (FRA)
**394** Double spread in black and white opening a portfolio in *Rolling Stone* in which the satirical cartoonist Ralph Steadman comments on the trial of Patty Hearst, with a text borrowed from Lewis Carroll. (USA)
**395** Full-page illustration from a series commissioned for an article in *Mims* magazine on family help and the elderly. Yellow and blue hands, pale face on a dark blue ground. (GBR)
**396** Collage for a project on P. T. Barnum used as an assignment by The Illustrators Workshop. (USA)
**397** Full-page illustration of an electric chair being painted, facing the opening of an article in *New Times* magazine on the imminent resumption of the death penalty in Georgia. (USA)

**393** Ganzseitige Schwarzweiss-Illustration aus einer humoristischen Monatsschrift; diese Nummer ist den menschlichen Lebensbedingungen gewidmet. Die Illustration ist Teil einer Folge, die zeigen soll, wie der Mensch ausgebeutet wird (die Hähnchen symbolisieren Arbeitskraft), bis er als leere, unbrauchbare Hülle auf einen Haufen geworfen wird. (FRA)
**394** Doppelseite aus einem in der Zeitschrift *Rolling Stone* erschienenen Portfolio des Karikaturisten Ralph Steadman zum Prozess gegen die Verlegertochter Patty Hearst, mit Zitaten von Lewis Carroll. (USA)
**395** Aus einer Serie von ganzseitigen Illustrationen zum Thema Gerontologie. Dieses Beispiel hier steht für vermehrte Hilfe für ältere Leute. Grell gelb beleuchtete Hände, totenblasses Gesicht, Grund in Dunkelblau. (GBR)
**396** Collage für ein Projekt über P. T. Barnum, das im Illustrators Workshop bearbeitet wurde. (USA)
**397** Illustration zum Artikel «Totenwache in Georgia», der die Wiedereinführung der Todesstrafe in Amerika diskutiert. (USA)

**393** Illustration pleine page tirée de *Satirix*, magazine humoristique mensuel; chaque numéro est consacré à un sujet particulier qu'un artiste illustre, celui-ci à la condition humaine. Cette illustration, qui fait partie d'une série, devrait symboliser l'homme qui est exploité jusqu'à ce qu'il ne reste plus rien qu'une dépouille qu'on jette. (FRA)
**394** Page double d'un portfolio du magazine *Rolling Stone*, dans lequel le caricaturiste satirique Ralph Steadman discute le procès contre la fille de l'éditeur Hearst, avec des textes empruntés à Lewis Carroll. (USA)
**395** Illustration figurant dans une série consacrée à la gérontologie. Cet exemple devrait symboliser l'importance de l'aide apportée aux vieux gens. Mains en jaune criard, visage livide, fond en bleu foncé. (GBR)
**396** Collage pour un projet sur P. T. Barnum (sujet exécuté dans le cadre d'un programme de l'Illustrators Workshop). (USA)
**397** Illustration d'un article intitulé «Veillée funèbre en Géorgie», discutant le rétablissement de la peine de mort aux Etats-Unis. (USA)

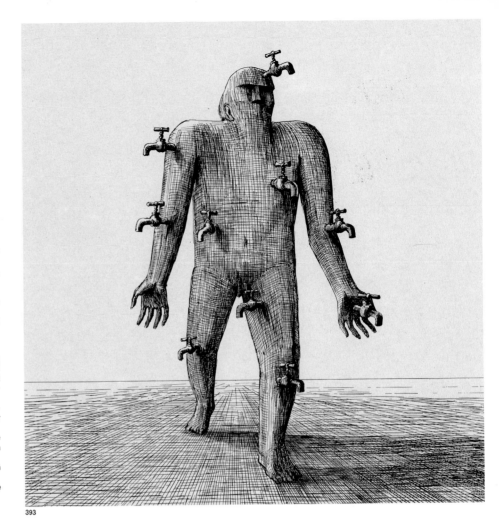
393

395

396

394

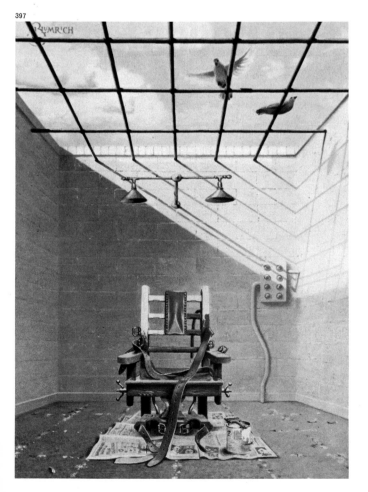

397

ARTIST / KÜNSTLER / ARTISTE:

393 Jacques Cardon
394 Ralph Steadman
395 Michael Trevithick
396 Fred Otnes
397 Christoph Blumrich

DESIGNER / GESTALTER / MAQUETTISTE:

393 Jacques Cardon
394 Greg Scott/William Johnson
395 Michael Trevithick/Roland Schenk

ART DIRECTOR / DIRECTEUR ARTISTIQUE:

393 L. Grand-Jouan
394 Roger Black
395 Roland Schenk
397 Steve Phillips

PUBLISHER / VERLEGER / EDITEUR:

393 Editions de l'Humour
394 Rolling Stone Magazine
395 Haymarket Publishing
397 New Times Magazine

**Magazine Illustrations**
Zeitschriften-Illustrationen
Illustrations de périodiques

398

399

401

402

**398** Full-page black-and-white illustration facing the opening of a science fiction story in *Rolling Stone* magazine. (USA)
**399** Full-page colour illustration for an interview with Eldridge Cleaver in *Rolling Stone*. (USA)
**400** Full-page colour illustration from *Rolling Stone* on the dangers of tissue cultures. (USA)
**401** Double page in *Rolling Stone* about a possible reunion of the Beatles. Black and white. (USA)
**402** Double spread in full colour opening an article in *Oui* magazine on the investigations into the assassination of John F. Kennedy. (USA)
**403** Illustration for an article on sport in the USA in the newspaper *O Estado de S. Paulo*. (BRA)
**404** Double-spread colour illustration of a milkman from the children's magazine *Sesame Street*. (USA)

**398** Illustration zu einer Science-Fiction-Geschichte in der Zeitschrift *Rolling Stone*. (USA)
**399** Vorwiegend in Blautönen gehaltene Illustration zu einem Interview der Zeitschrift *Rolling Stone* mit dem früheren Black-Panther-Führer Eldridge Cleaver. (USA)
**400** Zu einem Artikel in *Rolling Stone* über eine menschliche Gewebekultur, die sich auf unheimliche Art ausgebreitet hat. (USA)
**401** Erste Doppelseite eines Artikels über ein Come-Back-Konzert der Beatles. (USA)
**402** Zu einem Artikel über neue Erkenntnisse im Mordfall John F. Kennedy. Mehrfarbig. (USA)
**403** Illustration zu einem Artikel über Sport in den USA aus *O Estado de S. Paulo*. (BRA)
**404** Doppelseite aus einem Kinder-Magazin, hier zum Beruf des Milchmannes. (USA)

**398** Illustration accompagnant une histoire de science-fiction paru dans *Rolling Stone*. (USA)
**399** Première illustration d'une interview du magazine *Rolling Stone* avec l'ancien leader des Black Panthers – Eldridge Cleaver. Prédominance de tons bleus. (USA)
**400** D'un article du magazine *Rolling Stone* consacré à une culture de tissus humains qui se propage de façon effrayante. (USA)
**401** Page initiale d'un rapport sur une éventuelle réunion des Beatles. (USA)
**402** D'un article sur les nouvelles découvertes concernant l'assassinat de J.F. Kennedy. (USA)
**403** Illustration d'un article sur le sport aux E.-U., dans *O Estado de S. Paulo*. (BRA)
**404** Page double d'un magazine pour enfants, ici illustrant le métier du laitier. (USA)

400

403

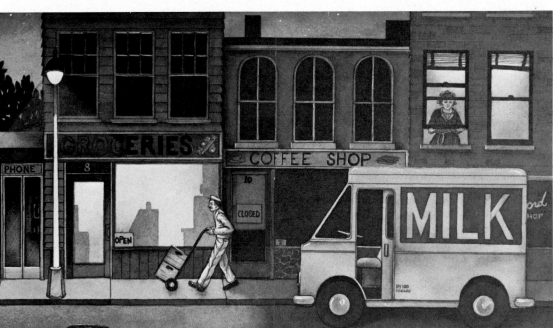

404

405

**405** Illustration in roughly actual size from a series of articles on astrology published in the magazine *Avenue*. (NLD)
**406, 407** Black-and-white pages as introductions to the chapters of a book entitled *You and Your Health* published by John Wiley & Sons, Inc. The two chapters deal with licit and illicit drugs and the dangers of tobacco. (USA)
**408, 409** Double spreads from articles published in the consumer magazine *Moneysworth*, with illustrations in green. The subjects are psychiatric treatment for dogs (mostly of rich owners) and the sevices offered to aging *gringos* by the maidens of Costa Rica. (USA)

**405** Illustration in Originalgrösse zu einer in der Zeitschrift *Avenue* erschienenen Artikelserie über Astrologie. (NLD)
**406, 407** Zwei ganzseitige Schwarzweiss-Illustrationen aus einer Artikelserie zum Thema Gesundheit. Abb. 406: über die Gefährlichkeit von Drogen und deren erlaubte und unerlaubte Anwendungsbereiche; Abb. 407 zu einem Artikel über Tabak und die Gefahren des Rauchens. (USA)
**408, 409** Doppelseiten aus einer Konsumenten-Zeitschrift. Die Zeichnungen (grün) illustrieren Artikel über Hundepsychiatrie (408) und Costa Rica, das Paradies der Lüstlinge (409). (USA)

**405** Illustration en grandeur nature accompagnant un article du magazine *Avenue* paru dans une série consacrée à l'astrologie. (NLD)
**406, 407** Deux illustrations pleines pages figurant dans une série d'articles sur la santé. Fig. 406: le danger des drogues et leur emploi licite et illicite; fig. 407: pour un chapitre sur le tabac et ses effets malsains. En noir et blanc. (USA)
**408, 409** Pages doubles d'un magazine économique. Les dessins (verts) illustrent des articles sur la psychiatrie du chien (408) et sur Costa Rica, le paradis des voluptueux (409). (USA)

ARTIST / KÜNSTLER / ARTISTE:

405 Hans Reizinger
406, 407 Cathy Hull
408, 409 Jerome Snyder

DESIGNER / GESTALTER / MAQUETTISTE:

408, 409 Herb Lubalin

ART DIRECTOR / DIRECTEUR ARTISTIQUE:

405 Dick de Moei
406, 407 Suzanne Bennett
408, 409 Tom Bodkin

AGENCY / AGENTUR / AGENCE – STUDIO:

408, 409 LSC & P Design Group, Inc.

PUBLISHER / VERLEGER / EDITEUR:

405 De Geillustreerde Pers N. V.
406, 407 John Wiley & Sons, Inc.
408, 409 Avant-Garde Media, Inc.

**Magazine Illustrations**
**Zeitschriften-Illustrationen**
**Illustrations de périodiques**

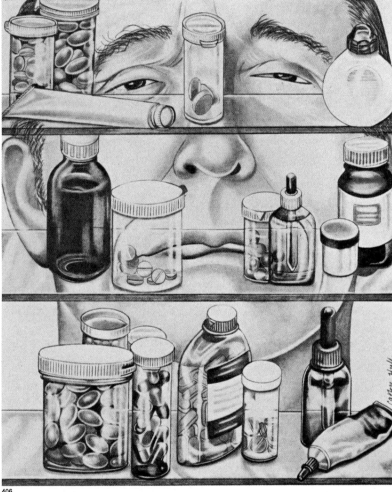

406

407

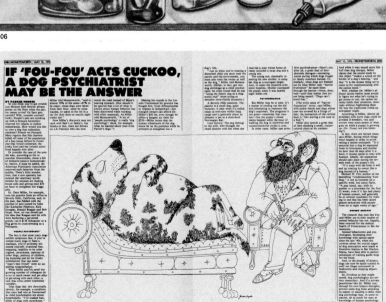

## IF 'FOU-FOU' ACTS CUCKOO, A DOG PSYCHIATRIST MAY BE THE ANSWER

408

## COSTA RICA: DIRTY OLD MAN'S PARADISE

409

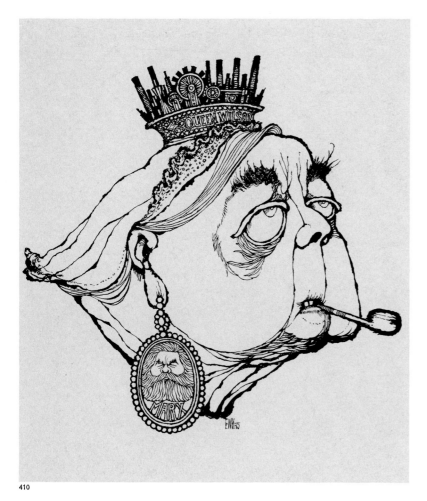

410

411

410–412 Caricatures from *Världens Store*, a book of 63 portraits of famous personalities by Ewert Karlson, published by Askild & Kärnekull. Here Harold Wilson (as Queen Victoria), the South African prime minister Vorster and Generalissimo Franco. (SWE)
413 Full-page illustration for an article in *Skeptic* magazine pleading that science and technology—and more particularly nuclear energy developments—should not be shackled. (USA)
414 Double spread with a labyrinth game from the children's magazine *Sesame Street*. Yellow maze, tent and type, green grass. (USA)
415 Illustration of the horse's laugh from a weekly magazine. Black and white. (JPN)
416 Pen-and-ink drawing as an illustration of an article in *Psychology Today* describing a family's psychological troubles and the therapy used to resolve them. (USA)

410–412 Karikaturen aus *Världens Store*, einer Publikation mit 63 Portraits bekannter Persönlichkeiten. Hier abgebildet sind Wilson, Vorster und Franco. (SWE)
413 Ganzseitige Illustration in Beige- und Grautönen zu einem Artikel des Nobelpreisträgers Seaborg. Er vertritt die Meinung, dass die wissenschaftliche und technische Entwicklung mit allen Mitteln vorangetrieben werden sollte, da es kein Zurück mehr geben kann. (USA)
414 «Wie gelangen wir in den Circus?» Doppelseitige Illustration aus dem Kinder-Magazin *Sesame Street*. Vorwiegend in Grün- und Gelbtönen gehalten. (USA)
415 Illustration aus einem wöchentlich erscheinenden Magazin. (JPN)
416 Illustration aus einer Monatsschrift über Psychologie zu einem Artikel über familiäre Probleme, die gegenüber Aussenstehenden totgeschwiegen werden. Schwarzweiss. (USA)

410–412 Caricatures de Wilson, Vorster et Franco tirées de *Världens Store*, une galerie de 63 portraits d'hommes célèbres. (SWE)
413 Illustration pleine page en tons beiges et gris accompagnant un article de Seaborg, lauréat du prix Nobel. D'après son opinion, l'évolution scientifique et technique devrait être poussée de toute force, car la situation actuelle ne permet plus de faire des pas en arrière; il faut tirer le maximum des connaissances acquises. (USA)
414 «Quel chemin faut-il prendre pour arriver au Cirque?» Illustration double page de *Sesame Street*, magazine pour enfants. Prédominance de tons verts et jaunes. (USA)
415 Illustration d'un magazine hebdomadaire. (JPN)
416 Illustration d'un magazine de psychologie mensuel. D'un article traitant de problèmes de famille qu'on ne discute pas avec des amis ou connaissances. Noir et blanc. (USA)

ARTIST / KÜNSTLER / ARTISTE:

410–412 Ewert Karlsson
413 Marshall Arisman
414 John O'Leary
415 Genpei Akasegawa
416 Hans-Georg Rauch

DESIGNER / GESTALTER / MAQUETTISTE:

410–412 Jan Bohman
413 Gordon Mortensen
414 Richard Weigand/John O'Leary
416 Hans-Georg Rauch

ART DIRECTOR / DIRECTEUR ARTISTIQUE:

413 Gordon Mortensen
414 Richard Weigand
416 Neil Shakery

AGENCY / AGENTUR / AGENCE – STUDIO:

414 John O'Leary
416 John Locke

PUBLISHER / VERLEGER / EDITEUR:

410–412 Askild + Kärnekull
413 Skeptic Magazine
414 Children's Television Workshop, Inc.
416 Psychology Today

414

Which way to the circus?
Ernie, Bert and Cookie Monster are trying to get to the circus tent.
Take a crayon and show Ernie the way.
Now help Bert. Can you help Cookie Monster?

16    17

**Magazine Illustrations**

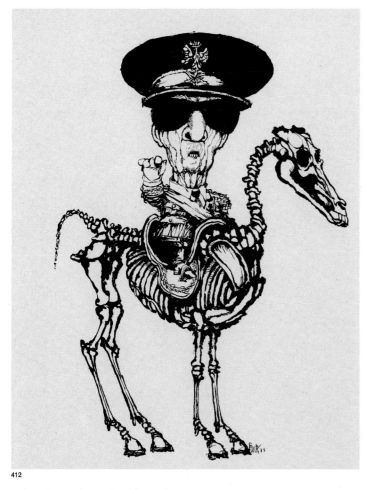

412

413

415

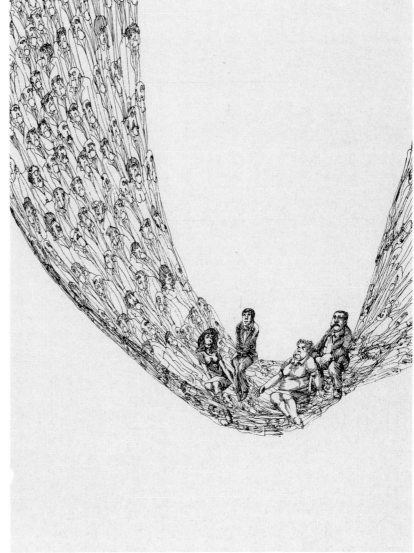

416

## Magazine Illustrations
## Zeitschriften-Illustrationen
## Illustrations de périodiques

**417** Full-page colour illustration in *Weekend Magazine* facing the opening of an article on recent advances in medical genetics. (CAN)
**418** Double spread opening a story about twins in *Ladies' Home Journal*. Full colour. (USA)
**419** Illustration in olive, black and white from an article in *Mims* magazine about helping to care for the elderly. (GBR)
**420, 421** From a London Calendar published in *The Illustrated London News*. Here referring to the Proms and the Chelsea Flower Show. Full colour. (GBR)
**422** Double spread from an article in *Road & Track* magazine which claims that car drivers identify their cars with their bodies. Red-brown and black. (USA)

**417** Illustration in Rostrot, Grün und Blau zu einem Artikel über die neuesten Erkenntnisse auf dem Gebiet der Genetik. Aus der wöchentlich erscheinenden Zeitschrift *Weekend Magazine*. (CAN)
**418** Doppelseite mit mehrfarbiger Illustration aus einer Frauenzeitschrift. Die Kurzgeschichte handelt von Zwillingen, die auf beängstigende Weise eine gedankliche Einheit bilden. (USA)
**419** Illustration in Olivgrün, Schwarz und Weiss aus einem in der Zeitschrift *Mims* erschienenen Artikel über die Einsamkeit und gesellschaftliche Abgeschiedenheit älterer Leute. (GBR)
**420, 421** Mehrfarbige Illustrationen aus Foremans «London Calendar», der in *The Illustrated London News* erscheint; hier für ein Promenadenkonzert und eine Blumenschau in Chelsea. (GBR)
**422** «Der Auto-Mensch.» Illustration in Braun und Schwarzweiss zu einem Artikel über Autofahrer, die sich vollständig mit ihrem Wagen identifizieren. (USA)

**417** Illustration accompagnant un article sur les découvertes les plus récentes dans le domaine de la génétique. Elément de l'hebdomadaire *Weekend Magazine*. Rouge brique, vert, bleu. (CAN)
**418** Page double avec illustrations en couleurs figurant dans un magazine féminin. La nouvelle traite de jumelles dont l'unité des pensées a atteint un degré inquiétant. (USA)
**419** Illustration en olive, noir et blanc parue dans le magazine *Mims*. Elément d'un article sur la solitude et l'isolement social des gens âgés. (GBR)
**420, 421** Deux exemples des illustrations de Michael Foreman réalisées pour le Calendrier londonien de l'*Illustrated London News*: concerts publics et floralies de Chelsea. (GBR)
**422** «L'homme-voiture.» Illustration en brun et noir-blanc figurant dans un article sur les automobilistes qui s'identifient complètement avec leurs voitures. (USA)

417

419

420

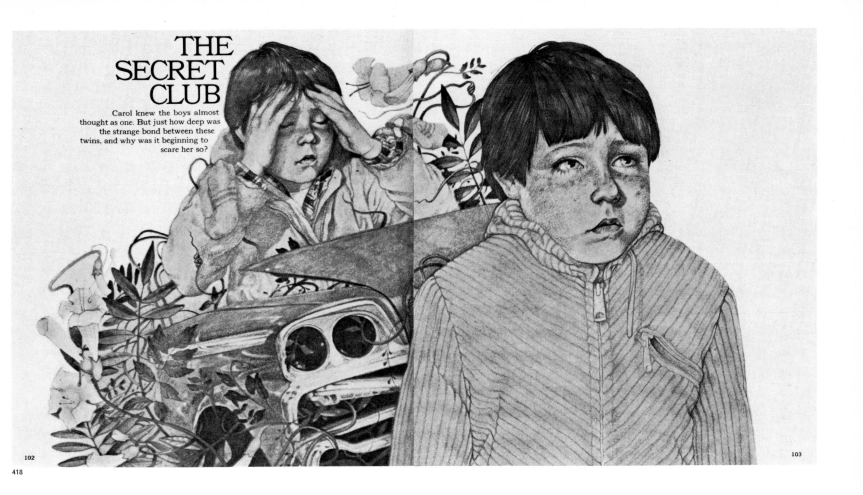

## THE SECRET CLUB

Carol knew the boys almost thought as one. But just how deep was the strange bond between these twins, and why was it beginning to scare her so?

102

103

418

421

422

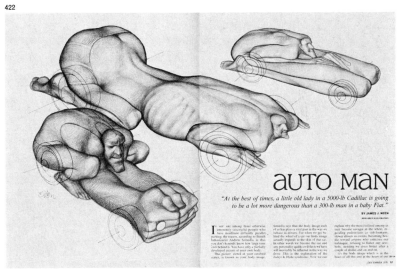

## AUTO MAN

"At the best of times, a little old lady in a 5000-lb Cadillac is going to be a lot more dangerous than a 300-lb man in a baby Fiat."

BY JAMES J. WEEN

DESIGNER / GESTALTER / MAQUETTISTE:

418 Donald A. Adamec
419–421 Michael Foreman
422 Dick Oden

ART DIRECTOR / DIRECTEUR ARTISTIQUE:

417 Jackie Young
418 Donald A. Adamec
419 Roland Schenk
420, 421 Adrianne Leman
422 William Motta

AGENCY / AGENTUR / AGENCE – STUDIO:

422 Dick Oden Illustration

PUBLISHER / VERLEGER / EDITEUR:

417 Montreal Standard Ltd.
418 Ladies' Home Journal
419 Haymarket Publishing
420, 421 The Illustrated London News
422 Road & Track

ARTIST / KÜNSTLER / ARTISTE:

417 Yves Simard
418 Julia Noonan
419–421 Michael Foreman
422 Dick Oden

423

424

425

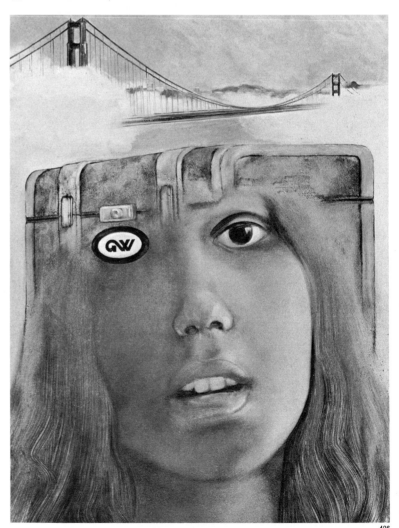

426

427

428

**423** Full-page colour illustration facing the opening of a story set in the province of Amazonas, Brazil. From the women's magazine *Freundin*. Full colour. (GER)
**424–426** Further full-page, full-colour illustrations facing openings of features in *Freundin*. The stories are a romantic thriller (Fig. 424), a tale of an elder sister who grows up (Fig. 425) and of a girl "with a second face" (Fig. 426). (GER)
**427, 428** Complete double page and detail of the colour illustration from a further story in *Freundin,* this time about a "listener behind the wall". (GER)
**429** Double spread opening a story by Oscar Wilde reprinted in *Freundin*. Full colour. (GER)

**423–429** Ganzseitige Illustrationen und Doppelseiten aus der vierzehntäglich erscheinenden Frauenzeitschrift *Freundin*. Abb. 423: «Der Amazonas kann sehr zärtlich sein» – eine Kurzgeschichte; Abb. 424: «Ein tödliches Versehen» – ein Krimi (in Beige- und Brauntönen, blutrot beschmierte Zeitungsseite); Abb. 425: «Ende einer Kindheit» – eine Kurzgeschichte (rosa, hellblau und gelb); Abb. 426: «Das Mädchen mit dem zweiten Gesicht» – eine Kurzgeschichte (Brauntöne, hellblauer Himmel); Abb. 427/428: Kurzgeschichte über eine Hausmeisterin, der nichts entging; Abb. 429: «Das Sternenkind» – eine Kurzgeschichte von Oscar Wilde (Schnee in kalten Blautönen). (GER)

**423–429** Illustrations pleines pages et pages doubles tirées du bimensuel féminin *Freundin*. Fig. 423: nouvelle sur une affaire amoureuse sur l'Amazone; fig. 424: roman policier (tons bruns et beiges, page de journal tachée de sang); fig. 425: nouvelle sur l'enfance passée (rose, bleu clair et jaune); fig. 426: nouvelle d'une jeune fille qui a un second visage (tons bruns, ciel bleu); fig. 427/428: nouvelle d'une concierge qui veille à ce que nulle chose ne lui échappe; fig. 429: nouvelle d'Oscar Wilde (neige en bleu froid). (GER)

ARTIST / KÜNSTLER / ARTISTE:

423 Hanno Rink/Rita Mühlbauer
424, 427, 428 Katrin Lindley
425 Edda Köchl
426 Josef Hozak
429 Karin Blume

ART DIRECTOR / DIRECTEUR ARTISTIQUE:

423–429 Eberhard Henschel

PUBLISHER / VERLEGER / EDITEUR:

423–429 Burda Verlag GmbH

**Magazine Illustrations**
**Zeitschriften-Illustrationen**
**Illustrations de périodiques**

429

430

ARTIST / KÜNSTLER / ARTISTE:

430, 431  Jane Bark
432, 433  Per Åhlin

DESIGNER / GESTALTER / MAQUETTISTE:

430–433  Femina Layout Dept.

AGENCY / AGENTUR / AGENCE – STUDIO:

430, 431  Jane Bark Productions AB

PUBLISHER / VERLEGER / EDITEUR:

430–433  Femina

**Magazine Illustrations**
**Zeitschriften-Illustrationen**
**Illustrations de périodiques**

431

432

433

**430—433** Double spread and details of the colour illustrations from fiction features published in the women's weekly magazine *Femina.* The references are to death in respectable circles (Fig. 430), to the methods of modern angels (Fig. 431) and to a story by the French writer Boris Vian (Fig. 432). (SWE)

**430—433** Doppelseite und Details verschiedener Illustrationen zu Erzählungen und Kurzgeschichten, die in der wöchentlich erscheinenden Frauenzeitschrift *Femina* veröffentlicht wurden. Abb. 430: über den Tod in frommen, ehrbaren Kreisen; Abb. 431: über die modernen Engel; Abb. 432: über eine Doppelseite laufende Illustration zu einer Erzählung von Boris Vian. (SWE)

**430—433** Page double et détails des illustrations couleurs de nouvelles publiées dans le magazine hebdomadaire féminin *Femina.* Les thèmes sont: la mort chez les bien-pensants (fig. 430), les anges modernes (fig. 431); fig. 432: illustration sur double page accompagnant un récit de Boris Vian. (SWE)

ARTIST / KÜNSTLER / ARTISTE:

434, 435, 438  Dick Oden
436, 437  Hermenegildo Sábat

DESIGNER / GESTALTER / MAQUETTISTE:

434, 435, 438  Dick Oden

ART DIRECTOR / DIRECTEUR ARTISTIQUE:

434, 435, 438  Elin Waite

AGENCY / AGENTUR / AGENCE – STUDIO:

434, 435, 438  Dick Oden Illustration

PUBLISHER / VERLEGER / EDITEUR:

434, 435, 438  Automobile Club of Southern
  California
436  Editorial AIRENE
437  Instituto Salesiano de Artes Gráficas

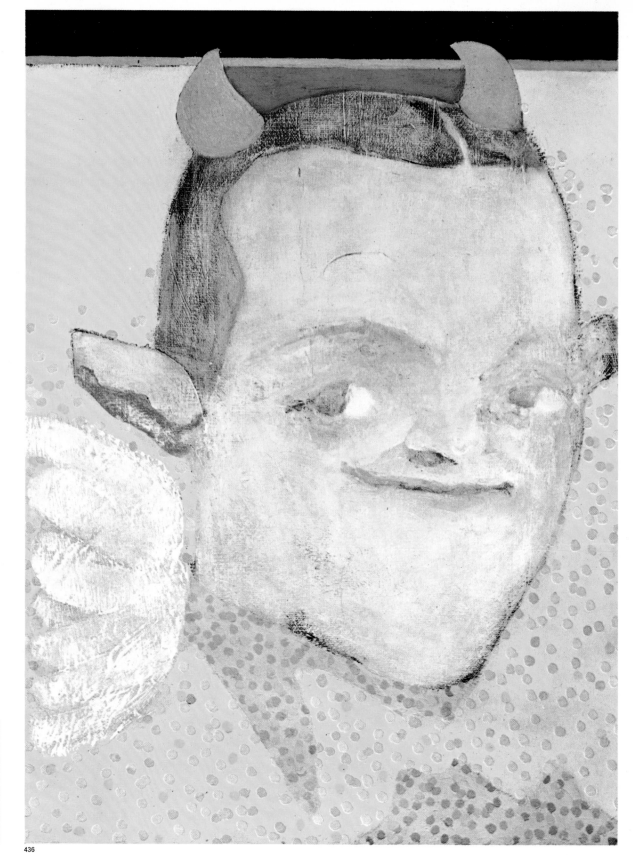

436

**434**

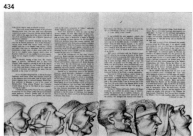

**435**

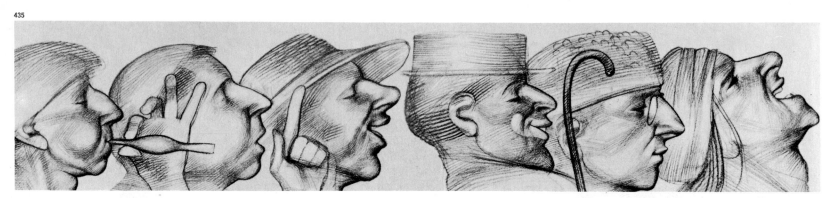

**434, 435** Double page and detail of the pencil illustration for an article on music in California published in *Westways* magazine. (USA)
**436** Cover of the Book *Yo Bix, tú Bix, él Bix,* in which the Brazilian artist Sábat pays graphic homage to Bix Beiderbecke, a trumpeter who made records from 1924 to 1930, dying at the age of only 28. (BRA)
**437** Double-spread illustration from *Scat,* an artist's interpretation of jazz, here with a caricature of Lennie Tristano. (BRA)
**438** Drawing illustrating a section on film from the same issue of *Westways* as in Figs. 434 and 435. The whole issue was illustrated in pencil by the same artist. (USA)

**434, 435, 438** Vollständige Doppelseite und zwei Illustrationen aus der Zeitschrift *Westways,* hier zum Artikel eines Komponisten und Musikprofessors über kalifornische Lieder und Musik und einem kurzen Rückblick über die Geschichte der Filmstadt Hollywood. (USA)
**436** Illustration aus der Publikation *Yo Bix, tú Bix, él Bix,* die der Künstler zu Ehren des Trompeters Bix Beiderbecke herausgab, der bereits mit 28 Jahren starb und, da er bei den Frauen wenig Erfolg hatte, versuchte, seine Gefühle in der Musik auszudrücken. (BRA)
**437** Seite aus einer Publikation, in welcher der Künstler verschiedene Jazzmusiker karikiert, hier Lennie Tristano. (BRA)

**434, 435, 438** Page double et deux illustrations parues dans le magazine *Westways.* Eléments de l'article d'un compositeur et professeur de musique sur les chansons californiennes et d'une rétrospective de l'histoire de Hollywood, centre de l'industrie cinématographique. (USA)
**436** Illustration de la publication *Yo Bix, tú Bix, él Bix,* hommage graphique à Bix Beiderbecke, un trompette des année vingt qui mourut à l'âge de 28 ans; son insuccès auprès des femmes le poussa à exprimer ses sentiments et son amour des Noirs dans sa musique. (BRA)
**437** Page d'une série d'interprétations du jazz, ici présentant un portrait de Lennie Tristano. (BRA)

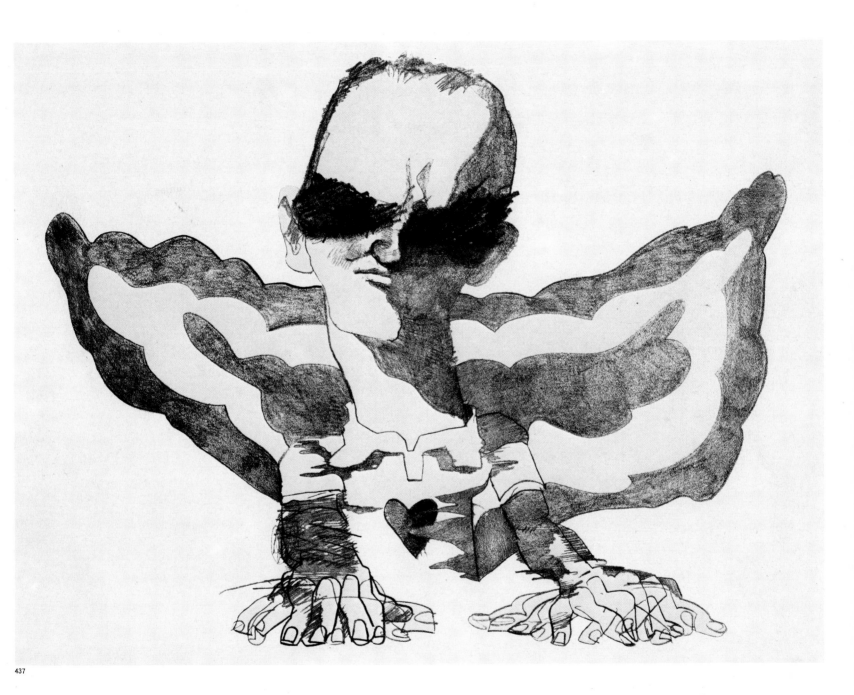

437

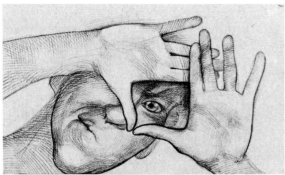

438

# Magazine Illustrations

ARTIST / KÜNSTLER / ARTISTE:

439 Larry Rivers
440 John O'Leary
441, 442 Jerome Podwil
443, 444 Hermenegildo Sábat

439

440

441

DESIGNER / GESTALTER / MAQUETTISTE:

440 Norm Schaefer
441, 442 Roy Moody

ART DIRECTOR / DIRECTEUR ARTISTIQUE:

439 Jack O'Grady
440 Arthur Paul/Norm Schaefer
441, 442 Arthur Paul

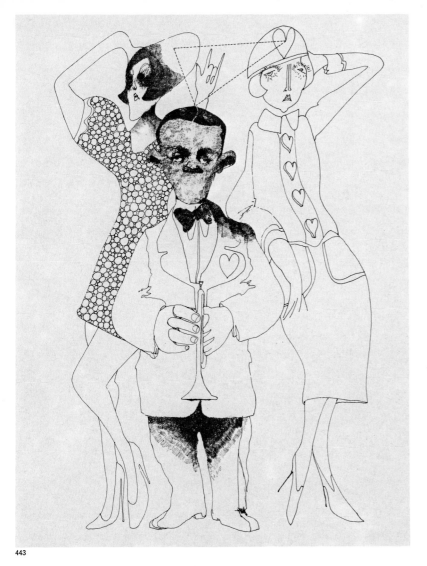

443

444

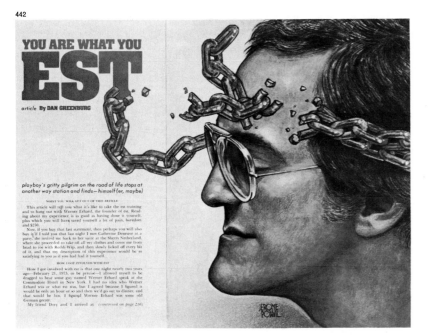

442

**439** Large sheet from a Bicentennial print collection. (USA)
**440** Illustration from *Playboy* magazine for an article about "the parts left out of the Patty Hearst trial". Full colour. (USA)
**441, 442** Page with closed and open gatefold from an article in *Playboy* about the "est" therapy for the treatment of stress. Fig. 441 on a red ground, Fig. 442, showing the breaking of the chain, on a pale green ground. (USA)
**443** Page from a book about the trumpeter Bix Beiderbecke, who, being unsuccessful with women, is said to have put all his feeling into his music. See Fig. 436. (BRA)
**444** Page from an interpretation of jazz by a Brazilian artist (see Fig. 437). This is a caricature of Bessie Smith. (BRA)

**439** Blatt aus einer anlässlich der 200-Jahrfeier der USA herausgegebenen Mappe. (USA)
**440** Mehrfarbige Illustration zu einem Artikel in der Zeitschrift *Playboy* über die im Patty-Hearst-Prozess «gestrichenen» Szenen. (USA)
**441, 442** Illustration mit Ausleger (geschlossen und offen gezeigt) zu einem Artikel über das Est-Programm, eine Therapie für Leute in Stresssituationen. Abb. 441: vor der Behandlung, roter Hintergrund; Abb. 442: während der Behandlung fallen die Ketten des psychischen Druckes; grüner, beruhigend wirkender Hintergrund. (USA)
**443** Ganzseitige Illustration aus der Publikation *Yo Bix, tú Bix, él Bix* (s. auch Abb. 436), die dem Trompeter Bix Beiderbecke gewidmet ist. (BRA)
**444** Seite aus Sábats Jazz-Interpretationen (s. Abb. 437), hier mit Bessie Smith. (BRA)

**439** Estampe tirée d'une collection consacrée au Bicentenaire des Etats-Unis. (USA)
**440** Illustration d'un article de *Playboy* présentant des scènes «sautées» du procès contre Patty Hearst. En polychromie. (USA)
**441, 442** Illustration à repli (montrée ouvert et fermé) accompagnant un article sur le programme Est, une thérapie pour les gens souffrant de perturbations psychiques. Fig. 441: avant le traitement, fond rouge; fig. 442: après le traitement, fond vert. (USA)
**443** Illustration d'une publication consacrée à Beiderbecke (voir aussi la fig. 436). (BRA)
**444** Page extrait d'un livre avec des interprétations du jazz de Sábat (voir fig. 437), ici avec une caricature de Bessie Smith. (BRA)

AGENCY / AGENTUR / AGENCE – STUDIO:

439 Jack O'Grady Communications, Inc.
440–442 John O'Leary

PUBLISHER / VERLEGER / EDITEUR:

440–442 Playboy Enterprises, Inc.
443 Editorial AIRENE
444 Instituto Salesiano de Artes Gráficas

445

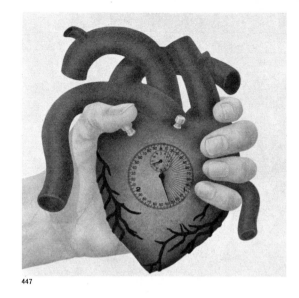

447

446

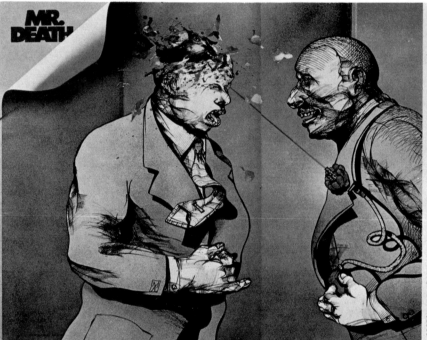

450

ARTIST / KÜNSTLER / ARTISTE:

445, 446, 448  Brad Holland
447  Jan Ten Hove
449  Richard Harvey
450  Marshall Arisman
451  Hans Ulrich Osterwalder
452  Wolfgang Fratzscher
453  Greg Wray

DESIGNER / GESTALTER / MAQUETTISTE:

445, 446  Bob Post
448, 450  Kerig Pope
449  Jean-Pierre Holley
452  George Guther
453  Roy Moody

ART DIRECTOR / DIRECTEUR ARTISTIQUE:

445, 446, 448, 450, 453  Arthur Paul
447  Dick De Moei
449  Don Menell
451, 452  Rainer Wörtmann

PUBLISHER / VERLEGER / EDITEUR:

445, 446  448, 450, 453  Playboy Enterprises, Inc.
447  De Geillustreerde Pers N.V.
449  Playboy Publications, Inc.
451, 452  Heinrich Bauer Verlag

452

448

449

451

453

**445, 446** Complete double page and detail of one colour illustration from a story of the Devil and a Polish peasant's wife in *Playboy* magazine. (USA)
**447** Illustration for an article in *Avenue* entitled "Perfectly fit in thirty minutes per week". Pink hand, purple heart. (NLD)
**448** Double spread opening an excerpt in *Playboy* from a novel about the future. (USA)
**449** Double spread opening a short story in *Playboy*. Pink and red shades. (USA)
**450** Double spread opening an article in *Playboy* on secret weapons for assassinations. Bluish and purplish shades. (USA)
**451** Double spread opening an article in the German *Playboy* on tricks for making money. Full colour. (GER)
**452** Double spread, chiefly in red and yellow shades, opening a story about the "weaker" sex in the German *Playboy*. (GER)
**453** Double spread opening an account published in *Playboy* of an episode in the war in Vietnam. Full colour. (USA)

**445, 446** Vollständige Doppelseite und mehrfarbige Illustration zu einem polnischen Märchen (Der Teufel und die Bäuerin). Die Illustration kann auf einen Karton aufgebügelt werden. (USA)
**447** Seite zu einem in der Zeitschrift *Avenue* erschienenen Artikel über Gesundheit. Rosa- und Lilatöne. (NLD)
**448** Erste Doppelseite aus *Playboy* zu den eigenartigen Memoiren des allerletzten amerikanischen Präsidenten. Mehrfarbig. (USA)
**449** Erste Doppelseite einer Kurzgeschichte. Rot, rosa. (USA)
**450** Zu einem Interview über die geheimen Waffen der CIA mit dem Ingenieur, der solche während 20 Jahren entwickelte. Dunkle Töne. (USA)
**451** Mehrfarbige Doppelseite aus der deutschen Ausgabe von *Playboy* zu einem Artikel über Spekulation. (GER)
**452** Illustration in Gelb- und Orangetönen zu einer im deutschen *Playboy* abgedruckten Erzählung von Stefan Heym. (GER)
**453** «Am 4. Juli geboren.» Im *Playboy* veröffentlichte Memoiren eines Marine-Offiziers über die Greuel des Vietnam-Krieges. Amerikanische Flagge als Hintergrund. (USA)

**445, 446** Page double complète et illustration polychrome qui y figure. Elément d'un conte polonais (Le diable et la paysanne) tiré du magazine *Playboy*. (USA)
**447** Page accompagnant un article sur la santé, paru dans le magazine *Avenue*. Tons roses et lilas. (NLD)
**448** Page double de *Playboy* introduisant les mémoires bizarres du dernier président des Etats-Unis. Polychrome. (USA)
**449** Page initiale d'un conte. Rouge et rose. (USA)
**450** Interview au sujet des armes secrètes de la CIA avec l'ingénieur qui a développé de telles armes pendant 20 ans. Illustration en tons foncés parue dans *Playboy*. (USA)
**451** Page double en couleurs de l'édition allemande de *Playboy*. L'article en question traite de la spéculation. (GER)
**452** Illustration accompagnant un récit de Stefan Heym, paru dans l'édition allemande de *Playboy*. Tons jaunes et orange. (GER)
**453** «Né le 4 juillet.» Mémoires d'un officier marin sur les atrocités de la guerre au Viêt-nam, publiées dans le magazine *Playboy*. Drapeau américain au fond. (USA)

**Magazine Illustrations**
**Zeitschriften-Illustrationen**
**Illustrations de périodiques**

454

DESIGNER / GESTALTER:
456, 457  Frank De Vino

ART DIRECTOR:
454–457  Joe Brooks

PUBLISHER / VERLEGER / EDITEUR:
454–457  Penthouse International Ltd.

456

**454** Yet another parody of the famous Grant Wood painting ("American Gothic"), this time facing an article in *Penthouse* on Jay Rockefeller. (USA)
**455** Double spread in full colour opening an interview in *Penthouse* with a scientist who believes in the human colonization of space. (USA)
**456, 457** Double spread opening a feature on Nelson Rockefeller in *Penthouse* and detail of the sculpture made of nylon fabric, polyester fibre and real hair. Full colour. (USA)

**454** Artikel über einen der Rockefeller-Neffen, der mit allen Mitteln versucht, US-Präsident zu werden. Die Abbildung parodiert das Gemälde «American Gothic» von Grant Wood. (USA)
**455** Zu einem Interview mit einem Physiker, der die Ansicht vertritt, dass bis im Jahr 2000 die ersten Leute im All leben werden, eine Lösung der Überbevölkerungsprobleme. (USA)
**456, 457** Doppelseite zu einem in der Zeitschrift *Penthouse* erschienenen Artikel über Nelson Rockefeller, mit Plastik aus Nylon, Polyester und echtem Haar. (USA)

**454** Article sur Jay Rockefeller qui fait jouer tous les ressorts pour devenir président des E.-U. L'illustration est une parodie de la peinture «American Gothic» de Grant Wood. (USA)
**455** Pour une interview avec un physicien qui est d'avis qu'en l'an 2000 on va peupler l'espace, solution partielle des problèmes écologiques et du surpeuplement. (USA)
**456, 457** Double page initiale d'un article sur Nelson Rockefeller dans *Penthouse* et détail de la sculpture en tissu nylon, fibre de polyester et cheveux véritables. (USA)

ARTIST / KÜNSTLER / ARTISTE:
454  Sean Earley
455  Shusei Nagaoka
456, 457  Judith Jampel/Klaus Lucka/ Linda Moss (Photo)

455

457

460

458

ARTIST / KÜNSTLER / ARTISTE:

458, 459 Alex Ebel
460 Frances Jetter
461 Mike Presley
462 Alex Gnidziejko
463 Wilson McLean
464, 465 Robert Giusti

DESIGNER / GESTALTER / MAQUETTISTE:

462 Don Menell
464, 465 Frank De Vino

ART DIRECTOR / DIRECTEUR ARTISTIQUE:

458, 459, 461, 463–465 Joe Brooks
460 Michael Brent
462 Don Menell

PUBLISHER / VERLEGER / EDITEUR:

458, 459, 461, 463–465 Penthouse
    International Ltd.
460 Institutional Investor Inc.
462 Playboy Publications, Inc.

**458, 459** Double page opening a story about a sorcerer in Malaysia in *Penthouse* magazine, and detail of the illustration. (USA)
**460** Black-and-white print illustrating a feature in a magazine which is published by Institutional Investor. (USA)
**461** Illustration (full colour) for an article in *Penthouse* about the heroin trade between Mexico and the United States. (USA)
**462** Double spread from *Playboy* about a young sculptor who uses himself as raw material—here having himself nailed to a *Volkswagen*. (USA)
**463** Full-page colour illustration facing the opening of an article in *Penthouse* about collaboration between the police and a truck-drivers' union. (USA)
**464, 465** Illustration (full colour) and corresponding double page from *Penthouse*. The feature is about a Korean religious leader at work in the US. (USA)

459

461

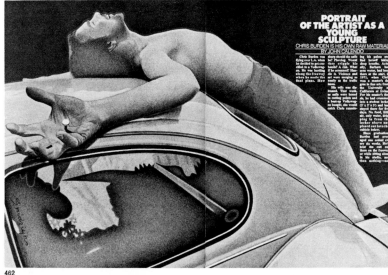

462

463

464

458,459 «Des Tigers Kleid.» Fiction-Story über einen malaysischen Regenmacher. (USA)
460 Schwarzweiss-Illustration aus einer Finanzzeitschrift. (USA)
461 Illustration aus der Zeitschrift *Penthouse* zu einem Bericht über den mexikanischen Heroin-handel. Braune Adler, jeder auf der Flagge seines Landes sitzend. (USA)
462 Doppelseite aus *Playboy* zu einem Bericht über einen jungen Bildhauer, der die ausgefallen-sten Ideen in die Tat umsetzt – hier liess sich auf einen VW nageln. (USA)
463 Aus einem Artikel in *Penthouse* über die furchterregende Verfilzung zwischen Polizei und zweifelhaften Elementen einer Fernfahrer-Gewerkschaft. Mehrfarbig. (USA)
464,465 Illustration und Doppelseite zu einem Bericht über Sun Myung Moon, Millionär und Sektenoberhaupt, dem immer mehr junge Leute hörig werden. Roter Teufel, gelbe Maske. (USA)

458,459 «Le poil du tigre.» Conte sur un magicien malais. (USA)
460 Illustration en noir et blanc figurant dans un magazine économique. (USA)
461 Illustration accompagnant un rapport dans le magazine *Penthouse* sur les trafiquants d'héroïne mexicains. Aigles bruns, chacun assis sur les couleurs de son pays. (USA)
462 Page double de *Playboy* illustrant le rapport sur un jeune sculpteur qui réalise les idées les plus extravagantes – ici il s'est fait clouer à une VW. (USA)
463 Illustration d'un article qui a paru dans le magazine *Penthouse* sur l'interpénétration effrayante de la police et d'éléments douteux d'un syndicat des routiers. (USA)
464,465 Illustration et page d'un rapport sur Sun Myung Moon, millionaire et leader d'une secte qui subjugue un nombre de jeunes toujours croissant. Diable rouge, masque jaune. (USA)

465

157

# Magazine Illustrations
## Zeitschriften-Illustrationen
## Illustrations de périodiques

466

ARTIST / KÜNSTLER / ARTISTE:

466 Lane Yerkes
467 Josse Goffin
468 Richard Hess
469 Seymour Chwast
470, 471 David Levine

DESIGNER / GESTALTER / MAQUETTISTE:

470 Walter Bernard

ART DIRECTOR / DIRECTEUR ARTISTIQUE:

466, 467 Joe Brooks
468–471 Milton Glaser/Walter Bernard

PUBLISHER / VERLEGER / EDITEUR:

466, 467 Penthouse International Ltd.
468–471 New York Magazine

# THE MISOGAMIST
### FICTION
### BY ANDRE DUBUS
It wasn't that he loved women less, but that he loved the Corps more.

In the summer of 1944 Roy Hodges was back from the Pacific. He was a staff sergeant, a drill instructor at the Recruit Depot at San Diego. He was twenty-six years old, and he was training eighteen-year-old boys. He was also engaged to marry Sheila Russell, who was twenty-six and had been waiting for eight years in Marshall, Tex., to marry him. At eighteen, and still virginal, she had given him a good-bye kiss that was sad, loving, and hopeful. She told him she would not go out with other boys while he was gone. After Boot Camp he went home on leave, and on the first night he took her virginity. She believed he was giving his, but he had bought out of it with a middle-aged whore when he was fifteen. He took her much more easily than he had expected. Every night for three weeks, and sometimes during the afternoons, he made love with her, and she aroused in him an excitement he had never felt before with a woman; nor did he

467

468

469

470

471

472

473

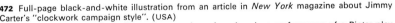

475

476

**472** Full-page black-and-white illustration from an article in *New York* magazine about Jimmy Carter's "clockwork campaign style". (USA)
**473** Page in subdued colours illustrating a review of an American performance of a Pinter play starring Sir John Gielgud and Sir Ralph Richardson. From *New York* magazine. (USA)
**474** Double-spread illustration of the Israeli rescue action in Entebbe, from *New York*. (USA)
**475** Sepia illustration for an article on stock options in *New York*. (USA)
**476, 477** Black-and-white illustration and corresponding page about a Polish restaurant serving *borscht*, from a regular gourmet feature by two designers in *New York* magazine. (USA)
**478, 479** Page and black-and-white illustration from a review in *New York* of the Western film *The Missouri Breaks*. (USA)

**472** Zu einem Artikel über Jimmy Carters sprichwörtliche Pünktlichkeit. Schwarzweiss. (USA)
**473** Ganzseitige Illustration zu einer Besprechung von Harold Pinters neuem Stück *Niemandsland*. Die Abbildung zeigt Harold Pinter und die beiden Hauptdarsteller, Gielgud und Richardson. (USA)
**474** Doppelseite aus einem illustrierten Bericht über die Geiselbefreiung der Israelis auf dem Flughafen von Entebbe. Aus der Zeitschrift *New York*. Mehrfarbig. (USA)
**475** Illustration zu einem Artikel über das Optionsrecht auf Aktien. Aus *New York*. (USA)
**476, 477** Illustration und Seite aus der Zeitschrift *New York*. Der Artikel berichtet über die in einem neu eröffneten polnischen Restaurant servierten Spezialitäten. Schwarzweiss. (USA)
**478, 479** Vollständige Seite und Schwarzweiss-Illustration aus einer Filmrezension, die auf das allgemein sinkende Niveau des Western hinweist. Aus der Zeitschrift *New York*. (USA)

**472** Illustration accompagnant un article sur la ponctualité presque proverbiale de Jimmy Carter. Elément en noir et blanc du magazine *New York*. (USA)
**473** Illustration pleine page pour la critique d'une nouvelle pièce de Harold Pinter. Les personnages représentent Harold Pinter et les deux interprètes principaux. (USA)
**474** Page double figurant dans un rapport illustré sur la libération des otages à Entebbe par les Israéliens. Elément du magazine *New York*. En polychromie. (USA)
**475** Illustration accompagnant un article consacré au droit d'option sur les actions. (USA)
**476, 477** Illustration et page où elle figure. D'une série de *New York* dont s'occupent deux graphistes gourmands – ils parlent ici de *borchtch* servi dans un restaurant polonais. (USA)
**478, 479** Page complète et illustration noir blanc qui y figure. D'une critique cinématographique discutant le déclin général du Western. (USA)

**Magazine Illustrations**
**Zeitschriften-Illustrationen**
**Illustrations de périodiques**

**Moment of Truth** Onrushing commandos kill four terrorists in first assault, including the German hijacker shown slumping near the front door. An Israeli youth, also at the entrance, is killed when mistaken for a terrorist. Ugandan cleaning woman, left front, runs out of bathroom and tries to surrender.

474

477

ARTIST / KÜNSTLER / ARTISTE:

472  Robert Grossman
473  Milton Glaser
474  Julian Allen
475  Paul Richer
476, 477  Milton Glaser
478, 479  Seymour Chwast

DESIGNER / GESTALTER / MAQUETTISTE:

472  Walter Bernard/Robert Grossman
473  Tom Bentkowski
474  Walter Bernard/Milton Glaser
476, 477  Milton Glaser

ART DIRECTOR / DIRECTEUR ARTISTIQUE:

472—479  Milton Glaser/Walter Bernard

PUBLISHER / VERLEGER / EDITEUR:

472—479  New York Magazine

478

479

480

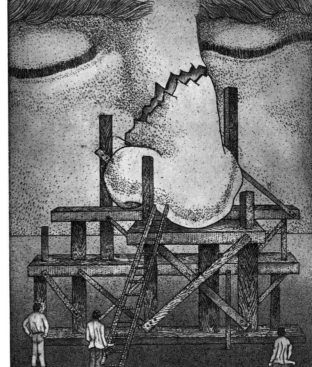

481

ARTIST / KÜNSTLER / ARTISTE:

480 Lanny Sommese
481 Christopher Spollen
482, 483 Jose Reyes
484 Eduard Prüssen
485 Don Weller
486 Phil Jordan
487 George Giusti

484

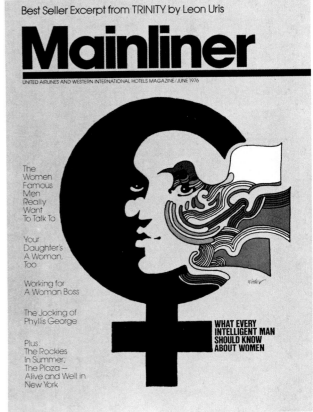

485

480 Front cover of the University of Rhode Island's magazine *Communication Quarterly*. Black on beige stock. (USA)
481 Full-page illustration in shades of yellow for an article in *Emergency Medicine* on the treatment of nasal injuries. (USA)
482, 483 Illustration in colour, and corresponding spread, introducing a series on handling emergencies in *Emergency Medicine*. (USA)
484 Black-and-white linocut illustration from the medical magazine *medizin heute*. (GER)
485 Cover of an issue of *Mainliner*, magazine of United Airlines and Western International Hotels, devoted to women. (USA)
486 Full-page illustration of a "good guy", known from Norse sagas and contractors' experience, from an article in the magazine *Construction Specifier*. Black and white. (USA)
487 Complete cover of *Topic*, a magazine of the arts. (USA)

480 Titelbild einer Vierteljahresschrift der Fakultät für Kommunikation der University of Rhode Island. Schwarz auf beigem Grund. (USA)
481 In Gelb- und Grüntönen gehaltene Illustration aus einer medizinischen Fachzeitschrift, zu einem Artikel über Nasenbrüche. (USA)
482, 483 Illustration und vollständige Doppelseite aus *Emergency Medicine*, zu einem Artikel über die Behandlung bewusstloser Patienten. (USA)
484 Linolschnitt zu einem in der Zeitschrift *medizin heute* veröffentlichten Artikel. (GER)
485 Umschlag der von einer Fluggesellschaft und Hotelkette gemeinsam herausgegebenen Monatsschrift *Mainliner*. Die ganze Nummer ist der Frau gewidmet. Mehrfarbig. (USA)
486 In einer Baufachzeitschrift erschienene Illustration zur «Sage des Charlie Goodguy», der sehr auf Fairness bedacht ist. Schwarzweiss. (USA)
487 Umschlag von *Topic*, einer Zeitschrift für zeitgenössische Kunst. (USA)

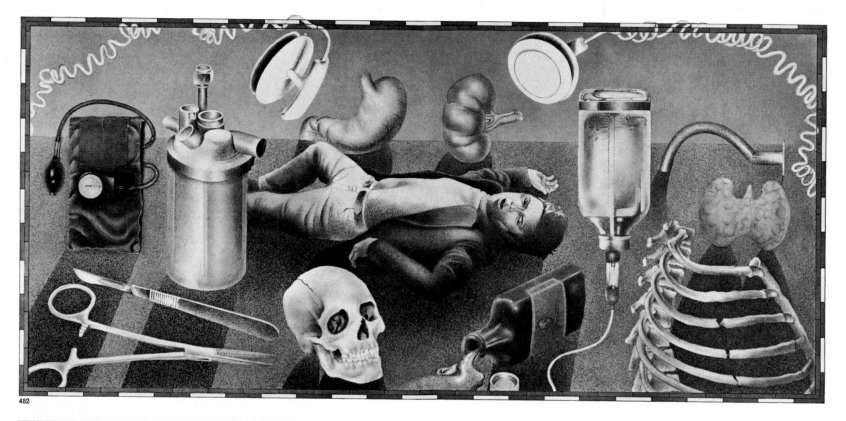

482

486

DESIGNER / GESTALTER / MAQUETTISTE:

480 Lanny Sommese
481—483 Tom Lennon
485 Don Weller

ART DIRECTOR / DIRECTEUR ARTISTIQUE:

480 Lanny Sommese
481—483 Ira Silberlicht/Tom Lennon
485 Chris Mossman
486 Phil Jordan
487 Joseph Baumer

AGENCY / AGENTUR / AGENCE – STUDIO:

485 Weller Institute for the Cure of Design
486 Beveridge & Assocs., Inc.

PUBLISHER / VERLEGER / EDITEUR:

480 Communication Quarterly
481—483 Fischer Medical Publications
484 Deutscher Ärzte Verlag
485 East/West Network
486 Construction Specification Institute
487 Topic Magazine

483

480 Couverture d'une revue trimestrielle de la faculté des communications de l'Université de Rhode Island. Noir sur fond beige. (USA)
481 Illustration tirée d'un périodique médical, accompagnant un article sur les fractures du nez. Prédominance de tons jaunes/verts. (USA)
482, 483 Illustration et page double où elle figure. Article d'*Emergency Medicine* sur le traitement de personnes évanouies. (USA)
484 Lino accompagnant un article qui a paru dans *medizin heute*, périodique médical. (GER)
485 Couverture d'un mensuel publié par une compagnie aérienne en coopération avec une chaîne d'hôtels. Ce numéro est entièrement consacré aux problèmes de la femme. En polychromie. (USA)
486 Illustration d'une revue professionnelle. «La légende de Charlie Goodguy», un type qui veille à la loyauté envers les clients. (USA)
487 Couverture de *Topic,* magazine d'art contemporain. (USA)

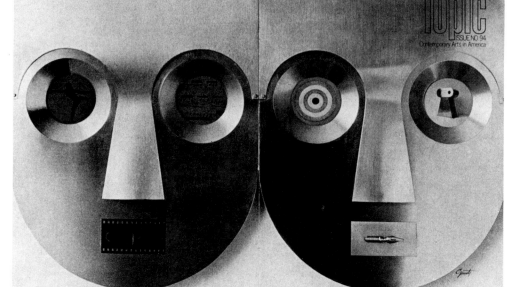

487

488

489

490

491

492

493

ARTIST / KÜNSTLER / ARTISTE:

489 Stanislaw Fernandes
490 Jack Unruh
491–493 Jack + Pam Lefkowitz
494 André Amstutz

DESIGNER / GESTALTER / MAQUETTISTE:

488 Robert Banks
489 John Vogler
490 Dennis Benoit
491–493 Jack + Pam Lefkowitz
494 André Amstutz

ART DIRECTOR / DIRECTEUR ARTISTIQUE:

488 Robert Banks
489 John Vogler
490 Dennis Benoit
491–493 Jack Lefkowitz
494 Norman Brownsword

AGENCY / AGENTUR / AGENCE – STUDIO:

488 U.S. Information Agency
489 Stanislaw Fernandes Solution
491–493 Jack Lefkowitz Inc.

PUBLISHER / VERLEGER / EDITEUR:

488 Economic Impact magazine
489 Business Week
490 Dallas Chamber of Commerce
491–493 Industrial Launderer
494 BBC Publications Ltd.

**488** Full-page illustration for an article on economic forecasting in the magazine *Economic Impact*. Black and white. (USA)
**489** Cover of an issue of *Business Week* containing an article on the future of Wall Street. Yellow street sign, red changes, tan background. (USA)
**490** Polychrome cover of a magazine issued by the Dallas Chamber of Commerce, here devoted to the State Fair of Texas. (USA)
**491–493** Covers of the magazine *Industrial Launderer*, all in flat colours. The references are to polluted air in factories, to inflammable textiles and to the preferential treatment given to white-collar workers. (USA)
**494** Illustration for a story from a series of books designed for children's education in conjunction with radio programmes. Roughly actual size. (GBR)

**488** Schwarzweiss-Illustration aus einem Wirtschaftsmagazin zu einem Artikel über wirtschaftliche Voraussagen. (USA)
**489** Mehrfarbiger Umschlag einer Finanzzeitschrift. Die Einbahntafel soll auf die Krise hinweisen, in welcher sich die amerikanische Wirtschaft im Moment befindet. (USA)
**490** Mehrfarbiger Umschlag der Zeitschrift *Dallas*. (USA)
**491–493** Titelblätter einer Fachzeitschrift. Abb. 491: Luftverschmutzung in Fabriken (mehrfarbig); Abb. 492: über die Brennbarkeit von Textilien (stahlblauer Grund); Abb. 493: über die Bevorzugung von Büroangestellten (weisser Kragen) gegenüber den Arbeitern (blauer Kragen). (USA)
**494** Illustration in Originalgrösse aus einer Publikationsreihe der BBC, die im Zusammenhang mit Bildungsprogrammen für Kinder herausgegeben wird. (GBR)

**488** Illustration en noir-blanc d'un magazine économique accompagnant un article sur les prévisions économiques. (USA)
**489** Illustration polychrome d'un périodique économique. Le panneau (sense unique ou quelle direction?) se rapporte à la crise actuelle de l'économie américaine. Polychrome. (USA)
**490** Illustration de couverture de la revue *Dallas*. (USA)
**491–493** Couvertures de revues professionnelles. Fig. 491: la pollution de l'air dans les usines (polychrome); fig. 492: les tissus inflammables (fond bleu acier); fig. 493: le traitement de faveur des employés (colle blanche) par rapport aux ouvriers (colle bleue) – chemises bleue et blanche. (USA)
**494** Illustration en grandeur nature d'une série de publications de la BBC, réalisées dans le cadre de ses programmes d'éducation pour enfants. (GBR)

**495** Illustration running over one and a third pages for an article on popular delusions published in the psychological magazine *Human Behavior*. (USA)
**496** Illustration for a title in the *Radio Times*. (GBR)
**497, 498** Silkscreen covers in colour for the magazine of printing and reproduction *Il Poligrafico Italiano*. On the one cover hands become human silhouettes, on the other they develop new features with a symbolic significance. (ITA)
**499** Black-and-white illustration for an article on costing in *Management Today*. (GBR)
**500** Page reviewing coming events in Chicago, from *Chicago Magazine*. In colour. (USA)
**501** Double spread with colour illustrations from the magazine *trotzdem* published by the City of Frankfurt for the handicapped. Here about a park and walks in Frankfurt. (GER)

**495** Illustration aus einer Zeitschrift für Psychologie, hier zu einem Artikel über die aussergewöhnlichen und doch so alltäglichen Selbsttäuschungen des Einzelnen. (USA)
**496** Illustration aus der *Radio Times*. Schwarzweiss. (GBR)
**497, 498** Mehrfarbige Umschläge einer polygraphischen Zeitschrift. Abb. 497: Hände verwandeln sich in Profile, wobei jedes seine eigene Geschichte hat; Abb. 498: die Hände symbolisieren den Teufel, Energie, Abwendung des Bösen und Verführung. (ITA)
**499** Illustration aus der Zeitschrift *Management Today* über Kostenberechnung. (GBR)
**500** Mehrfarbiger Veranstaltungskalender, der im *Chicago Magazine* veröffentlicht wird. (USA)
**501** Doppelseite mit mehrfarbigen Illustrationen aus der Zeitschrift *trotzdem*, die von der Stadt Frankfurt/M für die behinderten Mitbürger herausgegeben wird. (GER)

ARTIST / KÜNSTLER / ARTISTE:

495 Abe Gurvin
496 Wendy Hoile
497, 498 Giancarlo Iliprandi
499 Michael Foreman
500 Pat Dypold
501 Hans Jürgen Rau

DESIGNER / GESTALTER / MAQUETTISTE:

495 Abe Gurvin
496 Robert Priest/Wendy Hoile
501 Hans Jürgen Rau

ART DIRECTOR / DIRECTEUR ARTISTIQUE:

495 Annemarie Clarke
496 Robert Priest
497, 498 Giancarlo Iliprandi
499 Roland Schenk
500 Jack Lund
501 Hans Jürgen Rau

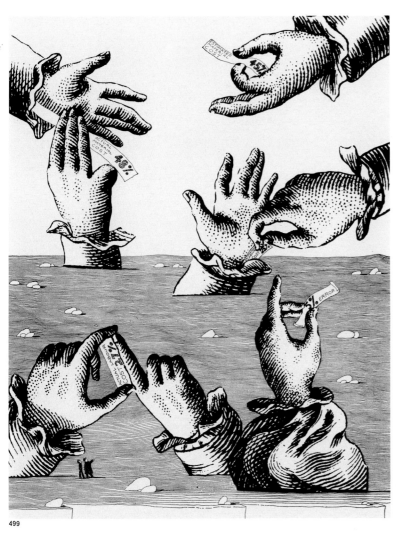

499

500

**495** Illustration tirée d'un périodique de psychologie. Elle accompagne un article sur les illusions auxquelles on succombe chaque jour. (USA)
**496** Illustration figurant dans le *Radio Times*. Noir et blanc. (GBR)
**497, 498** Couvertures (en couleurs) d'un magazine polygraphique. Fig. 497: les mains se transforment en profils, dont chacun a sa propre histoire; fig. 498: les mains prennent des contours ayant une signification symbolique. (ITA)
**499** Illustration du magazine *Management Today* sur le calcul des frais. (GBR)
**500** Page du *Chicago Magazine* avec calendrier des manifestations à Chicago. En couleurs. (USA)
**501** Conception d'une page double avec illustrations en couleurs du magazine *trotzdem* que la ville de Francfort s/M publie pour les handicapés. (GER)

AGENCY / AGENTUR / AGENCE – STUDIO:

495 Abe Gurvin
501 Studio und Edition Rau

PUBLISHER / VERLEGER / EDITEUR:

495 Human Behavior
496 Radio Times
497, 498 Il Poligrafico Italiano
499 Management Today
500 Chicago Magazine
501 Frankfurter Verein für soziale Heimstätten e. V. Paul Marx

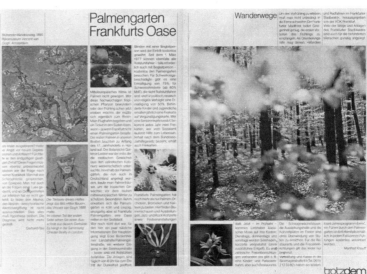

501

502

505

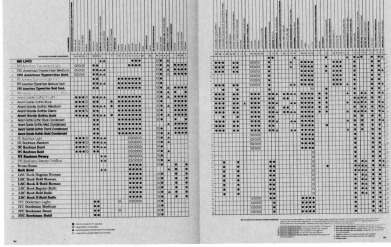

506

ARTIST / KÜNSTLER / ARTISTE:

502, 505  John Alcorn
503, 504  André Zenou
507  Geoffrey Moss
508  Tim
509  Randy Enos

DESIGNER / GESTALTER / MAQUETTISTE:

502, 505–507  Herb Lubalin
508  Jean-Régis Roustan
509  Tom Lennon

503

504

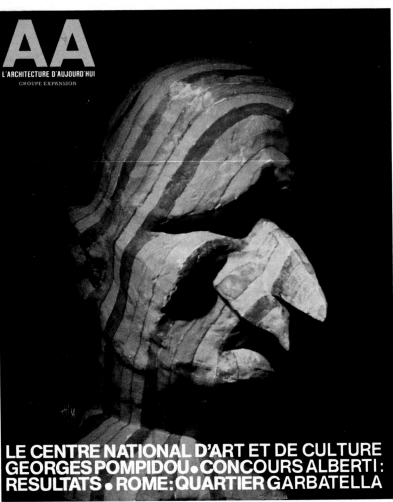

508

ART DIRECTOR / DIRECTEUR ARTISTIQUE:

502, 505–507  Herb Lubalin
508  Sylvain Canaux
509  Ira Silberlicht/Tom Lennon

AGENCY / AGENTUR / AGENCE – STUDIO:

502, 505–507  LSC&P Design Group, Inc.

PUBLISHER / VERLEGER / EDITEUR:

502, 505–507  International Typeface Corporation
503, 504  Citroën SA
508  Groupe Expansion
509  Fischer Medical Publications

168

U&lc. VOLUME 3, NUMBER 2, 1976

HERB LUBALIN, EDITORIAL & DESIGN DIRECTOR
AARON BURNS, EDITORIAL DIRECTOR
EDWARD RONDTHALER, EDITORIAL DIRECTOR
JACK ANSON FINKE, ASSOCIATE EDITOR
JEROME SNYDER, CONTRIBUTING EDITOR
ANNA McCUSKER, TONY DISPIGNA, ANDY DIODA, JOHN WILLIAMS,
LOWRY THOMPSON, MARK HUIE, ART & PRODUCTION EDITORS
JOHN PRENTKI, BUSINESS AND ADVERTISING MANAGER
EDWARD GOTTSCHALL, EDITORIAL/ADVERTISING COORDINATOR

U&lc IS PUBLISHED FOUR TIMES A
YEAR IN MARCH, JUNE, OCTOBER AND DECEMBER
BY INTERNATIONAL TYPEFACE CORPORATION
216 EAST 45TH STREET, NEW YORK, N.Y. 10017
A JOINTLY OWNED SUBSIDIARY OF
PHOTO-LETTERING, INC. AND LUBALIN, BURNS & CO. INC.
CONTROLLED CIRCULATION POSTAGE PAID AT NEW YORK,
N.Y. AND AT FARMINGDALE, N.Y.

BOARD OF DIRECTORS:
EDWARD RONDTHALER, CHAIRMAN
AARON BURNS, PRESIDENT
HERB LUBALIN, EXECUTIVE VICE PRESIDENT
JOHN PRENTKI, VICE PRESIDENT, GENERAL MANAGER
BOB FARBER, SENIOR VICE PRESIDENT
ED BENGUIAT, VICE PRESIDENT
STEPHEN KOPEC, VICE PRESIDENT

U.S. SUBSCRIPTION TO INDIVIDUALS $6.00—SINGLE COPIES $1.50
ELSEWHERE SUBSCRIPTION. $8.00, SINGLE COPIES $2.00.

## THE SAD STATE OF THE UNION
### GEOFFREY MOSS

"Symbols communicate. Word-bubbles, captions, and tags are unnecessary. The National pattern is dominated by conflict. The sources are endless. As long as one driver honks at another, or there's a fly on your nose, there'll be eventual battle."

Geoffrey Moss, the well-known satirist/illustrator has for years been wickedly depicting the national condition with a series of caption-less drawings enjoyed by readers of the Washington Post and a variety of other publications throughout the country. Unlike the President of the United States, Moss addresses his constituency, on the state of the union, with pictures, rather than words. And does so as a frequent contributor, besides his syndication, to such diverse publications as Time Magazine, Fortune, Horizon, American Heritage, Emergency Medicine and The New York Times. Also, unlike many of our political figures, he has an uncompromising viewpoint, untempered by the "straddle-fence" philosophy of pleasing all of the people all of the time. Insomuch as a reduction in size (essential for reproduction of so many drawings in U&lc) limits, in some instances, the full impact of the satirical content, the editors — ever ready to go all-out on behalf of our readers — have provided otherwise "unnecessary" captions.

THIS ARTICLE WAS SET IN ITC AMERICAN TYPEWRITER

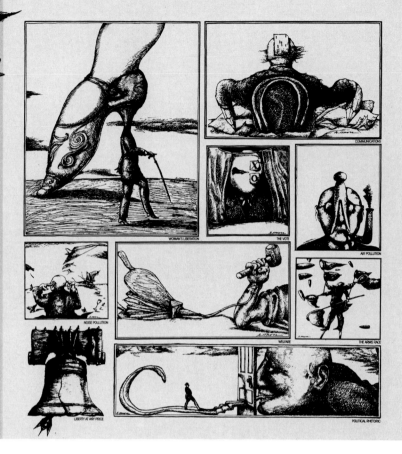

507

509

502, 505 Vignette and complete double spread of American speciality recipes from the magazine of typography U&lc. Black and white. (USA)
503, 504 Covers of two issues of the Citroën quarterly Le Double Chevron. Fig. 503 in silver on black, Fig. 504 in full colour showing a Citroën model in Vasarely's studio. (FRA)
506, 507 Further double spreads from U & lc. Fig. 506, on yellow paper, is part of a directory of typefaces available from the International Typeface Corporation, Fig. 507 part of a satirical graphic commentary on the State of the Union. (USA)
508 Cover of the magazine L'Architecture d'Aujourd'hui. The polychrome head refers to the new Pompidou Centre of art and culture in Paris. (FRA)
509 Full-page illustration from Emergeny Medicine: finger injuries from discus throwing. (USA)

502, 505 Illustration und Doppelseite aus U & lc, einer typographischen Zeitschrift, hier zu einem Artikel über amerikanische Gerichte mit amüsanten Namen. Schwarzweiss. (USA)
503, 504 Umschläge von zwei Ausgaben des Informationsbulletins von Citroën – Le Double Chevron. Abb. 503: die Illustration symbolisiert den «interplanetaren» Erfolg des Citroën CX, schwarz/silber; Abb. 504: Modell eines Citroën CX in Vasarelys Atelier. Mehrfarbig. (FRA)
506, 507 Weitere Seiten aus der typographischen Zweimonatszeitschrift U&lc: Doppelseite aus einem dieser Nummer beigehefteten Katalog über die Schriften der International Typeface Corp. (gelbes Papier) und Karikaturen zum Thema «Der traurige Zustand der Union». (USA)
508 Mehrfarbiges Titelblatt einer Zeitschrift für moderne Architektur. Diese Nummer enthält einen Artikel über das neue Pariser Kulturzentrum, das Centre Pompidou. (FRA)
509 Illustration zu einem in einer medizinischen Fachzeitschrift erschienenen Artikel über Verletzungen, die durch Wurfscheiben entstehen können. (USA)

502, 505 Illustration et page double d'un magazine typographique, ici pour un article consacré à des mets américains portant des noms amusants. En noir et blanc. (USA)
503, 504 Couvertures de deux numéros de Le Double Chevron, bulletin d'information de Citroën. Fig. 503: illustration symbolisant le succès «interplanétaire» de la Citroën CX (noir et argent); fig. 504: modèle de la Citroën CX dans l'atelier de Vasarely. Un commissaire priseur imagina de marier l'art moderne à l'auto en demandant à quelques grands peintres de décorer des maquettes de véhicules qui seront vendues aux enchères au profit de l'œuvre des Petits Lits Blancs. (FRA)
506, 507 Deux autres pages de la revue typographique U&lc: page double d'un catalogue inséré dans ce numéro et présentant les caractères de la International Typeface Corp. (papier jaune) et des caricatures accompagnant un article intitulé «L'état lamentable de l'Union». (USA)
508 Couverture polychrome de la revue L'Architecture d'Aujourd'hui. Ce numéro contient un article consacré au nouveau centre culturel de Paris – le Centre Pompidou. (FRA)
509 Illustration publiée dans un périodique médical pour un article sur les lésions du médius provoquées par les disques à jeter. (USA)

**Trade Magazines**
**Fachzeitschriften**
**Revues professionnelles**

510

511

513

514

**510–515** Full-page illustrations, all in full colour, facing the opening of articles in the magazine *Psychologie.* The subjects are: young people's reasons for taking drugs (Fig. 510), controlled breathing as an aid in attaining psychic balance (Fig. 511), the new cult of "biological" foods (Fig. 512), methods of mnemonic classification (Fig. 513), the life of the "wolf man" who was one of Freud's most famous patients (Fig. 514) and a scientific method of slimming (Fig. 515). (FRA)
**516, 517** Another example of a full-page illustration facing the opening of an article in the magazine *Psychologie,* with the complete double page. The illustration is this time in black and white, and the subject is the problems raised for the male partner by contraceptive measures. (FRA)
**518** Cover illustration, in full colour, of the magazine *Modern Medicine.* The subject is the use of insect poisons against human allergies. (USA)

**510–517** Ganzseitige Illustrationen und Doppelseite aus der Zeitschrift *Psychologie* zu folgenden Artikeln – Abb. 510: über das Drogenproblem bei Jugendlichen (mehrfarbig); Abb. 511: über den Zusammenhang von psychischem Gleichgewicht und richtiger Atmung (hellblauer Himmel, Lunge grün und hellrot); Abb. 512: über die neue Bewegung in Richtung von biologischer Nahrung (sandfarbener Grund, mattblauer Himmel, grüne Blätter); Abb. 513 über das Erinnerungsvermögen, im Altertum als reines Klassifizieren von Informationen im Gehirn betrachtet (gelbe Schädeldecke); Abb. 514: Geschichte und Analyse des Wolfsmanns, Freuds berühmtestem Patienten (mehrfarbig); Abb. 515: eine wissenschaftliche Methode zum Abmagern; Abb. 516/517: Empfängnisverhütung und die sich für den Mann ergebenden Probleme. (FRA)
**518** Umschlagillustration von *Modern Medicine* zu einem Artikel über den Gebrauch von Insektengiften für hyperallergische Patienten. Mehrfarbig. (USA)

512

516

ARTIST / KÜNSTLER / ARTISTE:

510 511, 514, 516, 517 Daniel Sinay
512 Georges Lemoine
513 Jean Alessandrini
515 Robert Grossman
518 Don Punchatz

ART DIRECTOR:

510–517 Daniel Sinay

AGENCY / AGENTUR / AGENCE:

510–517 Hollenstein Création

PUBLISHER / VERLEGER / EDITEUR:

510–517 Centre d'Etude et de
        Promotion de la lecture
518 Modern Medicine

517

515

**510–517** Illustrations pleines pages, toutes en couleurs, introduisant des articles publiés dans le magazine *Psychologie*. Les thèmes en sont: Pourquoi la drogue? L'ethnologue y voit un rite de passage de l'adolescence à l'âge adulte (fig. 510); Savez-vous respirer? L'équilibre psychique passe par l'équilibre respiratoire (fig. 511); Le refus de manger idiot. Après le culte de la voiture un nouveau culte: manger sain, manger «biologique» (fig. 512); L'art de la mémoire. Pour les anciens, notre cerveau était un palais dans lequel il fallait apprendre à classer les informations (fig. 513); L'homme aux loups – L'existence pathétique du plus célèbre patient de Freud (fig. 514); Une méthode scientifique pour maigrir (fig. 515); L'homme face à la contraception et les problèmes qui en résultent (fig. 516/517). (FRA)
**518** Illustration de couverture d'un périodique médical. Elle se rapporte aux poisons d'insectes utilisés contre les allergies humaines. (USA)

518

**519, 522** Full-colour covers of *Time* magazine. The issues contain articles on sex in tennis and the future of the Republican Party in America. (USA)
**520, 523** Covers of the weekly *L'Express*. The full-colour illustrations refer to rising prices and to the influence of Castro in Africa (see beard). (FRA)
**521** Cover of a Christmas number of *TV Guide*. Full colour. (USA)
**524** Cover of a magazine containing collections of stories. Red-striped shirt, blue hair, yellow ground. (JPN)
**525** Illustration in roughly actual size for the cover of a weekly magazine. (JPN)

**519, 522** Titelblätter des Nachrichtenmagazins *Time* zum Thema: «Sex und Tennis, das neue Kampffeld» und die Pleite der republikanischen Partei. Mehrfarbig. (USA)
**520, 523** Titelblätter des Wochenmagazins *L'Express*. Sie beziehen sich auf Artikel über Preisdruck und Afrika als Pulverfass (Castros Bart in der Form des afrikanischen Kontinents). (FRA)
**521** Mehrfarbiges Titelblatt eines TV-Programmheftes. (USA)
**524** Umschlag einer Zeitschrift. Gelber Grund, blaue Haare, rot-weiss gestreiftes Hemd. (JPN)
**525** Illustration in Originalgrösse, als Titelblatt eines Wochenmagazins verwendet. (JPN)

**519, 522** Couvertures du magazine d'information *Time*. Les thèmes: la sexualité et le tennis – le nouveau champ de bataille, et le débâcle du parti républicain. En polychromie. (USA)
**520, 523** Couvertures de l'hebdomadaire *L'Express*. Elles se réfèrent à des articles sur la politique des prix et l'influence de Castro en Afrique (barbe représentant l'Afrique). (FRA)
**521** Couverture couleur d'un programme de télévision. (USA)
**524** Couverture d'un magazine. Fond jaune, cheveux bleus, chemise rayée en rouge et blanc. (JPN)
**525** Illustration en grandeur nature figurant sur la couverture d'un magazine hebdomadaire. (JPN)

ARTIST / KÜNSTLER / ARTISTE:

519  Charles Saxon
520, 523  Tim
521  Ronald Searle
522  Jack Davis
524  Tadanori Yokoo
525  Aoi Fujimoto

DESIGNER / GESTALTER / MAQUETTISTE:

520, 523  Georges Lacroix
521  Ronald Searle
525  Aoi Fujimoto

ART DIRECTOR / DIRECTEUR ARTISTIQUE:

519, 522  David Merrill
520, 523  René Guyonnet
521  Jerry Alten
524  Tadanori Yokoo

AGENCY / AGENTUR / AGENCE – STUDIO:

521  John Locke

PUBLISHER / VERLEGER / EDITEUR:

519, 522  Time, Inc.
520, 523  Express-Union
521  Triangle Publications Inc.
524  Yomiuri-Shinbun-Sha
525  Futaba-Sha Co.

519

520
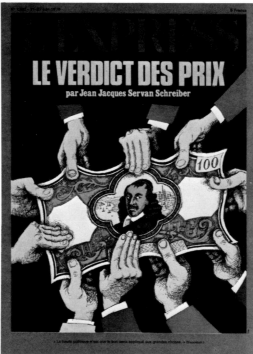

521

522

523

524
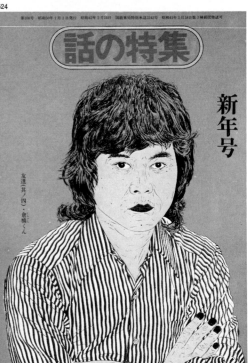

525

526

**Magazine Covers**
**Zeitschriftenumschläge**
**Couvertures de périodiques**

174

# DER SPIEGEL

**WAHL '76**

## Der Partner

SPIEGEL
Gespräch mit
FDP-Chef
Genscher

527

# DER SPIEGEL

**WAHL '76**

## Der Heraus-forderer

SPIEGEL
Gespräch mit
Helmut
Kohl

Schmutziger Fortschritt
**Seveso droht überall**

528

ARTIST / KÜNSTLER / ARTISTE:

526–529, 531  Jean Mulatier
530  Bill Nelson
532  Urs Maltry

DESIGNER / GESTALTER / MAQUETTISTE:

530  Steve Phillips

ART DIRECTOR / DIRECTEUR ARTISTIQUE:

526–529, 531  Eberhard Wachsmuth
530  Steve Phillips

PUBLISHER / VERLEGER / EDITEUR:

526–529, 531  Spiegel-Verlag
530  New Times Communications
532  Tages-Anzeiger AG

# DER SPIEGEL

Ost-Berlins Waffenhilfe
DDR-Soldaten
in Afrika

## Der Titel-verteidiger

SPIEGEL
Gespräch mit
Kanzler
Schmidt

**WAHL '76**

529

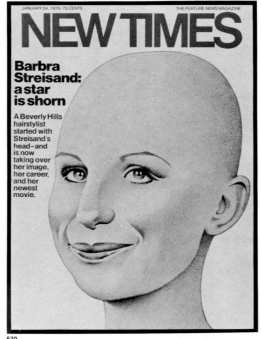

JANUARY 24, 1975 / 75 CENTS          THE FEATURE NEWS MAGAZINE

# NEW TIMES

## Barbra Streisand: a star is shorn

A Beverly Hills
hairstylist
started with
Streisand's
head – and
is now
taking over
her image,
her career,
and her
newest
movie.

530

526–529, 531 Illustration in actual size and four complete covers of the political magazine *Der Spiegel*, issued in succession at the time of the West German elections in 1976 and presenting the party leaders: Genscher as "the partner" (Fig. 527), Kohl as "the challenger" (Fig. 528), Helmut Schmidt as "the title-holder" (Fig. 529) and Strauss as "the godfather" (Figs. 526 and 531). (GER)
530 Cover of the magazine *New Times* with a portrait of the actress and singer Barbra Streisand, whose career has been taken over by a Beverly Hills hair stylist. (USA)
532 Cover of the weekly *Tages-Anzeiger Magazin*. The issue contained a feature on methods of stopping the waste of energy. Blue ground. (SWI)

526–529, 531 Illustration in Originalgrösse und vier Titelblätter des wöchentlich publizierten Nachrichtenmagazins *Der Spiegel*. Die Serie, die anlässlich der letzten Bundeskanzlerwahl erschien, brachte Artikel und Interviews zu parteipolitischen Fragen mit den Kanzlerkandidaten Schmidt (Abb. 529) und Kohl (Abb. 528) und den Führern der Koalitionsparteien, dem FDP-Parteivorsitzenden Genscher (Abb. 527) und dem CSU-Parteivorsitzenden Strauss (Abb. 526/531). (GER)
530 Umschlag der Zeitschrift *New Times*. Die Illustration bezieht sich auf einen Artikel mit dem Titel «Barbra Streisand: ein Star wurde geschoren»; er berichtet über einen Hair Stylist in Beverly Hills, der sich nun um ihre Karriere kümmert. (USA)
532 Titelblatt des Wochenendmagazins des *Tages-Anzeigers*. Die Illustration zu einem Artikel über Massnahmen gegen die Energieverschwendung soll symbolisieren, wie wenig in dieser Hinsicht unternommen wird. Vorwiegend in Blautönen. (SWI)

526–529, 531 Illustration en grandeur originale et quatre couvertures du magazine d'information *Der Spiegel*. La série a été publiée à l'occasion de l'élection du chancelier de la République fédérale d'Allemagne avec des articles sur le programme politique et des interviews avec les dirigeants des partis: Genscher, le partenaire (fig. 527), Kohl, le challenger (fig. 528), Helmut Schmidt, le défenseur du titre (fig. 529) et Strauss, le parrain (fig. 526 et 531). (GER)
530 Couverture du magazine *New Times*. L'illustration se réfère à un article intitulé: Barbra Streisand, une vedette à la tête chauve. On se moque du fait qu'un hair stylist de Beverly Hills s'occupe dorénavant de sa carrière. (USA)
532 Couverture du supplément hebdomadaire du *Tages-Anzeiger*. L'illustration, se rapportant à un article sur les démarches d'économie d'énergie devrait symboliser que les responsables n'entreprennent rien dans cette direction. Tons bleus. (SWI)

# DER SPIEGEL

**WAHL '76**

Franz Josef Strauß

## Der Pate

SPIEGEL-REPORT:
**Die Nicht-Wähler entscheiden**

531

# TAGES ANZEIGER MAGAZIN

532

535

536

537

534

533

533, 534 Two covers of the humorous magazine *National Lampoon*. The one refers to the explosive impact of the magazine, the other to Elvis Presley as he approaches middle age. Full colour. (USA)
535, 536 Two covers of the satirical magazine *Szpilki*: Mona Lisa and sister (black and yellow on red), and the danger of feeding hungry dogs (yellow and brown on black). (POL)
537 Cover art for *The New York Times Magazine*. "If France's Michelin rated our restaurants…", a feature on the quality of food served in American restaurants. (USA)
538, 539 Cover art for the magazine *Newsweek,* with the complete cover. A feature in this issue was devoted to the subject of gossip. (USA)

533, 534 Zwei Titelblätter der humoristischen Monatszeitschrift *National Lampoon*. Abb. 533: der «einschlagende» Erfolg der Zeitschrift; Abb. 534: der alternde Elvis Presley. Mehrfarbig. (USA)
535, 536 Titelblätter der satirischen Zeitschrift *Szpilki*. Mehrfarbig. (POL)
537 Umschlag einer Ausgabe des illustrierten Magazins der *New York Times*. Der Artikel «Wenn Frankreichs Michelin unsere Restaurants bewerten müsste…» – mit einer Anspielung auf den Reiseführer Guide Michelin – vergleicht die europäische und amerikanische Küche. (USA)
538, 539 Illustration und vollständiger Umschlag des Nachrichtenmagazins *Newsweek* zum Thema «Klatsch». (USA)

533, 534 Deux couvertures du mensuel humoristique *National Lampoon*. Fig. 533: l'effet éclatant du magazine; fig. 534: Elvis Presley entre deux âges. En polychromie. (USA)
535, 536 Couvertures du magazine satirique *Szpilki*. En polychromie. (POL)
537 Couverture d'un numéro du supplément hebdomadaire du *New York Times*. «Si le guide Michelin français se mettait à classer nos restaurants…» (USA)
538, 539 Détail de l'illustration et couverture complète où elle figure. Elément du magazine d'information *Newsweek* se rapportant à un article sur le commérage. (USA)

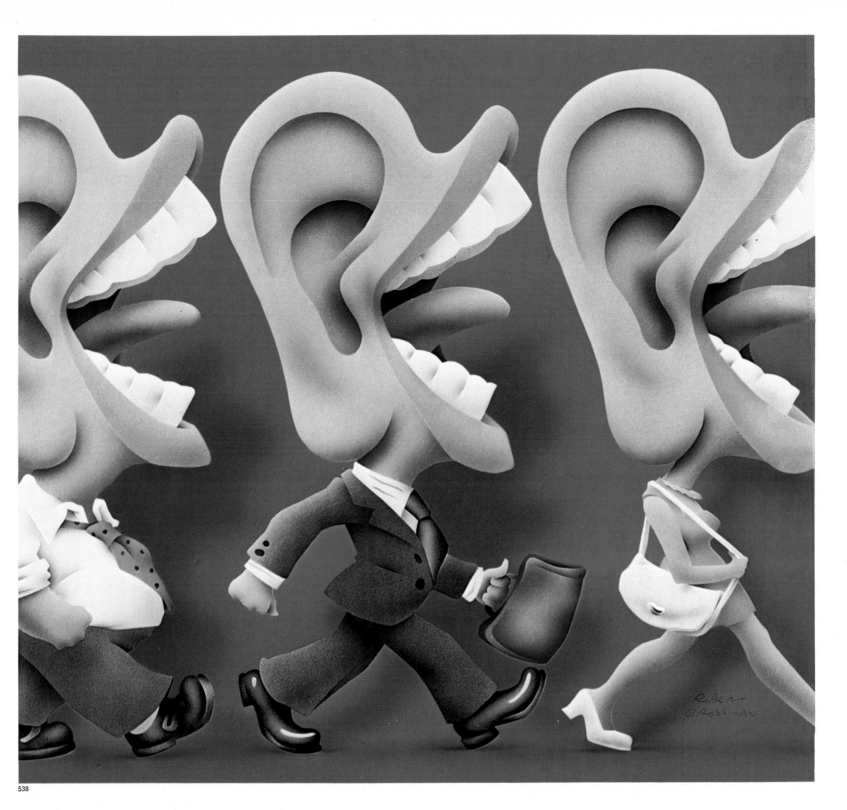

538

539

ARTIST / KÜNSTLER / ARTISTE:

533 Page Wood
534 John Youssi
535 Alain le Quernec
536 Zygmunt Zaradkiewicz
537–539 Robert Grossman

DESIGNER / GESTALTER / MAQUETTISTE:

533, 534 Peter Kleinman
535, 536 Alicja Bobrowska

ART DIRECTOR / DIRECTEUR ARTISTIQUE:

533, 534 Peter Kleinman
535, 536 Maria Byskiniewicz
537 Ruth Ansel
538, 539 Ron Meyerson/Robert Engle

PUBLISHER / VERLEGER / EDITEUR:

533, 534 National Lampoon/Twenty-First Century
        Communications, Inc.
535, 536 Szpilki
537 The New York Times
538, 539 Newsweek

**Magazine Covers**
**Zeitschriftenumschläge**
**Couvertures de périodiques**

540

ARTIST / KÜNSTLER:

540, 541 Tibor Helényi
542 Eugene Hoffman

DESIGNER / GESTALTER:

540, 541 Györgi Kemény

ART DIRECTOR:

540, 541 Györgi Kemény
542 Eugene Hoffman

AGENCY / AGENTUR:

542 Eugene Hoffman

PUBLISHER / VERLEGER:

540, 541 Interpress
542 Leisure Living

**540, 541** Detail of the artwork and complete cover of *Interpress Magazin*. The title of the picture is "Moving Forts". (HUN)
**542** Cover in roughly actual size of the magazine *Leisure Living*. The issue contains an article on the work of the artist, who specializes in three-dimensional metal artefacts. (USA)

**540, 541** Illustration in Originalgrösse und vollständiges Titelblatt des *Interpress Magazins*. Die Abbildung trägt den Titel «Die beweglichen Festungen». (HUN)
**542** Titelblatt (in Originalgrösse) der Zeitschrift *Leisure Living,* die einen Artikel über den Künstler enthält. Komposition in Eisen. (USA)

**540, 541** Illustration en grandeur nature et couverture complète de l'*Interpress Magazine*. L'illustration est intitulée «Les forteresses mobiles». (HUN)
**542** Couverture (grandeur nature) du magazine *Leisure Living*. Ce numéro contient un article sur l'artiste Eugene Hoffman, spécialisé en compositions tridimensionnelles en métal. (USA)

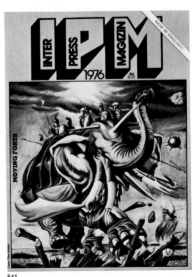

541

543

ARTIST / KÜNSTLER / ARTISTE:

543, 544  Etienne Delessert
545, 548  Barth
546  Eugène Mihaesco
547  Jacqui Morgan
549  Lou Myers
550  Ronald Searle

DESIGNER / GESTALTER / MAQUETTISTE:

547  Don McClain/Stanley Hochstadt

ART DIRECTOR / DIRECTEUR ARTISTIQUE:

543, 544  Pierre Berard
545, 548  Franz Mächler
546  Lee Lorenz
547  Jerry Joseph

PUBLISHER / VERLEGER / EDITEUR:

543, 544  Télérama
545, 548  Nebelspalter Verlag
546, 549, 550  The New Yorker
547  Society Audio Consultants

544

545

546

547

548

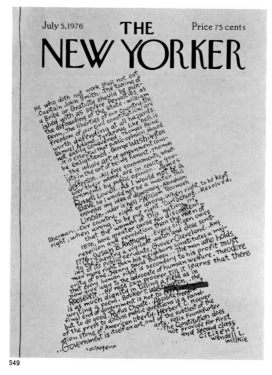

549

550

**Magazine Covers**
**Zeitschriftenumschläge**
**Couvertures de périodiques**

**543, 544** "The J Day of music." Artwork in roughly actual size and complete cover of the magazine *Télérama*, a weekly containing radio and television programmes. (FRA)
**545, 548** Two covers for the humorous weekly *Nebelspalter*: a "housewife's recipe" (green suit, red and white tablecloth), and a polydactyl secretary listening to her master's voice (green typewriter, blue dress, yellow ground). (SWI)
**546, 549, 550** Three covers of the weekly magazine *The New Yorker*. Fig. 546 in coloured pencil on blue ground, showing that everything in our civilization belches steam amd smoke; Fig. 549 a head with blue eye and red mouth consisting of great statements by famous Americans; Fig. 550 in subdued colours depicting the bird that has been driven from the skies by men's aviation and has taken to the road. (USA)
**547** Cover of *Sac's Audio Primer*, house organ of the Society of Audio Consultants. Artwork in pastel shades. (USA)

**543, 544** Illustration in Originalgrösse und vollständiger Umschlag der Zeitschrift *Télérama*, ein wöchentlich erscheinender Veranstaltungskalender. (FRA)
**545, 548** Zwei Titelblätter der humoristischen Wochenzeitschrift *Nebelspalter*. Abb. 545: rot-weiss karierte Tischdecke, «eingemachter» Mann in grünem Anzug; Abb. 548: Tippmamsell in blauem Kleid, grüne Maschine, gelber Grund. (SWI)
**546, 549, 550** Titelblätter der Zeitschrift *The New Yorker*. Abb. 546: bemalter Bleistift auf Blau, der zeigt, dass alles in unserer Zivilisation Rauch und Dampf speit; Abb. 549: Zitate berühmter Amerikaner zum Thema Menschenrechte in der Form eines Kopfes; Abb. 550: der Vogel, der vom Flugzeug aus der Luft vertrieben wurde und nun zu Fuss geht. (USA)
**547** Umschlag der Hauszeitschrift eines Beraterteams, das sich auf die Installation von Aufnahme- und Wiedergabegeräten spezialisiert hat. Illustration in Pastellfarben. (USA)

**543, 544** Illustration en grandeur originale et couverture complète du magazine *Télérama*, un calendrier des manifestations qui paraît chaque semaine. (FRA)
**545, 548** Deux couvertures de l'hebdomadaire humoristique *Nebelspalter*. Fig. 545: «La recette de la ménagère», nappe carrée en rouge et blanc, homme «conservé» en vert; fig. 548: secrétaire polydactyle en robe bleue écoutant la voix du maître. (SWI)
**546, 549, 550** Couvertures du magazine *The New Yorker*. Fig. 546: crayon coloré, démontrant que tout ce que notre civilisation produit vomit de la fumée et de la vapeur; fig. 549: citations de célèbres personnages américains au sujet des droits de l'homme, arrangées sous forme de tête; fig. 550: l'oiseau qui est chassé du ciel par l'aviation et reprend la route. (USA)
**547** Couverture du journal d'entreprise d'un groupe de conseillers spécialisés dans l'installation d'appareils d'enregistrement et de reproduction. Composition en tons pastels. (USA)

**551–554** Covers of *The New York Times Magazine,* all in full colour. The references are to an article by Norman Mailer on President Carter (Fig. 551), the prospects of George Wallace (Fig. 552), the stuggle of *Bell Telephone* against computer firms (Fig. 553), and a feature on Ronald Reagan (Fig. 554). (USA)
**555, 556** Artwork and complete cover of an issue of *The New York Times Magazine* containing an article on an aggressive truck-drivers' union. (USA)
**557** Complete cover of an issue of *Neue Berliner Illustrierte* devoted to tourism. (GDR)

**551–556** Titelblätter des illustrierten Wochenmagazins der *New York Times*. Die Illustrationen beziehen sich auf folgende Artikel: Abb. 551: Norman Mailer versucht hinter Carters Lächeln zu kommen; Abb. 552: George Wallace – ein letztes Hurra?; Abb. 553: Mutter Bell *(Bell Telephone)* zieht in die Schlacht – über die politische Einflussnahme der Multinationalen; Abb. 554: Ronald Reagan – Schlagabtausch in New Hampshire; Abb. 555/556: Verfilzung von Polizei und Fernfahrergewerkschaft. (USA)
**557** Geöffneter Umschlag der *Neuen Berliner Illustrierten* mit einem Reisemagazin. (GDR)

**551–556** Couvertures du supplément hebdomadaire du *New York Times*. Les illustrations se rapportent aux articles suivants: Fig. 551: Norman Mailer tâche à comprendre le sourire de Jimmy Carter; fig. 552: George Wallace – le dernier hourra?; fig. 553: Maman Bell *(Bell Telephone)* s'en va-t-en guerre – sur l'influence politique des industries multinationales; fig. 554: Ronald Reagan – échange de coups à New Hampshire; fig. 555/556: l'interpénétration de la police et d'éléments douteux d'un syndicat des routiers. (USA)
**557** Couverture complète d'une revue illustrée avec un supplément de voyage. (GDR)

551

552

553

554

555

556

557

ARTIST / KÜNSTLER / ARTISTE:

551  Andy Warhol
552, 554  Roger Law/Peter Fluck
553  Seymour Chwast
555, 556  James McMullan
557  Klaus Segner, Gruppe 4

DESIGNER / GESTALTER / MAQUETTISTE:

554  Ruth Ansel
557  Klaus Segner

ART DIRECTOR / DIRECTEUR ARTISTIQUE:

551–556  Ruth Ansel
557  Gerhard Schmidt

PUBLISHER / VERLEGER / EDITEUR:

551–556  The New York Times
557  Neue Berliner Illustrierte

558

563

ARTIST / KÜNSTLER / ARTISTE:

558  Benton Silverman
559, 560  Milton Glaser
561  Richard Hess
562  Tadanori Yokoo
563  Antoni Boratynski
564  Zuzanna Lipinska
565  Andrzej Krajewski

DESIGNER / GESTALTER / MAQUETTISTE:

558  Milton Glaser/Walter Bernard
559–561  Milton Glaser

ART DIRECTOR / DIRECTEUR ARTISTIQUE:

558–561  Milton Glaser/Walter Bernard
562  Tadanori Yokoo
563–565  Lech Zahorski

PUBLISHER / VERLEGER / EDITEUR:

558–561  New York Magazine
562  Jigen-Sha
563–565  Polish Interpress Agency

559

560

564

565

558 Cover of a special issue of *New York* magazine devoted to the story of New York's relations to the cinema. (USA)
559, 560 Complete cover and art in roughly actual size from an issue of *New York* magazine containing a feature on gossip. (USA)
561 Cover of *New York*. The issue features an article on Kissinger as a loser. (USA)
562 Magazine cover with red title on gold, red and gold flames, purple and gold triangle, blue horizon, dull gold sea. (JPN)
563–565 Three complete covers of the magazine *Poland*, all in full colour. The motifs—flying carpet and cat—are freely chosen. Fig. 565 is entitled "Interesting reading". (POL)

558 «Sie sollten unbedingt ins Filmgeschäft einsteigen.» Umschlag in matten Farben für eine Nummer der Zeitschrift *New York* zu einem Artikel über die Beziehung New Yorks zum Film. (USA)
559, 560 Vollständiger Umschlag und Detail der Illustration in Originalgrösse. Sie bezieht sich auf einen Artikel mit dem Titel «Warum alle über Klatsch reden». (USA)
561 Vorwiegend in dunklen Tönen gehaltenes Titelblatt der Zeitschrift *New York* zu einem Artikel über Kissinger mit dem Titel «Der grosse Vermittler als Verlierer». (USA)
562 Zeitschriftenumschlag. Sonnenuntergangsstimmung auf dem Meer, rote Flammen. (JPN)
563–565 Geöffnete Umschläge in bunten Farben für das illustrierte Kulturmagazin *Polen*, das in verschiedenen Sprachen herausgegeben wird. (POL)

558 Couverture en couleurs atténuées d'un numéro du magazine *New York* pour un article sur les relations de New York avec le cinéma. (USA)
559, 560 Couverture complète et détail de l'illustration qui y figure. Elle se réfère à un article intitulé «Pourquoi est-ce que tout le monde parle du commérage?». (USA)
561 Couverture du magazine *New York* se rapportant à un article sur Kissinger, intitulé «Le médiateur d'hier est le perdant d'aujourd'hui». Prédominance de tons foncés. (USA)
562 Couverture de magazine. Coucher du soleil, flammes rouges. (JPN)
563–565 Recto et verso de trois couvertures de *Pologne*, magazine culturel illustré publié en différentes langues. En couleurs vives. (POL)

**Magazine Covers**
**Zeitschriftenumschläge**
**Couvertures de périodiques**

561

562

566

567

568

House Organs
Hauszeitschriften
Journaux d'entreprise

ARTIST / KÜNSTLER / ARTISTE:

566 Milton Glaser
567–569 Seymour Chwast
570 Michael Hostovich
571 David Croland
572 Joyce MacDonald

DESIGNER / GESTALTER / MAQUETTISTE:

566–572 Seymour Chwast

ART DIRECTOR / DIRECTEUR ARTISTIQUE:

566–572 Seymour Chwast

AGENCY / AGENTUR / AGENCE – STUDIO:

566–572 Push Pin Studios

PUBLISHER / VERLEGER / EDITEUR:

566–572 Push Pin Graphic Inc.

**566, 567, 569, 570** Illustration, cover and two full-page illustrations from an issue of *Push Pin Graphic*, house organ of the Push Pin Studios, devoted to mothers. Figs. 566 and 569 show Aubrey Beardsley's and Juan Gris' mothers, from a series of imaginary mothers of famous artists, while Fig. 570 groups a few belongings of Hieronymus Bosch's mother. Fig. 567 is the cover of the issue, in pastel shades except for the red horned cap. (USA)
**568, 571, 572** Cover and two pages from an issue of *Push Pin Graphic* devoted to the chicken. Fig. 571 shows "the latest from Paris", Fig. 572 has an illustration of a chicken kitchen. (USA)

**566, 567, 569, 570** Ganzseitige Illustrationen und Umschlag (farbig) einer Publikation der *Push Pin Studios*. Diese Nummer ist den Müttern gewidmet. Abb. 566 zeigt Aubrey Beardsleys Mutter, Abb. 569 Juan Gris' Mutter, Abb. 570 Hieronymus Boschs Mutter mit ihren Lieblingsgegenständen. Schwarz-weiss. (USA)
**568, 571, 572** Umschlag und zwei Doppelseiten aus einer Publikation der Push Pin Studios. Diese Nummer ist ausschliesslich den Hühnern gewidmet. Die Illustrationen zeigen den «letzten Schrei» der Pariser Modeschöpfer (Abb. 571) und die Hühnerküche (Abb. 572). (USA)

**566, 567, 569, 570** Illustrations pleines pages et couverture (polychrome) d'une publication des Push Pin Studios. Ce numéro a été consacré aux mères. Fig. 566: la mère d'Aubrey Beardsley, dessin à la plume de Milton Glaser; fig. 569: la mère de Juan Gris par Seymour Chwast; fig. 570: la mère de Hieronymus Bosch avec ses objets préférés, par Michael Hostovich. (USA)
**568, 571, 572** Couverture et deux pages doubles d'une autre publication des Push Pin Studios, consacrée exclusivement aux poules. Les illustrations présentent la dernière création de Paris (fig. 571) et la cuisine des poules (fig. 572). (USA)

JUAN GRIS' MOTHER BY SEYMOUR CHWAST

569

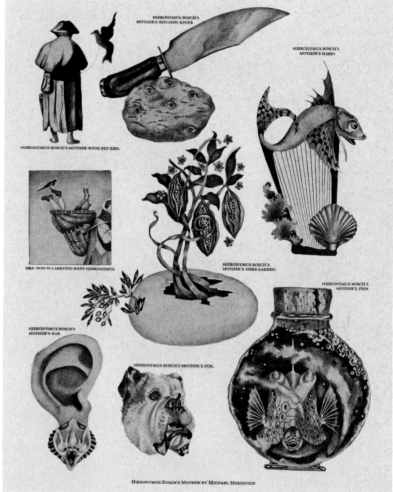

HIERONYMUS BOSCH'S MOTHER BY MICHAEL HOSTOVICH

570

571

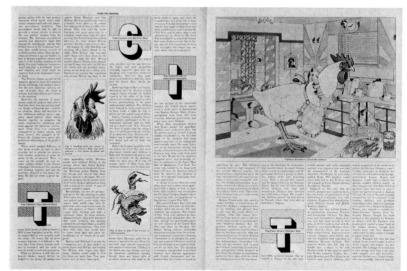

572

573

573 Medieval feast in black on cream, cover illustration for *Restaurants of Dallas* published by the Dallas Chamber of Commerce. Local animals take part in the feast. (USA)
574 Illustration from a house organ of Newspaper Enterprise Association. (USA)
575, 576 Page and spread from booklets of satirical linocuts issued by the artist. They illustrate flats for old people with shared bathroom, and violence among schoolchildren. (GER)
577, 578 Cover and double spread from *The Five Minute Hour*, a *Geigy* paper sent to psychiatrists. The subjects are the psychiatrist in "middlescence" and the psychology of clothing. (USA)
579, 580 Illustration in full colour (for a story of an ancient Persian treatment of rheumatoid arthritis) and corresponding double page from a number of *The Five Minute Hour*. (USA)

573 Umschlagillustration der Hauszeitschrift der Handelskammer von Dallas. Cremefarben. (USA)
574 Illustration aus der Publikation einer Zeitungsvereinigung. Mehrfarbig. (USA)
575, 576 Seite und Doppelseite aus zwei Ausgaben der *Donkey-Post*, einer Hauszeitschrift, die in 40 Exemplaren für Freunde des Graphikers Prüssen herauskommt. Die beiden Linolschnitte beziehen sich auf ein Gemeinschaftsbad für alte Leute und das Quälen einzelner Schüler. Auf gelbem, resp. grünem Papier gedruckt. (GER)
577–580 Seiten, Doppelseiten und Detail einer Illustration aus verschiedenen Ausgaben von *The Five Minute Hour*, einer vierteljährlich erscheinenden Zeitung von *Geigy* für Ärzte und Psychiater. Mehrfarbige Illustrationen auf gelblichem, resp. hellgrauem Papier. (USA)

573 Illustration de couverture d'un magazine de la chambre de commerce de Dallas. (USA)
574 Illustration figurant dans une publication d'une association de journaux. Polychrome. (USA)
575, 576 Page et page double de deux éditions de *Donkey-Post*, magazine petit format à tirage limité (40 exemplaires) adressé aux amis du graphiste Prüssen. Les linos se réfèrent à un bain commun pour les âgés et à la violence qu'exercent les élèves entre eux. Imprimé en noir sur papier jaune, respectivement vert. (GER)
577–580 Page, page double et détail de l'illustration de differentes éditions de *The Five Minute Hour*, un journal trimestriel de *Geigy* distribué aux médecins et psychiatres. Illustrations en couleurs sur papier jaunâtre, respectivement grisé. (USA)

574

# House Organs
## Hauszeitschriften
## Journaux d'entreprise

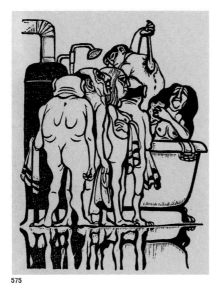

575

Sich zur Wehr setzend
zog der
in die Enge getriebene
das Messer
und stach einen seiner
Peiniger
in den Hals.
All das nicht aufregend,
denn höchstbundesrichterlich
ist festgestellt, daß
„gruppenweises Verfolgen

und Quälen"
einzelner Schüler
untereinander
„nicht ungewöhnlich" sei.
Wie wahr, wie wohl,
wie beruhigend geklärt
ist somit dieses Geschehen
zwischen Kindern
des ersten Schuljahres
auf dem Schulhof.

576

ARTIST / KÜNSTLER / ARTISTE:

573 Jack Unruh
574 Rudy Hoglund
575, 576 Eduard Prüssen
577, 578 Cliff Condak
579, 580 Alan Cober

DESIGNER / GESTALTER:

573 Dennis Benoit
574 Rudy Hoglund
575, 576 Eduard Prüssen
577–580 Bob Paganucci

ART DIRECTOR:

573 Dennis Benoit
574 Rudy Hoglund
577–580 Bob Paganucci

AGENCY / AGENTUR / AGENCE:

574 Newspaper Enterprise
Association

PUBLISHER / VERLEGER / EDITEUR:

573 Dallas Chamber of Commerce
574 Newspaper Enterprise
Association
575, 576 Donkey-Press
577–580 Geigy Pharmaceuticals

The Psychiatrist in "Middlescence"

Geigy

577

Habilogenics:
The Psychology of Clothing
Comes Out of the Closet

578

579

**Another tale from the
Persian Nights.**

**Going negative to get
a positive relaxing effect.**

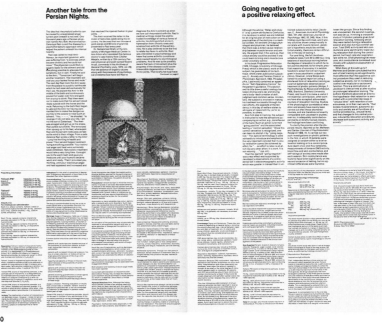

580

**Jetting to market**

Pegasus

581

582

583

584

586

587

**581** Double spread from the *Mobil* house magazine *Pegasus* on jet travel for businessmen. (GBR)
**582** "Come on, it's round." Complete cover of *Pegasus*, figures in colour. (GBR)
**583, 584** Covers of the *Upjohn* house magazine *Scope*. Trees as snowmen in the landscape and a pale blue-green featureless carpet laid over the flowering meadows. (JPN)
**585** Illustration in pastel shades for an article on medical services for air passengers in the *Roche* house magazine *Hexagon*. (SWI)
**586, 587** Covers of the house magazine of Tokyu Electric Car Co. Ltd. (JPN)
**588** Egyptian wall hanging (tan figure, green, black and white headdress) on the cover of an issue of the *Exxon* house magazine *The Lamp* containing an article on Egypt. (USA)
**589, 590** Complete double page and one illustration in actual size (referring to Renoir's *La Grande Illusion*) from an article in *The Lamp* about the television broadcasting of 100 film classics sponsored by *Exxon*. (USA)

**581** Doppelseite aus der *Mobil*-Hauszeitschrift *Pegasus*. Thema: Jetreisen für Geschäftsleute. (GBR)
**582** «Kommt mit, es ist rund.» Umschlag einer Ausgabe von *Pegasus*. (GBR)
**583, 584** Umschläge der Hauszeitschrift einer pharmazeutischen Fabrik: Schneemänner stehen als Bäume in der Gegend, und ein langweiliger, monotoner Teppich legt sich über die Landschaft. (JPN)
**585** In der *Roche*-Hauszeitschrift *Hexagon* erschienene Illustration zum Thema «ärztliche Vorsorge und Verantwortung für Flugpassagiere». (SWI)
**586, 587** Zwei Umschläge der Hauszeitschrift eines Industriekonzerns. Mehrfarbig. (JPN)
**588** Ägyptischer Wandteppich (braune Figur, Haartracht grün, schwarz und weiss) als Umschlagillustration der *Exxon*-Hauszeitschrift *The Lamp*. Das Heft enthält einen Artikel über Ägypten. (USA)
**589, 590** Doppelseite und Illustration in Originalgrösse – zu Jean Renoirs Film *Die grosse Illusion* – aus der Hauszeitschrift *The Lamp*. Der Artikel über Meisterwerke berühmter Filmregisseure kündigt eine von *Exxon* unterstützte TV-Retrospektive mit 100 Filmklassikern an. (USA)

**581** Page double de *Pegasus*, journal d'entreprise de la *Mobil*, sur les voyages en jet pour les hommes d'affaires. (GBR)
**582** «Venez voir, elle est ronde.» Couverture de la revue d'entreprise de la *Mobil*. (GBR)
**583, 584** Couvertures de la revue d'une entreprise de produits pharmaceutiques. Les bonhommes de neige devraient symboliser des arbres; un tapis monotone est déroulé au-dessus d'un paysage en fleur. (JPN)
**585** Illustration de *Hexagon*, revue d'entreprise de *Roche*, se rapportant à un article sur le service médical dans les avions. (SWI)
**586, 587** Couvertures polychromes de la revue d'une entreprise industrielle. (JPN)
**588** Tapisserie égyptienne (figure brune, chevelure en vert, noir et blanc) sur la couverture de *The Lamp*, revue d'entreprise de *Exxon*. Elle se rapporte à un article sur l'Egypte. (USA)
**589, 590** Page double et illustration en grandeur nature (se référant à *La Grande Illusion* de Jean Renoir) figurant dans un article sur une rétrospective télévisée de 100 chef-d'œuvres de grands metteurs en scène, patronnée par *Exxon*. (USA)

589

585

588

590

ARTIST / KÜNSTLER / ARTISTE:

581, 582 Michael Foreman
583, 584 Yoji Kuri
585 Marcus Hodel
586, 587 Hirata Yorikazu
588 Charles N. Barnard (Photo)
589, 590 Robert Andrew Parker

DESIGNER / GESTALTER / MAQUETTISTE:

585 Marcus Hodel
586, 587 Hirata Yorikazu
588–590 Harry O. Diamond

ART DIRECTOR / DIRECTEUR ARTISTIQUE:

581, 582 Derek Birdsall
585 Jacques Hauser
586, 587 Hirata Yorikazu
588–590 Harry O. Diamond

AGENCY / AGENTUR / AGENCE – STUDIO:

581, 582 Omnific Ltd.

PUBLISHER / VERLEGER / EDITEUR:

581, 582 Mobil Oil Co.
583, 584 Kodansha Ltd.
585 F. Hoffmann-La Roche
586, 587 Tokyu Elektric Car Co., Ltd.
588–590 Exxon Corporation

**House Organs
Hauszeitschriften
Journaux d'entreprise**

591

592

593

594

595

**591–593, 595** Cover art in actual size, corresponding cover, double page and a further cover of *The Family in Distress*, a *Geigy* publication with excerpts from the medical press mailed to doctors. Figs. 591–593 refer to changing family roles as affected by women's liberation. (USA)
**594** Illustration for an article in *Pastimes*, house magazine of *Eastern Airlines*. Subject: the benefits of a good memory. Black and white. (USA)

**591–593, 595** Illustration in Originalgrösse, Umschläge und Doppelseite aus einer regelmässig erscheinenden Zeitung von *Geigy* für Ärzte. Diese Publikationsserie ist der Familie gewidmet, die sich durch den veränderten Lebensstil der Jungen, die Emanzipation der Frau und die neuen Erziehungsmethoden in einer Krise befindet. (USA)
**594** «Ein gutes Gedächtnis macht sich bezahlt.» Illustration aus einer Ausgabe der Hauszeitschrift der *Eastern Airlines* zu einem Artikel über Profitsteigerung dank einem guten Gedächtnis. Schwarzweiss. (USA)

**591–593, 595** Illustration en grandeur nature, couvertures et page double d'un journal que *Geigy* adresse aux psychiatres. Cette série de publications est consacrée à la famille qui subit actuellement un changement total; les jeunes, cherchant un style de vie plus libérale en ce qui concerne les relations et l'éducation, ne l'acceptent plus sous sa forme traditionnelle et se trouvent alors dans une période transitoire assez problématique. (USA)
**594** Illustration accompagnant un article de la revue d'entreprise de *Eastern Airlines* sur les avantages d'une bonne mémoire. (USA)


ARTIST / KÜNSTLER / ARTISTE:

591–593  Rick McCollum
594  Cathy Hull
595  Norm Walker

DESIGNER / GESTALTER / MAQUETTISTE:

591–593, 595  John DeCesare

ART DIRECTOR / DIRECTEUR ARTISTIQUE:

591–593, 595  John DeCesare
594  Marty Pederson

AGENCY / AGENTUR / AGENCE – STUDIO:

594  Pederson Design

PUBLISHER / VERLEGER / EDITEUR:

591–593, 595  Geigy Pharmaceuticals
594  Eastern Airlines

ARTIST / KÜNSTLER / ARTISTE:
596—600 Josse Goffin

DESIGNER / GESTALTER:
596—600 Patrick Gueva

ART DIRECTOR:
596—600 Patrick Gueva

AGENCY / AGENTUR / AGENCE:
596—600 Partner SA

599

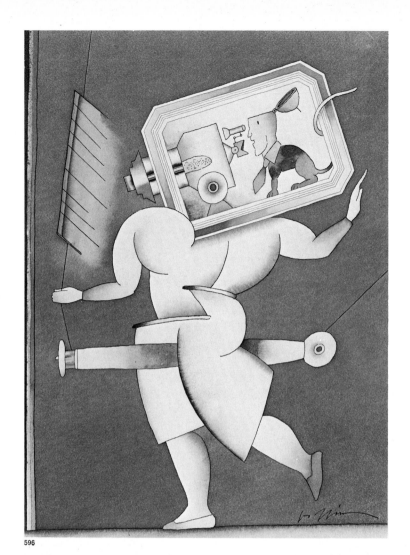

596

**596—600** Four of the full-page colour illustrations, and one double page, from a booklet entitled "Social and Human Aspects of a Modern Enterprise", published by *Esso Belgium*. The illustrations face articles on the four years of existence of a staff council (Fig. 596), the role and philosophy of *Exxon* as shareholder (Fig. 597), the social experience of union delegates (Fig. 598) and the move towards employee participation (Figs. 599, 600). (BEL)

**596—600** Ganzseitige Illustrationen und Doppelseite aus dem Jahresbericht der *Esso* Belgien, zum Thema «soziale und menschliche Aspekte eines modernen Unternehmens». Die Illustrationen beziehen sich auf folgende Berichte – Abb. 596: die vierjährige Tätigkeit eines Gremiums, in welchem Abgeordnete der höheren Kader vertreten sind; Abb. 597: Rolle und Geschäftspolitik der *Exxon* in ihrer Funktion als Aktionärin; Abb. 598: die gesellschaftspolitischen Erfahrungen der Gewerkschaftsvertreter; Abb. 599/600: Bestrebungen in Hinsicht auf die Mitbestimmung der Beschäftigten. (BEL)

**596—600** Quatre illustrations pleines pages (en couleur) et page double figurant dans un rapport de l'*Esso Belgique*, intitulé «Aspects sociaux et humains d'une entreprise moderne». Les illustrations se rapportent aux articles suivants: Quatre années d'existence du Conseil des Cadres (fig. 596); rôle et philosophie d'*Exxon* en tant qu'actionnaire (fig. 597); l'expérience sociale des délégués syndicaux (fig. 598); où en sommes-nous en matière de participation? (fig. 599/600). (BEL)

597

598

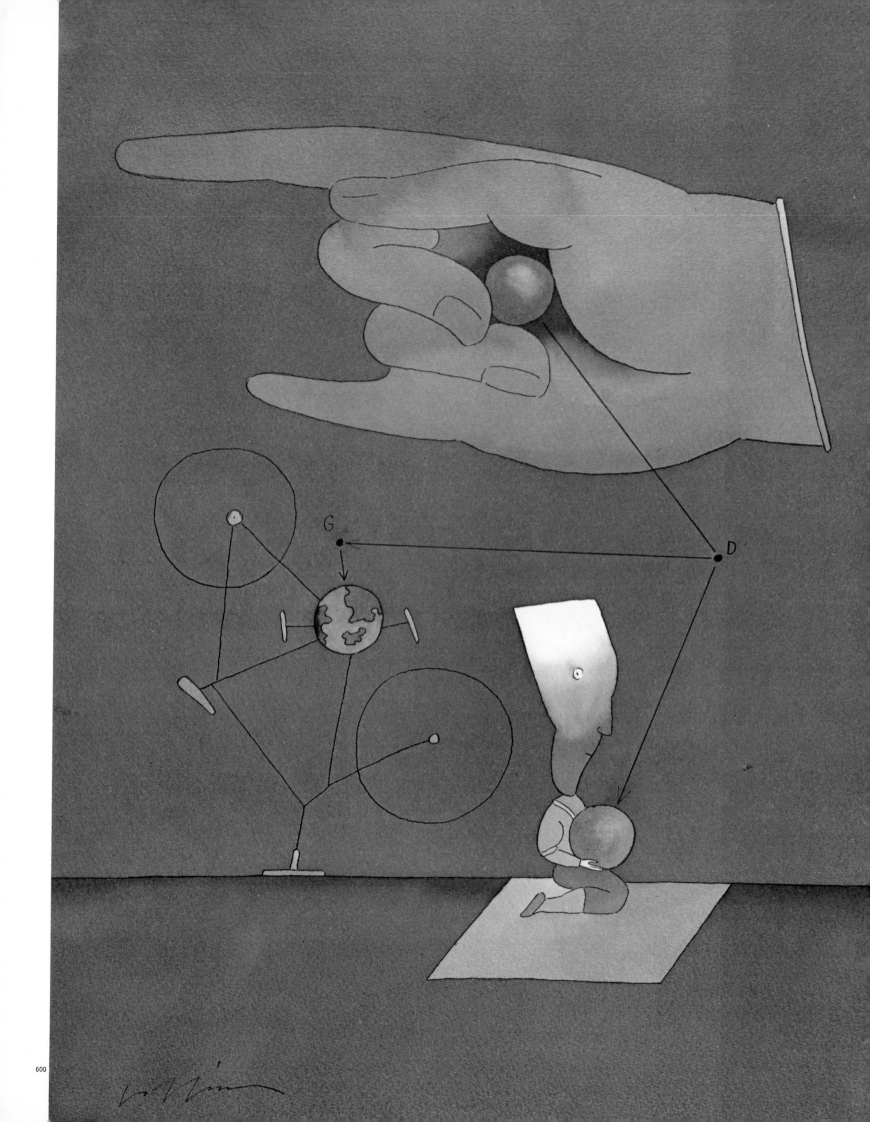

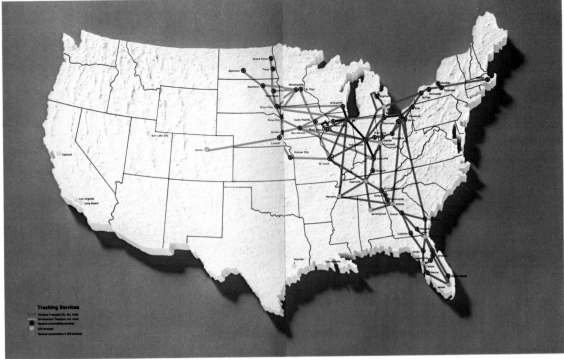

601

ARTIST / KÜNSTLER / ARTISTE:

601  Joe Boone
602  Edward G. Jenkins
603, 604  Wynn Medinger
605  Barth Pruim
606, 607  Mike Kelly
608  Archie Lieberman

DESIGNER / GESTALTER / MAQUETTISTE:

601  Larry A. Profancik/Bill Swearingen
602  Edward X. Redings
603, 604  Gottschalk + Ash Ltd.
605  Walter Rusznyak
606, 607  Mike Kelly
608  Norman Perman
609  Morton Goldsholl

ART DIRECTOR / DIRECTEUR ARTISTIQUE:

601  Larry A. Profancik/Bill Swearingen
602  Edward X. Redings
603, 604  Fritz Gottschalk
605  Koos LeGrange
606, 607  Mike Kelly
608  Norman Perman
609  Morton Goldsholl

AGENCY / AGENTUR / AGENCE – STUDIO:

601  PW Inc., Swearingen Graphics Div.
603, 604  Gottschalk + Ash Ltd.
605  Design Unit (Pty) Ltd.
606, 607  BBDM Inc.
608  Norman Perman
609  Wright & Manning Inc./Goldsholl Associates

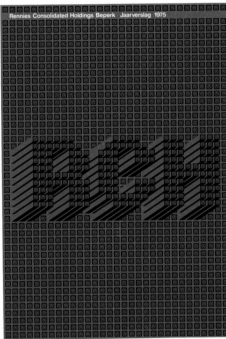

605

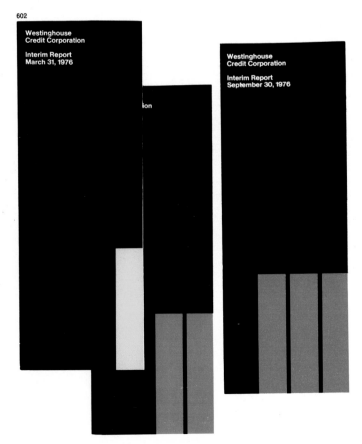

602

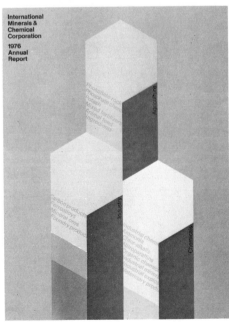

606

**Annual Reports**

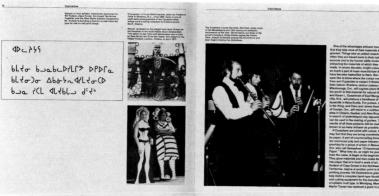

603

604

Planning for growth.

606

607

Researching the problems.

Brown Group, Inc. Annual Report for 1975

609

**601** Double spread from the 1975 annual report of the Texas Gas Transmission Corporation showing their trucking services in the States. (USA)
**602** Interim reports of the Westinghouse Credit Corporation for three quarters of 1976. (USA)
**603, 604** Double pages from the 18th annual report of The Canada Council; Fig. 603 relates to experimental projects, Fig. 604 lists contributions to conferences. Black and white. (CAN)
**605** Cover of the 1975 annual report of Rennies Consolidated Holdings, a diversified company. The pattern is built up from the company trade mark. (SAF)
**606, 607** Double pages from an annual review of the University of Health Sciences, Chicago Medical School. Illustrations (symbolizing growth and research) in red, blue and black. (USA)
**608** Cover of an annual report of International Minerals & Chemical Corp. Pastel shades. (USA)
**609** Cover of the 1975 annual report of the Brown Group, Inc. (USA)

**601** Verteilernetz aus dem Jahresbericht eines Unternehmens der petrochemischen Industrie. (USA)
**602** Drei der vierteljährlich erscheinenden Berichte eines Kreditinstituts. (USA)
**603, 604** Zwei Doppelseiten aus dem Jahresbericht des Canada Council, einer Institution zur Förderung der Kunst, der Geistes- und Sozialwissenschaften. (CAN)
**605** Umschlag des Geschäftsberichts 1975 einer Holdinggesellschaft. Für die Umschlaggestaltung wurden die Schutzmarke und die Initialen verwendet. (SAF)
**606, 607** Doppelseiten aus dem Jahresrückblick der medizinischen Fakultät der Universität Chicago zum Ausbau des Gesundheitsdienstes (606) und über medizinische Forschung (607). (USA)
**608** Umschlag des Jahresberichts eines diversifizierten Industriekonzerns. Die Säulen repräsentieren die Jahresumsätze der drei Hauptzweige. Hellblau, lila, hellgrün, grau. (USA)
**609** Umschlag des Geschäftsberichts 1975 der Brown Group, Inc. (USA)

**601** Réseau publié dans le rapport annuel d'une entreprise de pétrochimie. (USA)
**602** Trois des rapports trimestriels d'un établissement de crédit. (USA)
**603, 604** Deux pages doubles figurant dans le rapport annuel du Canada Council, une institution pour la promotion des arts, des lettres et des sciences sociales. (CAN)
**605** Couverture du rapport annuel '75 d'un holding. Le design consiste en une combinaison de la marque déposée et des initiales de la société. (SAF)
**606, 607** Pages doubles du rapport annuel de la faculté de médecine de l'Université de Chicago avec référence au développement du service sanitaire et aux recherches médicales. (USA)
**608** Couverture du rapport annuel d'une entreprise industrielle diversifiée. Les colonnes représentent les chiffres d'affaires annuels des trois branches principales. (USA)
**609** Couverture du rapport annuel 1975 du Brown Group, Inc. (USA)

610

611

612

## Annual Reports

**610, 611** Double spreads with colour illustrations of new housing estates in Singapore and Hong Kong from the 1975 annual report of The Hongkong and Shanghai Banking Corporation, which contains an essay on housing. (HKG)
**612** Cover (polychrome on black) of the 1976 annual report of Eastern Asia Navigation Co. Ltd. It shows (in Dragon Year) an old Chinese embroidery of dragons above a stylized sea. (HKG)
**613, 615** Two of a series of enamel paintings used as full-page illustrations in the 1975 annual report of Koor Industries Ltd., Israel's largest industrial complex. (ISR)
**614** Cover of the 1975 annual report of Monogram Industries, Inc. Red, yellow and light blue drawing on dark blue, silver name. (USA)
**616** Cover of a fifteen-month report of Imasco Ltd. Blue, green and grey on white. (CAN)
**617** Page from the 1975 annual report of the PolyGram Group, showing the company organization. (NLD)

**610, 611** Doppelseiten aus dem Jahresbericht der Hong Kong and Shanghai Banking Corporation. Mehrfarbige Illustrationen von Blocks mit Sozialwohnungen in Hong Kong und Singapur. (HKG)
**612** Umschlag des Geschäftsberichts einer ostasiatischen Schiffahrtsgesellschaft für «das Jahr des Drachens». Das Sujet stammt von einer alten chinesischen Tapisserie mit dem königlichen Drachen über einem stilisierten Meer. (HKG)
**613, 615** Ganzseitige Illustrationen aus dem Jahresbericht 1975 des Industriekonzerns der israelischen Arbeitergewerkschaft Histadrut. Mehrfarbige Emailgemälde. (ISR)
**614** Umschlag des Jahresberichts eines Industrieunternehmens. Illustration in Rot, Gelb und Hellblau auf Dunkelblau, Name in Silber. (USA)
**616** Umschlag eines Geschäftsberichts über 15 Monate, was aus dem Design hervorgeht. Hellgrau, blau und grün. (CAN)
**617** Seite aus dem Jahresbericht von *PolyGram*. Die Graphik zeigt ein Organigramm der in dieser Gruppe zusammengeschlossenen Firmen. Schwarzweiss. (NLD)

**610, 611** Pages double du rapport annuel de la Hong Kong and Shanghai Bank. Illustrations polychromes de constructions d'H.L.M. à Hong Kong et Singapore. (HKG)
**612** Couverture du rapport annuel d'une compagnie maritime de l'Asie orientale pour l'année du dragon. Le sujet de cette ancienne tapisserie chinoise représente le dragon royal au-dessus d'une mer stylisée. (HKG)
**613, 615** Illustrations pleines pages du rapport annuel 1975 de la société industrielle du syndicat ouvrier israélien Histadrut. En polychromie. (ISR)
**614** Couverture du rapport annuel d'une entreprise industrielle. Illustration en rouge, jaune et bleu clair sur fond bleu foncé, nom en argent. (USA)
**616** Couverture d'un rapport pour 15 mois. Gris pâle, bleu et vert. (CAN)
**617** Page du rapport annuel de *PolyGram*. Le design représente un organigramme des entreprises réunies dans ce groupe. En noir et blanc. (NLD)

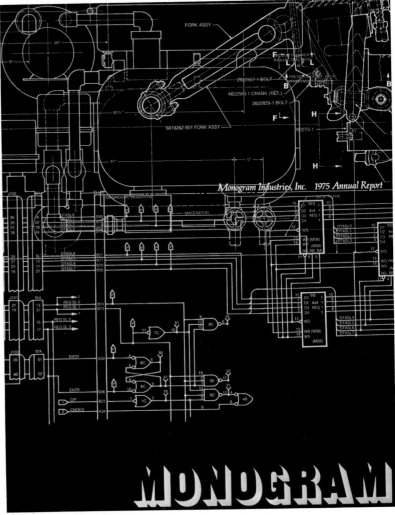

614

613

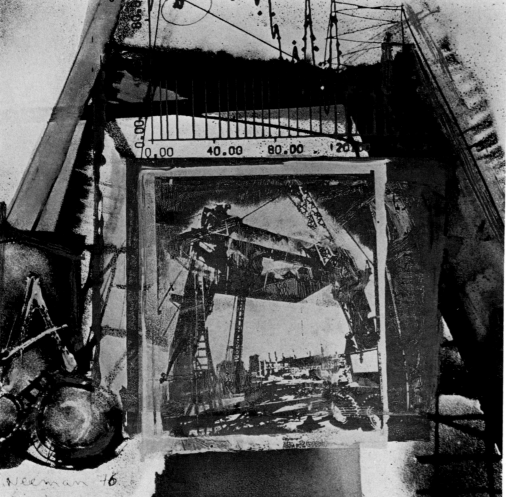

615

ARTIST / KÜNSTLER / ARTISTE:

610, 611 Norman MacDonald
612 John Nye (Photo)
613, 615 Ruth Ne'eman
614 Stephan Stanley
617 Martin Andersch

DESIGNER / GESTALTER / MAQUETTISTE:

610–612 Henry Steiner
613, 615 Ilan Hagari
614 Dawson Zaug
616 Ernst Roch
617 Klaus Müller-Neuhof

ART DIRECTOR / DIRECTEUR ARTISTIQUE:

610–612 Henry Steiner
613, 615 Yael Shalit
614 Reginald Jones
616 Ernst Roch
617 Herbert Winter

AGENCY / AGENTUR / AGENCE – STUDIO:

610–612 Graphic Communication Ltd.
613, 615 Forum Public Relations
614 Unigraphics
616 Design Collaborative
617 H. W. Gemmecke

616

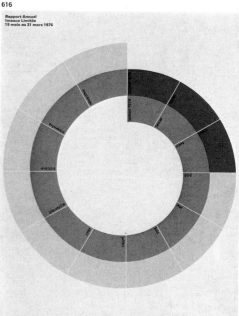

617

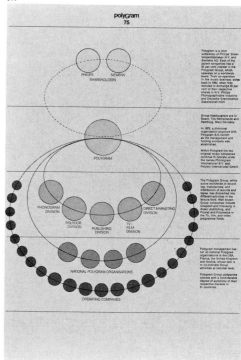

199

618 Page facing a shipping section in an annual report of Cyprus Mines Corp. (USA)
619, 621 Illustrations from the annual report of a bank which commissions artists to "humanize" the dry facts of banking. Here banknote design and bank secrecy are "humanized" with faces drawn from history and from German banknotes. (GER)
620 Double spread from the *Hoechst* annual report for 1975 with illustrations in shades of blue incorporating diagrams that supply data on company operations. (GER)
622 Complete cover with gatefold of an annual report of International Flavors and Fragrances, Inc. The illustrations relate to the human energy system. (USA)

618 Illustration aus einem Jahresbericht der Cyprus Mines Corp. (USA)
619, 621 Aus dem Geschäftsbericht '75 der *Bank für Gemeinwirtschaft*, die namhafte Künstler beauftragt, die trockene Bankmaterie so umzusetzen, dass menschliche Bezüge sichtbar werden. Hier versinnbildlicht: Geldschöpfung und Bankgeheimnis. (GER)
620 Doppelseite (weiss/blau) aus dem Jahresbericht '75 der Hoechst AG mit Darstellung des Weltumsatzes nach Wirtschaftsgebieten und der Unternehmensleitung. (GER)
622 Umschlag mit doppeltem Ausleger des Jahresberichtes eines Unternehmens der Aroma- und Geruchstoff-Branche. (USA)

618 Illustration d'un rapport annuel de la Cyprus Mines Corp. (USA)
619, 621 Illustrations du rapport annuel d'une banque qui demande chaque année à un artiste de renom de «humaniser» les affaires bancaires. Ici elles se réfèrent à la création de monnaie et au secret de banque. (GER)
620 Page double (blanc/bleu) du rapport annuel '75 de la Hoechst SA présentant les chiffres d'affaires d'après les régions économiques et le management du groupe. (GER)
622 Couverture à repli double du rapport annuel d'une entreprise travaillant dans le secteur d'arômes et d'odorants. (USA)

618

620

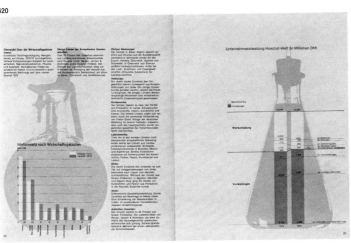

619

ARTIST / KÜNSTLER / ARTISTE:

618 Richard Krogstad
619, 621 Michael Mathias Prechtl
620 Nacke + Flink
622 Barbara Nessim

DESIGNER / GESTALTER / MAQUETTISTE:

618 Richard Krogstad
619, 621 Michael Mathias Prechtl
620 Heinrich Stamm
622 Brian O'Neill

ART DIRECTOR / DIRECTEUR ARTISTIQUE:

618 Robert Steinle
620 Heinrich Stamm
622 Brian O'Neill

AGENCY / AGENTUR / AGENCE – STUDIO:

618 Advertising Designers, Inc.
620 Graph. Atelier/Werbeabteilung Hoechst AG
622 Davis, Delaney, Arrow

**623** Cover of a children's book (Let the Children Have a Go) about riding on pieces of furniture. (GER)
**624** Paperback cover (full colour) for a humorous book by a popular comedian. (GBR)
**625** Cover of a book of short thrillers and detective stories for young readers. (GER)
**626** Paperback cover (full colour) for a book about the well-known pop group. (GBR)
**627** Paperback cover of a book about English punctuation. Title in blue and red. (GBR)
**628** Dust jacket of a book about a man who turned into a tree. Black on buff, white frame. (SWI)
**629, 631** Two covers from a range of inexpensive paperbacks intended for the student market, here for essays on communication by body motion (blue and red arrows) and for a work on dictatorship and democracy (black and white). (GBR)
**630** Dust jacket of a psychological book on man as a caring creature. Black and purple lettering, red heart. (USA)
**632** Cover of a novel (Light over White Rocks) about life in a remote valley. Black and red on tan. (GDR)

**623** Kinderbuch, das die unwahrscheinliche Geschichte der Möbelreiter erzählt, die die Stadt umkrempeln. (GER)
**624** Umschlag eines humoristischen Taschenbuches. (GBR)
**625** Umschlag eines Jugendbuches mir 13 Kurzkrimis verschiedener Autoren. (GER)
**626** Mehrfarbiger Umschlag eines Taschenbuches von Hank Harrison über eine bekannte Pop-Gruppe. (GBR)
**627** Umschlag eines *Penguin*-Taschenbuches über die Regeln der Satzzeichensetzung. Titel in Rot und Blau. (GBR)
**628** Schutzumschlag (braun und senfgelb) für einen Roman: ein Büroangestellter wächst und wächst, bis er auf verschiedenen Irrwegen im Wald seine Bleibe und Freiheit findet. (SWI)
**629, 631** Aus einer Taschenbuchreihe für Studenten. Abb. 629: über Bewegungsabläufe im Körper (schwarzweiss, rote und blaue Pfeile); Abb. 631: über die gesellschaftspolitischen Hintergründe von Diktatur und Demokratie (schwarzweiss). (GBR)
**630** Schutzumschlag für das Werk eines führenden Psychoanalytikers. Schwarz, rot und magenta. (USA)
**632** Schutzumschlag eines Romans über das Schicksal von drei Personen in einem Bergtal. Rot, dunkelgelb, schwarz. (GDR)

**623** Couverture d'un livre d'enfant racontant l'histoire étrange d'un groupe chevauchant des meubles et transformant ainsi de fond en comble la ville entière. (GER)
**624** Couverture d'un livre de poche humoristique. (GBR)
**625** Couverture d'un livre pour la jeunesse avec 13 romans policiers de différents auteurs. (GER)
**626** Couverture polychrome d'un livre de poche de Hank Harrison sur un groupe pop bien connu. (GBR)
**627** Couverture d'un livre de poche *Penguin* sur les règles de la ponctuation. Titre en rouge et bleu. (GBR)
**628** Jaquette (brun et jaune moutarde) pour un roman, traitant d'un employé qui ne cesse plus de grandir; ayant été exclu de la société humaine il retrouve sa liberté dans le bois. (SWI)
**629, 631** D'une série de livres de poche pour étudiants. Fig. 629: sur la cybernétique (noir-blanc, flèches rouges et bleus); fig. 631: sur les critères socio-politiques de la dictature et de la démocratie (noir et blanc). (GBR)
**630** Jaquette pour l'œuvre d'un psychanaliste de renom. Noir, rouge et magenta. (USA)
**632** Jaquette d'un roman sur la vie de trois personnes dans une vallée de montagne. Rouge, jaune foncé et noir. (GDR)

ARTIST / KÜNSTLER / ARTISTE:

623, 625  Heinz Edelmann
624  Mike Terry
626  Chris Moore
628  Oskar Weiss
632  Klaus Segner

DESIGNER / GESTALTER / MAQUETTISTE:

623, 625  Heinz Edelmann
624, 626  John Munday
627  Alan Fletcher
629, 631  John McConnell
630  Herb Lubalin
632  Klaus Segner

ART DIRECTOR / DIRECTEUR ARTISTIQUE:

624, 626  John Munday
627  Alan Fletcher
628  Oswald Dubacher
629, 631  John McConnell
630  Lidia Ferrara
632  Günter Jacobi

AGENCY / AGENTUR / AGENCE – STUDIO:

627, 629, 631  Pentagram

PUBLISHER / VERLEGER / EDITEUR:

623, 625  C. Bertelsmann Verlag
624, 626  Star Books
627, 629, 631  Penguin Books Ltd.
628  Ex Libris Verlag AG
630  Alfred A. Knopf
632  Mitteldeutscher Verlag

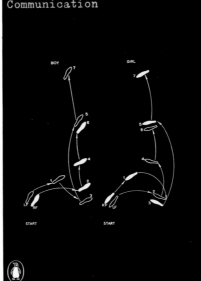

627

A brief guide to punctuation/G.V.Carey

Jean-Charles Rémy
L'ARBORESCENCE

628

Ray L.Birdwhistell
Kinesics and Context
Essays on Body-Motion
Communication

629

CARING

WILLARD GAYLIN

630

Barrington Moore Jr
Social Origins of
Dictatorship
and Democracy

631

632

Licht über weißen Felsen

Liselotte
Welskopf-
Henrich

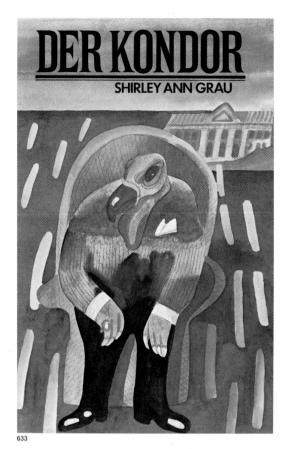

# DER KONDOR
## SHIRLEY ANN GRAU

A Crime Club Selection

Innocent Bystander
George Bagby

start — engelska för dig
Rolig och effektiv
modern och annorlunda
radio och tv-kurs
Studeras enskilt eller i grupp
Sveriges Radios Vuxenundervisning
Sveriges Radios förlag
Brevskolan

ISBN 91-522-1368-4

start 6

Engelsk fortsättningskurs för vuxna
Dennis Gotobed Stig Eriksson
Illustrerad av Torsten Bergentz

**633** Dust jacket of a novel about a rich old man and his black butler. Full colour. (GER)
**634** Complete paperback cover of a romance about an attempted kidnapping in an express at the turn of the century. Full colour with green carriages. (USA)
**635** Dust jacket of a detective story set in New York. Black and white knife, brown metronome, red blood. (USA)
**636** Complete cover of an English course for adults published to accompany a programme of the Swedish radio. Mainly yellow and red shades. (SWE)
**637** Cover of a collection of spicy tales from Bavaria (The Bavarian Decameron). Full colour. (GER)
**638** Front and spine of the dust jacket of a German edition of the successful humorous novel about the doings in a French village. Full colour with blue jacket, brown hat. (GER)
**639, 640** Complete dust jacket, with spine, and detail of the artwork for the collected works of a humorous author who writes stories in German dialect. (GER)

**633** Mehrfarbiger Schutzumschlag eines Romans: ein einsamer Reicher verbringt seinen Lebensabend mit einem Negerbutler, der für ihn den Kondor verkörpert – den Totenvogel, der den Reichtum dieser Welt ins Jenseits trägt. (GER)
**634** Geöffneter Taschenbuchumschlag eines Abenteuerromans, der im Petersburg–Cannes-Express spielt. Mahrfarbig. (USA)
**635** «Der unschuldige Passant». Schutzumschlag für einen Kriminalroman. Braunes Metronome, rote Blutlache. (USA)
**636** Kompletter Umschlag für einen Englischkurs für Erwachsene, der vom Schwedischen Radio ausgestrahlt wurde. Vorwiegend in Gelb- und Rottönen. (SWE)
**637** Mehrfarbiger Schutzumschlag eines Werkes mit Schwänken und Schnurren gegen Griesgram, von Prechtl illustriert. (GER)
**638** Schutzumschlag (mit Rücken) für einen Schelmenroman, der im Nest Clochemerle im Beaujolais spielt. (GER)
**639, 640** Schutzumschlag (mit Rücken) und Detail der Illustration für Spoerls Gesammelte Werke, herausgegeben von der *Büchergilde Gutenberg* und illustriert von M. M. Prechtl. (GER)

**633** Jaquette polychrome d'un roman intitulé «Le condor» racontant l'histoire d'un riche solitaire qui passe ses dernières années avec un domestique noir qui, pour lui, personnifie le condor, l'oiseau des morts qui porte les richesses de ce monde à l'au-delà. (GER)
**634** Couverture complète d'un livre de poche. Roman d'aventures se passant dans l'express Petersbourg–Cannes. Polychrome. (USA)
**635** «La passant candide.» Jaquette pour un roman policier. Métronome brun, tache de sang en rouge. (USA)
**636** Couverture complète d'un cours d'anglais pour adultes de la Radio suédoise. Jaune prédominant, tons rouges. (SWE)
**637** Jaquette polychrome d'un livre de contes drôlatiques de Bavière (le «décaméron bavarois»). (GER)
**638** Jaquette (avec dos) pour un roman picaresque qui se passe à Clochemerle au Beaujolais. (GER)
**639, 640** Jaquette (avec dos) et détail de l'illustration pour les œuvres complets d'un écrivain humoristique allemand. (GER)

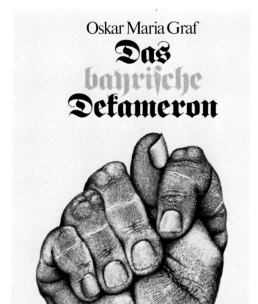

637

638

ARTIST / KÜNSTLER / ARTISTE:

633 Hennes Maier
634 Stanislaw Zagorski
635 Cathy Hull
636 Torsten Bergentz
637–640 Michael Mathias Prechtl

DESIGNER / GESTALTER / MAQUETTISTE:

633 Hennes Maier
634 Stanislaw Zagorski
637–640 Michael Mathias Prechtl

ART DIRECTOR:

634 H. Levine
635 Rallou Hamshur

PUBLISHER / VERLEGER / EDITEUR:

633, 637, 639, 640 Büchergilde
        Gutenberg
634 Harcourt Brace, Jovanovich, Inc.
635 Doubleday & Co., Inc.
636 Sveriges Radios Förlag
638 Europäische Bildungsgemeinschaft

639

640

641

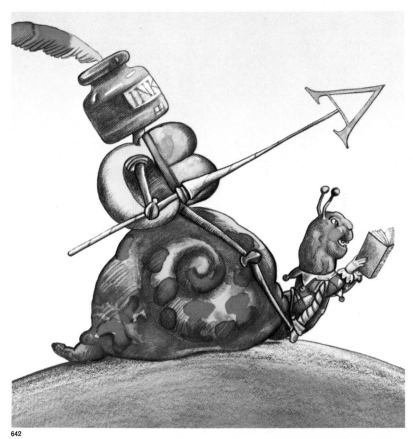

642

643

644

ARTIST / KÜNSTLER / ARTISTE:

641 H. U. Steger
642 Michael Foreman
643, 644 Wayne Anderson
645 Etienne Delessert
646–648 Kjell Ivan Anderson

DESIGNER / GESTALTER:

641 H. U. Steger
643, 644 Wayne Anderson
645 Etienne Delessert
646–648 Kjell Ivan Anderson

ART DIRECTOR:

643, 644 Wayne Anderson

PUBLISHER / VERLEGER:

641 Diogenes Verlag AG
642 Penguin Books Ltd.
643, 644 Jonathan Cape
645 Gertraud Middelhauve
      Verlag
646–648 Zindermans

ANNE VAN DER ESSEN · ETIENNE DELESSERT

# DIE MAUS UND DIE SCHMETTERLINGE

EIN UMWELTBUCH FÜR KINDER

MIDDELHAUVE

645

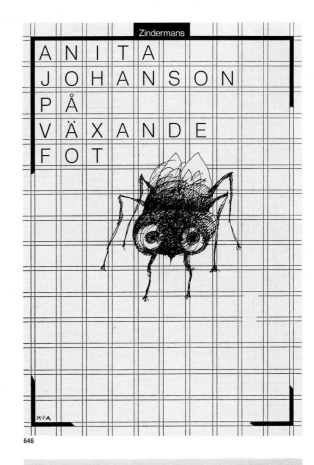

Zindermans

ANITA
JOHANSON
PÅ
VÄXANDE
FOT

646

**641** Cover of a children's book (When Kubaki Comes) about two children who go for a trip round the world with an old horse. (SWI)
**642** Design for the cover of a *Penguin* anthology of comic and curious verse. (GBR)
**643, 644** Cover of a children's story of a mysterious world in which a bluebird lays an egg, and detail of the artwork. Swiss edition of *Ratsmagic*, published by *Jonathan Cape*. (SWI)
**645** Cover of a children's book about the environment (The Mouse and the Butterflies). Full colour. (GER)
**646** Black-and-white cover of a collection of lyric poetry. (SWE)
**647** Jacket of a detective novel (Murderess). In the rectangle, red figure on a yellow ground, black title. (SWE)
**648** Jacket of a detective novel (Murder in Memory). Book in colour, red blood. (SWE)

**641** Kartonierter Umschlag mit Farbillustration für ein *Diogenes*-Kinderbuch über eine Weltreise mit dem Pferd Kubaki. (SWI)
**642** Zeichnung für den Umschlag einer *Penguin*-Anthologie der komischen Poesie. (GBR)
**643, 644** Vollständiger Umschlag und Illustration in Originalgrösse für die deutsche Ausgabe eines englischen Kinderbuches. (SWI)
**645** Titelbild eines Bandes, der in der Reihe «Umweltbücher für Kinder» des *Middelhauve Verlags* erschien. Mehrfarbig. (GER)
**646** Schwarzweiss-Umschlag eines Taschenbuches mit moderner Lyrik. (SWE)
**647** Schutzumschlag eines Kriminalromans Name des Autors und Titel auf gelbem Grund, Figur in Orange, Rest schwarzweiss. (SWE)
**648** Schutzumschlag für einen Kriminalroman. Buch in Hellbraun und Schwarz, roter Blutfleck. (SWE)

**641** Couverture cartonnée avec illustration en couleur pour un livre d'enfant sur un voyage autours du monde avec le cheval Kubaki. (SWI)
**642** Composition pour la couverture de l'anthologie *Penguin* de poésie cocasse. (GBR)
**643, 644** Couverture et illustration (grandeur nature) de l'édition allemande d'un livre d'enfant anglais. (SWI)
**645** Couverture du livre «Le souris et les papillons» paru en français dans la série écologique des éditions *Gallimard*. (GER)
**646** Couverture en noir et blanc d'un livre de poche de poésie moderne. (SWE)
**647** Jaquette d'un roman policier. Nom d'auteur et titre sur fond jaune, figure en orange, design en bas en noir et blanc. (SWE)
**648** Jaquette d'un roman policier. Livre en brun et noir, tache de sang rouge. (SWE)

Zindermans

# KG Matiason
# Mördaren

647

Zindermans

# Jan Broberg
# Mord i minne

12 kapitel
om deckare
och deckar
författare

648

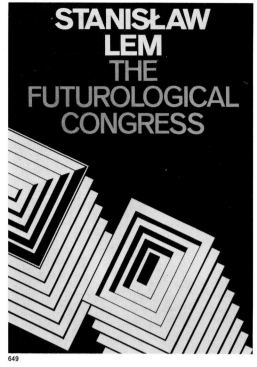

**STANISŁAW LEM THE FUTUROLOGICAL CONGRESS**

649

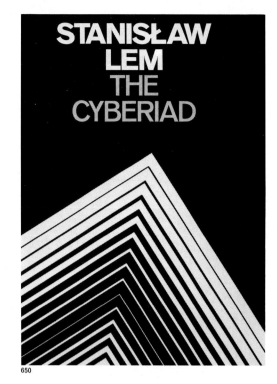

**STANISŁAW LEM THE CYBERIAD**

650

**Georg Büchmann Geflügelte Worte**

Gesamtausgabe

651

Queneau *Zazie dans le métro*

654

Cendrars *La main coupée*

655

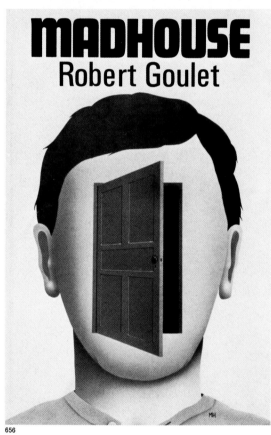

**MADHOUSE** Robert Goulet

656

**649, 650** Dust jackets of two science fiction works by the same Polish author, both black and white, the one with a red and the other with a yellow title. (GBR)
**651** Dust jacket for a collection of "winged words". Pale green and white on dark blue. (SWI)
**652** Cover of an "idea book" issued by *Xerox*. (USA)
**653** Cover of a paperback collection of Sicilian tales in Norwegian translation. (NOR)
**654** Cover of a paperback novel about the Parisian métro by a French author. Full colour. (FRA)
**655** Cover of a paperback novel (The Severed Hand). Flower in red and green, green grass. (FRA)
**656** Dust jacket of a book about the author's stay in a Mallorcan mental home. Shades of brown. (GBR)
**657** Cover of a paperback selection of a Polish playwright's dramas and stories. Full colour. (POL)
**658** Dust jacket of a book about the history of beards. Black and white. (USA)

**649, 650** Einheitlich gestaltete Schutzumschläge für zwei Werke eines polnischen Autors. Design schwarzweiss, Titel in Orange, resp. Gelb. (GBR)
**651** Schutzumschlag einer Ausgabe von Georg Büchmanns *Geflügelten Worten*. Blauer Grund, grüne Schrift. (SWI)
**652** Umschlag eines Ideen-Buches, das von der Xerox Corporation herausgegeben wurde. (USA)
**653** Mehrfarbiger Umschlag für die in einer Taschenbuchreihe in norwegischer Übersetzung herausgekommenen Sizilianischen Erzählungen von Danilo Dolci. (NOR)
**654, 655** Umschläge für zwei in einer Taschenbuchreihe erschienene Romane. Mehrfarbig. (FRA)
**656** Schutzumschlag eines Werkes, in dem der Autor über seine Erlebnisse in einem Irrenhaus auf Mallorca berichtet. (GBR)
**657** Umschlag eines Taschenbuches des Dramatikers Slawomir Mrozek. Blau-grau-grüner Hintergrund. (POL)
**658** Schutzumschlag für eine faszinierende Geschichte über die Bärte im Spiegel der Jahrhunderte. (USA)

**649, 650** Jaquettes de conception uniforme pour les ouvrages d'un auteur polonais. Design en noir et blanc, titre en orange, resp. jaune. (GBR)
**651** Jaquette d'un livre contenant la collection complète des citations de Georg Büchmann. Fond bleu, typo verte. (SWI)
**652** Couverture d'un «livre d'idées» publié par la Xerox Corporation. (USA)
**653** Couverture en couleur du livre «La Sicile raconte» de Danilo Dolci qui a paru dans une série de poche en traduction norvégienne. (NOR)
**654, 655** Couverture de deux romans parus dans une série de poche. En couleurs. (FRA)
**656** Jaquette du roman d'un écrivain qui décrit les expériences qu'il a faites dans un asile d'aliénés sur l'île de Majorque. (GBR)
**657** Couverture d'un livre de poche de l'auteur dramatique Slawomir Mrozek. Fond en tons bleus, grisés et verts. (POL)
**658** Jaquette pour un livre sur l'histoire fascinante de la barbe vue à travers les époques. (USA)

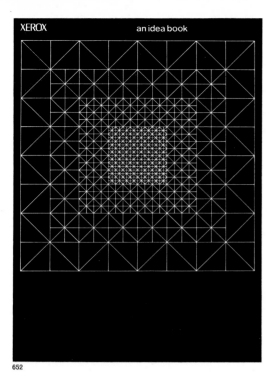

652

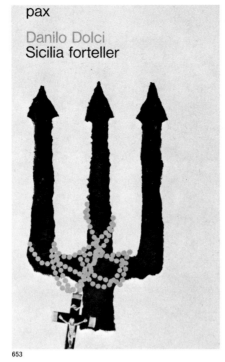

653

ART DIRECTOR / DIRECTEUR ARTISTIQUE:

651 Oswald Dubacher
652 John D. Hough/Tom Geismar
654, 655 Massin
656 Chris Davidson
658 Harris Lewine

AGENCY / AGENTUR / AGENCE – STUDIO:

652 Chermayeff & Geismar Associates
656 John Calder (Publishers) Ltd.
658 LSC&P Design Group Inc.

PUBLISHER / VERLEGER / EDITEUR:

649, 650 Secker & Warburg Ltd.
651 Ex Libris Verlag AG
652 Xerox Corp.
653 Pax Forlag
654, 655 Gallimard
656 Calder & Boyars Ltd.
657 Wydawnictwo Literackie
658 Harcourt, Brace, Jovanovich, Inc.

657

658

ARTIST / KÜNSTLER / ARTISTE:

649, 650 Philip Mann
653 Bruno Oldani
654, 655 Henri Galeron
656 Michael Hasted
657 Zofia Darowska
658 Alan Peckolick

DESIGNER / GESTALTER / MAQUETTISTE:

649, 650 Philip Mann
651 Alfred Bauer
652 Tom Geismar
654, 655 Massin
656 Michael Hasted
658 Alan Peckolick

**659** Complete book cover. Pink face, blue disc. (JPN)
**660** Cover of a children's book about a king and his pet. Drawing in full colour. (GBR)
**661, 662** Two dust jackets from a series, here for works by Shaw and Beckett. Full-colour artwork, names in dark purplish brown. (GER)
**663** Cover of a paperback. Green hair, maroon shirt, yellow tie, brown and blue ground. (GBR)
**664** Dust jacket with Indian motif. Red body, gold lettering. (JPN)
**665** Dust jacket of a book by a witness of the assassination of Abraham Lincoln. Typography in black, red and blue. (USA)
**666** Dust jacket of a novel. Printed in black and orange. (SWI)
**667** Complete dust jacket of a novel. Reds and browns. (SWE)
**668** Dust jacket of a retelling of the story of the Indian girl Pocahontas. Full colour, title red and yellow. (USA)

**659** Schutzumschlag. Rosa Kopf, Hintergrund schwarz und rot. (JPN)
**660** Mehrfarbiger Umschlag eines Kinderbuches über einen Zauberer, der die schlafenden Haustiere verzauberte und einsperrte. (GBR)
**661, 662** Aus einer einheitlich gestalteten Serie von Schutzumschlägen für Sammelbände von Shaw und Beckett. Mehrfarbige Illustration, Name des Autors in dunklem Weinrot. (GER)
**663** Taschenbuch. Grünes Haar, braunes Hemd, gelbe Kravatte. (GBR)
**664** Mehrfarbiger Schutzumschlag. (JPN)
**665** Für einen Augenzeugenbericht über den Mord an Lincoln und die Verschwörung von 1865. Rot, blau und schwarz auf Beige. (USA)
**666** Schutzumschlag für einen Roman. Orange, braun. (SWI)
**667** Schutzumschlag für einen Roman von Anthony Burgess. (SWE)
**668** Für einen Roman. Brauntöne, Titel in Rot und Gelb. (USA)

**659** Jaquette complète. Visage rose, disque bleu. (JPN)
**660** Couverture d'un livre d'enfant racontant l'histoire d'un roi et de ses animaux domestiques. Illustration en couleurs. (GBR)
**661, 662** Deux jaquettes de conception uniforme figurant dans une série, ici pour les œuvres de Shaw et de Beckett. Composition en couleurs, noms en rouge brunâtre. (GER)
**663** Couverture d'un livre de poche. Cheveux verts, chemise brune, cravate jaune, fond brun et bleu. (GBR)
**664** Jaquette avec motif indien. Corps rouge, typo dorée. (JPN)
**665** Jaquette d'un livre sur l'assassinat d'Abraham Lincoln, écrit par un témoin oculaire. Typo en noir, rouge et bleu. (USA)
**666** Jaquette d'un roman. Imprimé en noir et orange. (SWI)
**667** Jaquette complète pour un roman. Tons bruns et rouges. (SWE)
**668** Jaquette d'un livre racontant l'histoire de la jeune fille indienne Pocahontas. En couleurs, titre en rouge et jaune. (USA)

ARTIST / KÜNSTLER / ARTISTE:

659, 664 Tadanori Yokoo
660 David McKee
661, 662 Design-Team München
663 Brian Grimwood
666 Oskar Weiss
667 Per Ahlin
668 Richard Hess

DESIGNER / GESTALTER / MAQUETTISTE:

659, 664 Tadanori Yokoo
660 David McKee
661, 662 Design-Team München
663 Brian Grimwood
665 Ira Treichberg

661

662

664

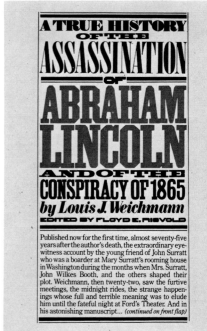
665

659

660

663

666

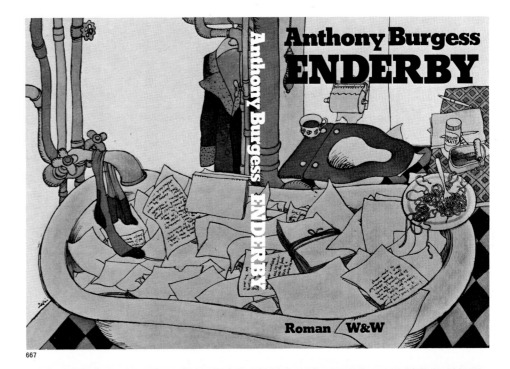

667

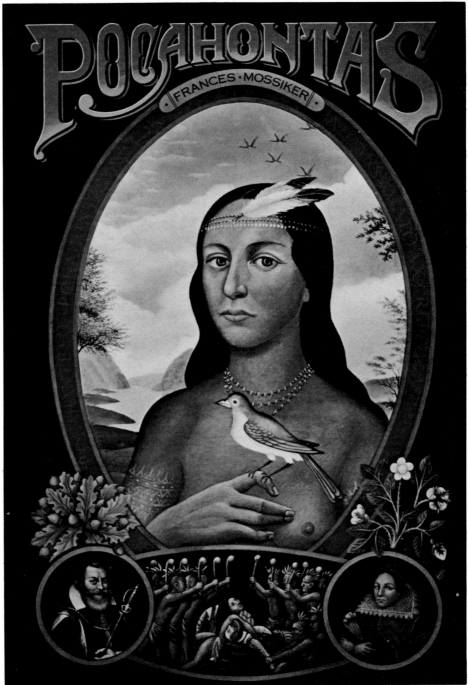

668

ART DIRECTOR / DIRECTEUR ARTISTIQUE:

661, 662 Design-Team München
663 Mike Dempsey
665, 668 Lidia Ferrara
666 Oswald Dubacher

PUBLISHER / VERLEGER / EDITEUR:

659 Yomiuri Shinbun-Sha
660 Abelard-Schuman Ltd.
661, 662 Deutscher Bücherbund
663 Collins Publishers
664 Kodan-Sha
665, 668 Alfred A. Knopf, Inc.
666 Ex Libris Verlag AG
667 Wahlström & Widstrand

**Book Covers**
**Buchumschläge**
**Couvertures de livres**

# 4

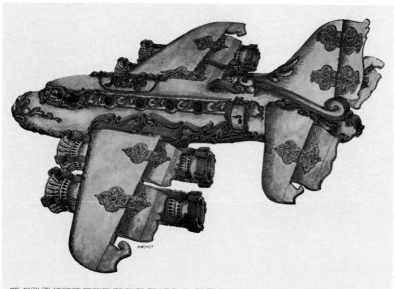

669

**669** Sheet from a large calendar for the *Repro* photoengraving company ("*Repro* takes off"). The colour sheets show fantastic variations on the aeroplane. (BRA)
**670–673** Illustration pages (printed in black and tan) and one complete opening of a small booklet of weights and measures issued by Lachema N. P., Brno. Fig. 670 faces pressure units, Fig. 673 units of matter in moles. Fig. 672 faces the introductory text. (CSR)
**674–676** Illustrations and one complete sheet from an *Esso* calendar devoted to petrol saving and showing footwear through the ages (here Egyptian, Greek, Roman and twentieth-century). (BRA)
**677, 678** Sheet for December from a calendar issued in Nuremberg and entitled "Nuremberg in Twelve Pictures". Full colour. (GER)

**669** Seite aus dem grossformatigen Kalender einer Lithoanstalt. Die Farbblätter stellen phantastische Variationen von Flugzeugen dar. (BRA)
**670–673** Seiten und vollständige Doppelseite aus einem Adressbüchlein mit Kalender. Die Illustrationen beziehen sich auf die auf den gegenüberliegenden Seiten gedruckten Umrechnungstabellen für Masse und Gewichte, hier für Druckmessung (670) und Stoffmengen (673). (CSR)
**674–676** Illustrationen und Blatt aus einem *Esso*-Kalender zum Thema Benzinsparen. Unter dem Motto «*Esso* gibt dem ältesten Vehikel die Ehre» präsentiert er Fussbekleidung aus verschiedenen Epochen, hier aus dem alten Aegypten, Griechenland und Rom und aus dem 20. Jahrhundert. (BRA)
**677, 678** Dezemberbild aus dem Kalender «Nürnberg in 12 Bildern von M. M. Prechtl». (GER)

**669** «*Repro* prend son essor.» Feuillet d'un calendrier grand format pour l'atelier de photogravure *Repro*, avec des variations fantasmagoriques sur le thème de l'avion. (BRA)
**670–673** Pages et page double complète tirées d'un carnet d'adresses avec calendrier. Les illustrations se rapportent aux barèmes de conversion des pages d'en face, ici aux unités de pression (fig. 670) et à la masse de corps en moles (fig. 673). (CSR)
**674–676** Illustrations et feuillet complet d'un calendrier *Esso* sur le thème des économies d'essence. Titre: «Hommage d'*Esso* au plus ancien véhicule» – la chaussure à travers les âges. Ici: l'Egypte, la Grèce, Rome et le 20ᵉ siècle. En polychromie. (BRA)
**677, 678** Feuillet de décembre du calendrier nurembergeois de M. M. Prechtl. (GER)

674

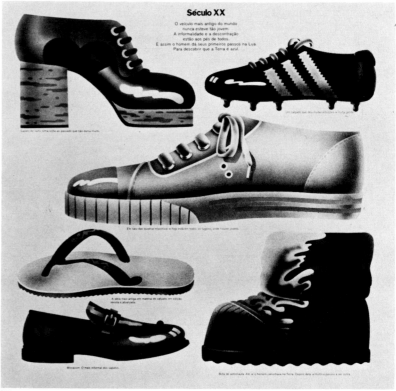

675

ARTIST / KÜNSTLER / ARTISTE:

669 Claudio Sendin
670–673 Vlasta Zábransky
674–676 Oliveira Monte
677, 678 Michael Mathias Prechtl

DESIGNER / GESTALTER / MAQUETTISTE:

669 Claudio Sendin
670–673 Vlasta Zábransky

ART DIRECTOR / DIRECTEUR ARTISTIQUE:

669 Claudio Sendin
674–676 Vítor Lemos

AGENCY / AGENTUR / AGENCE – STUDIO:

674–676 McCann-Erickson

676

Calendars / Kalender
Calendriers

670

672

673

671

677

678

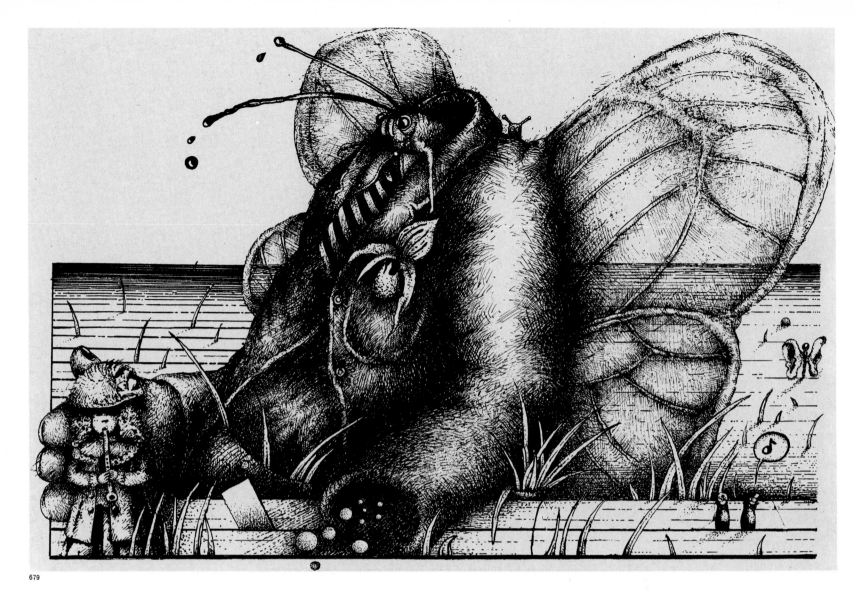

679

680

681

**679** Sheet for August from a calendar published in the humorous magazine *Szpilki*. (POL)
**680** Double page from an *Olivetti* desk diary for 1977 in Italian and English. (ITA)
**681** Double-spread colour illustration from an *Olivetti* appointments calendar for 1977. (ITA)
**682** Wall calendar for the Italian type-foundry *Nebiolo*. (ITA)
**683** Sheet of a wall calendar for a graphic design and photography studio in Stuttgart. The colour circle shrinks as the year progresses and the die-cut sheets are turned. The calendar was a co-production of two German companies with the Museum of Modern Art, New York. (GER)
**684** Sheet from a three-year gardening almanac with tips and space for the gardener's own notes. Published by Alfred A. Knopf. Pale green design on calendar table. (USA)

**679** Blatt aus einem von der satirischen Zeitschrift *Szpilki* veröffentlichten Kalender. (POL)
**680** Doppelseite aus einem in hellgraues Wildleder gebundenen Pultkalender. (ITA)
**681** Doppelseite aus einem Terminkalender von *Olivetti*, der jedes Jahr von einem namhaften Künstler illustriert wird. (ITA)
**682** Wandkalender einer Schriftgiesserei für das Jahr 1975. (ITA)
**683** Kalender, der als Co-Produktion von Kulzer & Co., dem Museum of Modern Art (New York) und Domberger KG unter dem Titel «Color Circle 77» erschien. Die ausgestanzten Kreise verkleinern sich von Monat zu Monat gegen die Mitte hin. (GER)
**684** Aus einem Garten-Almanach mit 3jährigem Kalender. Hellgrün, schwarz, beiges Papier. (USA)

**679** Feuillet d'un calendrier publié par le magazine satirique *Szpilki*. (POL)
**680** Page double d'un calendrier de bureau, relié en cuir chamoisé gris. (ITA)
**681** Page double d'un calendrier de bureau *Olivetti*. Chaque année on demande à un artiste de renom d'illustrer ce calendrier. (ITA)
**682** Calendrier mural pour 1975, publié par *Nebiolo*, fonderie de caractères. (ITA)
**683** Calendrier, publié en co-production par Kulzer & Cie, le Musée d'Art Moderne, New York, et Domberger KG sous le titre «Color Circle 77». Les cercles découpés se réduisent sur chaque feuillet mensuel. (GER)
**684** D'un almanach de jardin avec calendrier pour trois ans. Vert et noir sur papier teint. (USA)

# Calendars / Kalender / Calendriers

ARTIST / KÜNSTLER / ARTISTE:

679 Andrzej Mleczko
681 Horst Janssen
682 Rinaldo Del Sordo / Giuseppe Berlinghieri
683 Gebhardt + Lorenz
684 Stephanie Tevonian

DESIGNER / GESTALTER / MAQUETTISTE:

680 Camilla Masciadri
681 Enzo Mari
683 Gebhardt + Lorenz
684 Stephanie Tevonian

ART DIRECTOR / DIRECTEUR ARTISTIQUE:

680 Franco Bassi
681 Giorgio Soavi
682 Rinaldo Del Sordo/Giuseppe Berlinghieri
684 Betty Anderson

AGENCY / AGENTUR / AGENCE – STUDIO:

682 Studio Giob

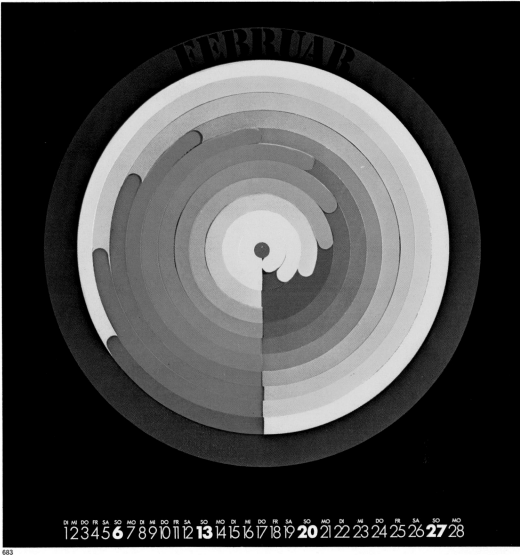

683

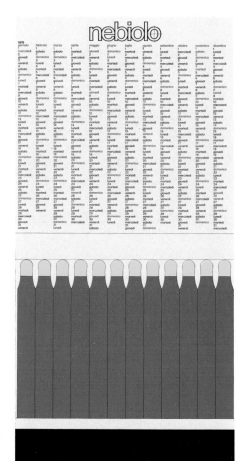

682

684

685

ARTIST / KÜNSTLER / ARTISTE:

685, 686 Christine Chagnoux
688 Migone + Izquierdo
689–697 Ziraldo Pinto
698, 699 Reynold Ruffins

DESIGNER / GESTALTER / MAQUETTISTE:

685, 686 Christine Chagnoux
688 Edgardo Gimenez
698, 699 Reynold Ruffins

686

**685, 686** Illustration and complete sheet from a wall calendar with twelve motifs by a French illustrator of children's books. Each motif is also available as a poster. (NLD)
**687** Sheet from a *Mogurt* calendar. Yellow truck, blue ground. (GER)
**688** "Time to grow into a good harvest." Sheet for May from a calendar for *Esso*. Three-dimensional cockerel in full colour. (ARG)
**689–697** Illustrations for a *Winthrop* calendar, each relating to a different pharmaceutical. (BRA)
**698, 699** Sheet (full colour) and complete opening of a riddle calendar for children published by Charles Scribner's Sons. (USA)

**685, 686** Illustration in Originalgrösse und vollständiges Blatt aus dem Kalender eines Poster-Verlegers. Die in diesem Kalender abgebildeten Sujets einer bekannten französischen Kinderbuch-Illustratorin sind alle auch als Poster erhältlich. (NLD)
**687** Blatt aus einem Kalender. Gelber Wagen, blauer Grund.
**688** «Die Zeit, in welcher eine gute Ernte wächst.» Mai-Blatt aus einem *Esso*-Kalender, mit dreidimensionalem Hahn in bunten Farben. (ARG)
**689–697** Illustrationen aus dem Kalender einer pharmazeutischen Fabrik. Jede Abbildung spielt auf ein bestimmtes Medikament an. (BRA)
**698, 699** Mehrfarbige Illustration und geöffneter, spiralgehefteter Wandkalender mit «tierischen» Rätseln für Kinder. (USA)

**685, 686** Illustration en grandeur originale et feuillet complet d'un calendrier avec des motifs réalisés par une illustratrice française de livres d'enfant. Chacun est en vente sous forme d'affiche décorative. (NLD)
**687** Feuillet d'un calendrier. Voiture jaune, fond bleu.
**688** «Le temps pour cultiver une bonne récolte.» Le coq, composé de divers céréales, noix et graines avec des rouages d'une montre comme pieds, devrait illustrer le slogan de cette feuille d'un calendrier *Esso*. (ARG)
**689–697** Illustrations pour le calendrier d'une entreprise de produits pharmaceutiques, chacune se rapportant à un autre remède. (BRA)
**698, 699** Illustration couleur et calendrier mural à reliure spirale avec des devinettes «animales». (USA)

687

688

689–697

698

699

ART DIRECTOR / DIRECTEUR ARTISTIQUE:

688  Edgardo Gimenez
689–697  Wilson McCord
698, 699  Reynold Ruffins

AGENCY / AGENTUR / AGENCE – STUDIO:

688  Martinez Vadé Publicidad
689–697  International Advertising Agency

**Calendars / Kalender
Calendriers**

club de tiro el trull

700

rangée

701

escargot

702

703

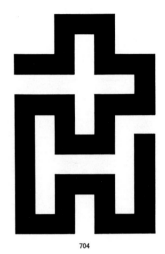

704

706

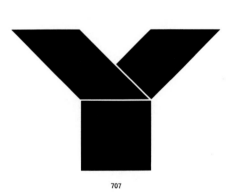

707

709

710

712

713

Trade Marks
Schutzmarken
Marques et emblèmes

705

715

708

711

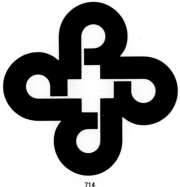

714

ARTIST / KÜNSTLER / ARTISTE:

703 Clyde Hogg/Larry Bishop

DESIGNER / GESTALTER / MAQUETTISTE:

700 Pere Ariño
701, 702 Takenobu Igarashi
703 Clyde Hogg
704 Joseph Moore
705 Karl Hartig/Arnold Saks
706 Ron Hughes
707 Akitosh Sato
708 Ivan Dvoršak
709 Enric Huguet
710 Roger Cook/Don Shanosky
711 Dean Lindsay
712 Marty Neumeier
713 Hans Hartmann
715 Yusaku Kamekura

ART DIRECTOR / DIRECTEUR ARTISTIQUE:

701, 702 Takenobu Igarashi
703 Clyde Hogg
704 Joseph Moore
705 Arnold Saks
706 Ron Hughes
709 Enric Huguet
710 Roger Cook/Don Shanosky
711 Dean Lindsay
713 Publizitätsdienst SBB
715 Yusaku Kamekura

AGENCY / AGENTUR / AGENCE – STUDIO:

700 Estudi Ariño
701, 702 Takenobu Igarashi Design
703 Daniel, Riley & Hogg
704 Logowitz & Moore Design Associates
705 Arnold Saks Inc.
706 Unigraphics
709 Enric Huguet
710 Cook & Shanosky Associates, Inc.
711 Center for Advanced Research in Design
712 Marty Neumeier
713 Publizitätsdienst SBB

**700** Logotype for the "El Trull" shooting club. (SPA)
**701** Logotype for a French restaurant. (JPN)
**702** Logotype for a restaurant serving snails. (JPN)
**703** Logotype for the Birmingham Americans, an American football team. Red, white and blue. (USA)
**704** Emblem for the Harvard School of Public Health. (USA)
**705** Trade mark for the Transnitro Corp., nitrogen import and export. (USA)
**706** Symbol for Federal Energy Conservation. (USA)
**707** Trade mark for a design enterprise, Yonemiya Co. Ltd. (JPN)
**708** Symbol for Univerza v Mariboru, Maribor. (YUG)
**709** Trade mark for Empresa SA, water, gas and heating installations. (SPA)
**710** Symbol for the UN Centre for Housing, Building & Planning. (USA)
**711** Symbol for a civic organization concerned with the commercial development of the town of Wilmette, Illinois. (USA)
**712** Trade mark and logotype for Real Estate Masters. (USA)
**713** Symbol for Swiss Federal Railways incorporating the Swiss cross. (SWI)
**714** Symbol for a Presbyterian medical centre. (USA)
**715** Symbol for a federation of agricultural cooperatives. (JPN)

**700** Schriftzug für einen Schiessverein. (SPA)
**701** Logo eines französischen Restaurants. (JPN)
**702** Schriftzug für ein französisches Restaurant. (JPN)
**703** Für eine Fussballmannschaft. Blau, rot und weiss. (USA)
**704** Symbol einer Schule für Sozialhelfer und Pflegepersonal. (USA)
**705** Firmenzeichen eines Stickstoff-Importeurs/Exporteurs. (USA)
**706** Symbol und Mahnzeichen, das für das von der staatlichen Energiekommission durchgeführte Energiesparprogramm verwendet wird. (USA)
**707** Markenzeichen von *Yonemiya*, einer Designfirma. (JPN)
**708** Schutzmarke der Univerza v Mariboru. (YUG)
**709** Schutzmarke einer Installations- und Sanitärfirma. (SPA)
**710** Symbol: United Nations Center for Housing, Building & Planning. (USA)
**711** Symbol einer gemeinnützigen Vereinigung zur Förderung und Belebung des Geschäftsviertels von Wilmette, Illinois. (USA)
**712** Firmenzeichen eines Häuser- und Grundstückmaklers. (USA)
**713** Symbol der Schweizerischen Bundesbahnen. (SWI)
**714** Symbol für ein medizinisches Zentrum. (USA)
**715** Symbol einer Vereinigung für landwirtschaftliche Zusammenarbeit. (JPN)

**700** Logo pour une association de tir. (SPA)
**701** Logo pour un restaurant français. (JPN)
**702** Logo pour le restaurant français *Escargot*. (JPN)
**703** Emblème d'une équipe de football. Bleu, rouge et blanc. (USA)
**704** Symbole d'une école pour assistants sociaux et gardes-malades. (USA)
**705** Marque déposée d'une maison d'import-export d'azote. (USA)
**706** Symbole et signe de rappel que la commission nationale d'énergie utilise pour son programme d'économie de l'énergie. (USA)
**707** Symbole de *Yonemiya*, un studio de design. (JPN)
**708** Marque déposée de l'Univerza v Mariboru. (YUG)
**709** Marque déposée d'une entreprise pour installations sanitaires. (SPA)
**710** Symbole: United Nations Center for Housing, Building & Planning. (USA)
**711** Symbole d'une association publique pour la promotion et le développement du quartier des affaires de Wilmette, Illinois. (USA)
**712** Emblème d'un agent immobilier. (USA)
**713** Symbole des Chemins de fer suisses, avec la croix suisse. (SWI)
**714** Symbole d'un centre médical. (USA)
**715** Symbole d'une association pour la promotion de la coopération dans l'agriculture. (JPN)

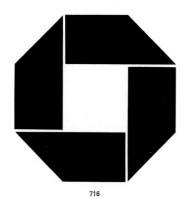

716

717

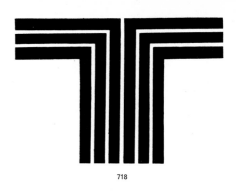

718

720

721

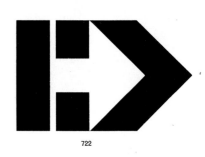

722

724

725

726

DESIGNER / GESTALTER / MAQUETTISTE:

716, 721, 725, 727 Tom Geismar
717 Stephen Harding
718 Pierre Rousselet
719 Eduardo Cánovas
720 John + Barbara Casado
722 John Nash
723 Michael Vanderbyl
724 Yusaku Kamekura
726 João Lauro
728 Bob Paganucci
729 Udo Lauffer
730 Ivan Chermayeff
731 Arnold Saks

ART DIRECTOR / DIRECTEUR ARTISTIQUE:

716, 721, 725, 727 Tom Geismar
717 Blair Good
718 Pierre Rousselet
720 John Casado
724 Yusaku Kamekura
728 Bob Paganucci
729 Udo Lauffer
730 Ivan Chermayeff
731 Arnold Saks

AGENCY / AGENTUR / AGENCE — STUDIO:

716, 721, 725, 727, 730 Chermayeff & Geismar
Associates
717 Aubrey Lee Associates
718 Carlos Duailibi, Pierre Rousselet
Propaganda S.A.
719 Estudio Cánovas
720 Casado Design Ltd.
723 Michael Vanderbyl Graphic Design
729 Lauffer + Dalke Propaganda
731 Arnold Saks Inc.

719

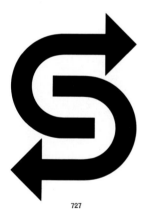

723

**716** Trade mark for the Chase Manhattan Bank. (USA)
**717** Trade mark for a *Westinghouse* nuclear steam supply system, in this case Model 414. (USA)
**718** Trade mark for Tropical Ltda., an import firm. (BRA)
**719** Trade mark for the *Bagò* pharmaceutical laboratory. (ARG)
**720** Symbol for the Center for Educational Renewal in Los Angeles. (USA)
**721** Symbol for the US National Park Service. (USA)
**722** Trade mark for Interlink Development Ltd., a marketing and product development company. (GBR)
**723** Symbol for The Court, a sports ground with tennis courts and handball facilities. (USA)
**724** Symbol for the Japan Crafts Industry Association. (JPN)
**725** Trade mark for Screen Gems, Inc., a company supplying cinema and television films. (USA)
**726** Emblem for the publishing house *Editora Vozes*. (BRA)
**727** Trade mark for Seatrain Lines, Inc., a transport service. (USA)
**728** Proposal for a symbol for a new antispastic pharmaceutical developed by *Geigy*. (USA)
**729** Emblem for homes run by the Evangelical churches under the name of Pella e Bethania. (BRA)
**730** Trade mark for G. F. Business Equipment. The mark is designed to permit animated presentation. (USA)
**731** Symbol for General Learning, an educational enterprise, suggesting a guided passage. (USA)

729

727

**716** Firmenzeichen der Chase Manhattan Bank. (USA)
**717** Schutzmarke – hier für das Modell 414 – für ein von *Westinghouse* entwickeltes, mit Atomkraft betriebenes Energieerzeugungssystem. (USA)
**718** Firmensignet des Importeurs Tropical Ltda. (BRA)
**719** Signet einer pharmazeutischen Fabrik. (ARG)
**720** Symbol eines Zentrums in Los Angeles, das sich mit Bildungsreform befasst. (USA)
**721** Symbol für den amerikanischen National-Park-Service. (USA)
**722** Markenzeichen der Interlink Development Ltd., einer Marketing- und Produktentwicklungsfirma. (GBR)
**723** Symbol für eine Sportanlage mit Tennisplätzen und Handballfeldern. (USA)
**724** Symbol einer Vereinigung zur Förderung des japanischen Kunsthandwerks. (JPN)
**725** Schutzmarke eines Lieferanten von Fernsehfilmen. (USA)
**726** Firmensignet des Verlags *Editora Vozes*. (BRA)
**727** Schutzmarke einer Transportfirma. (USA)
**728** Entwurf für ein Symbol für ein neues Produkt von *Geigy* mit krampflösender Wirkung. (USA)
**729** Signet der evangelischen Pella- und Bethanienheime. (BRA)
**730** Schutzmarke für eine Büroeinrichtungsfirma. Die Marke ist so gestaltet, dass sie auch als Mobile verwendet werden kann. (USA)
**731** Signet von General Learning, einem Unternehmen, das auf dem Bildungssektor tätig ist. (USA)

730

728

**716** Marque déposée de la Chase Manhattan Bank. (USA)
**717** Marque déposée pour le modèle 414 d'un système *Westinghouse* pour la production d'énergie nucléaire. (USA)
**718** Marque déposée de la société d'importation Tropical Ltda. (BRA)
**719** Symbole d'une entreprise de produits pharmaceutiques. (ARG)
**720** Symbole d'un centre à Los Angeles qui s'occupe de la réforme de l'enseignement. (USA)
**721** Marque déposée de l'Office des parcs nationaux des Etats-Unis. (USA)
**722** Marque déposée de Interlink Development Ltd., une société pour le marketing et le développement de produits. (GBR)
**723** Symbole d'un centre sportif avec des courts de tennis et des terrains de handball. (USA)
**724** Symbole d'une association pour la promotion des arts et métiers du Japon. (JPN)
**725** Marque déposée d'un fournisseur de films TV. (USA)
**726** Emblème des Editions *Editora Vozes*. (BRA)
**727** Marque déposée d'une entreprise de transport. (USA)
**728** Projet pour l'emblème d'un nouveau produit *Geigy* qui a des effets antispasmodiques. (USA)
**729** Emblème des foyers évangéliques Pella e Bethania. (BRA)
**730** Marque déposée d'une maison d'équipements de bureau. La marque peut être utilisée comme sculpture mobile. (USA)
**731** Symbole de General Learning, une société qui travaille dans le domaine pédagogique. (USA)

731

732

733

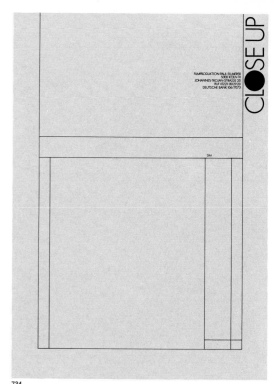

734

NEED

736

Near East
Emergency
Donations, Inc.

737

738

732 Letterhead for Ham Pye Film Productions Ltd. Ham pie in pale pink and grey-brown shades. (GBR)
733 Letterhead for a literary café in Munich. (GER)
734 Invoice for a film production company. Type matter in black, red lines. (GER)
735 Stationery for Tony Page Associates, an advertising agency. Tips of pencils in various colours. (GBR)
736, 737 Logotype and letterhead for Near East Emergency Donations, Inc., an aid organization for refugees that is sponsored by *Time-Life*. (USA)
738 Letterhead for Bushby-McIntire Associates, general contractors. Saw ochre and silver, real cut. (USA)
739, 740 Letterhead for the Methodist Medical Center of Illinois, with its emblem (printed orange on the stationery). (USA)
741 Stationery for Rug Tufters, Inc. Company name printed in brown with orange R. (CAN)
742, 743 Stationery for *Studio Three D*, printed in grey, with detail of the symbol. (USA)

732 Briefkopf der *Ham Pye* Filmproduktions-Gesellschaft. Kuchenstücke in Hellbraun und Rosa. (GBR)
733 Briefbogen der Literatenkneipe *Litfass* in München. (GER)
734 Rechnungsformular einer Filmproduktions-Gesellschaft. Schwarze Schrift, rote Linien. (GER)
735 Briefbogen einer Werbeagentur. Spitzen der Malstifte in verschiedenen Farben. (GBR)
736, 737 Signet und Briefkopf für eine von *Time-Life* unterstützte Flüchtlingshilfe-Organisation, die in den Kriegsgebieten des Nahen Ostens arbeitet. (USA)
738 Briefbogen eines Bauunternehmens. Vom obern Rand her bis zum Sägeblatt schräg eingeschnitten. (USA)
739, 740 Briefbogen (hellgraues Papier) und Signet (rot) für ein medizinisches Zentrum. (USA)
741 Briefbogen mit Umschlag für Rug Tufters, Inc. Orangerotes Signet, braune Schrift. (CAN)
742, 743 Briefbogen mit Umschlag und Signet für das graphische Atelier *Studio Three D*. (USA)

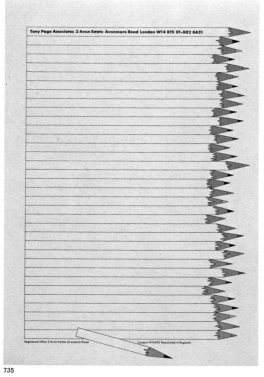

DESIGNER / GESTALTER / MAQUETTISTE:

732  Maurice Hamblin
733, 734  Heinz Bähr
735  Tony Page
736, 737  Arnold Saks
738  Roger Cook/Don Shanosky
739, 740  James V. Neill
741  Peter Adam
742, 743  Stan Baker

ART DIRECTOR / DIRECTEUR ARTISTIQUE:

735  Tony Page
736, 737  Arnold Saks
738  Roger Cook/Don Shanosky
739, 740  James V. Neill
741  Gottschalk + Ash Ltd.
742, 743  Stan Baker

AGENCY / AGENTUR / AGENCE — STUDIO:

732  Format Arts
735  Tony Page Associates
736, 737  Arnold Saks Inc.
738  Cook & Shanosky Assoc. Inc.
739, 740  James V. Neill
741  Gottschalk + Ash Ltd.
742, 743  Studio Three D

735

741

739

740

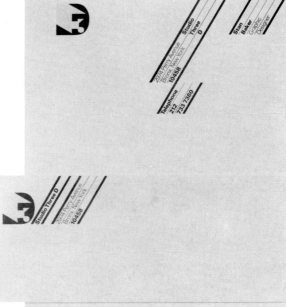

742

743

**732** En-tête de *Ham Pye* (tarte au jambon), société de production cinématographique. En brun clair et rose. (GBR)
**733** En-tête d'un bistro littéraire à Munich. (GER)
**734** Facture d'une société de production cinématographique. Typo noire, lignes rouges. (GER)
**735** Papier à lettres d'une agence publicitaire. Pointes des crayons en différentes couleurs. (GBR)
**736, 737** Logo et en-tête de Near East Emergency Donations, Inc., organisation d'aide aux réfugiés du Proche Orient soutenu par *Time-Life*. (USA)
**738** Papier à lettres d'une maison de construction. Feuille coupée en haut par la scie en brun et argent. (USA)
**739, 740** En-tête (papier grisé) et symbole (rouge) pour un centre médical. (USA)
**741** Papier à lettres et enveloppe pour Rug Tufters, Inc. Symbole orange, typo brune. (CAN)
**742, 743** En-tête avec enveloppe et marque déposée de l'atelier graphique *Studio Three D*. (USA)

**Trade Marks / Letterheads
Schutzmarken / Briefköpfe
Marques et emblèmes / En-têtes**

225

744

745

ARTIST / KÜNSTLER / ARTISTE:

744 John Casado
745 Ernest Witzig/Martin Rodi
746, 748 Ernest Witzig
747 Emanuel Bosshart/Ernest Witzig
749 Emanuel Bosshart
750 Takashi Fujita
751 Alfredo Mastellaro

DESIGNER / GESTALTER / MAQUETTISTE:

744 John Casado

ART DIRECTOR / DIRECTEUR ARTISTIQUE:

744 John Hyde
745 Michel Logoz/Peter Strickler
746 Pierre Jeanmonod
747 Peter Strickler/Pierre Jeanmonod
748, 749 Peter Strickler
750 Hiroshi Yokoo
751 Alfredo Mastellaro

AGENCY / AGENTUR / AGENCE – STUDIO:

744 Casado Design, Ltd.
745–749 Roth & Sauter SA
751 Studio Mastellaro

746

747

**744** Bottle styling for three white and rosé *Jacaré* wines from California. Labels in Art Nouveau style. (USA)

**745** Labels for a bottle of Ticinese grappa (woodcut of a medieval still, sepia and red) and for a bottle of herb spirits (in the style of old Swiss peasant painting). (SWI)

**746–749** Labels and bottles for wines marketed in Switzerland. Fig. 746 for a red wine label in gold on matt black; Fig. 748 for a Portuguese rosé, red, brown, black and gold; Fig. 749 for a white wine dedicated to St. Joder or Theodule, patron saint of the Valais who once performed a miracle to ward off a bad grape harvest; the other wine shown in Fig. 747 celebrates the 500th anniversary of the Battle of Grandson. (SWI)

**750** Bottle styling with grape relief on the glass for a *Suntory* fancy rosé. (JPN)

**751** Labels for three different *Frascati* wines. (ITA)

748

750

749

751

**744** Drei mehrfarbige Etiketten (Jugendstil) für *Jacaré*-Rosé- und Weissweine. (USA)

**745** Flaschen- und Etikettgestaltung für einen Tessiner Grappa und einen Kräuterschnaps. Das Etikett links zeigt eine Grappabrennerei nach einam alten Holzschnitt, das Etikett rechts ahmt den Stil alter Bauernmalerei nach (olivgrün und rot auf hellbeigem Grund). (SWI)

**746–749** Drei Etiketten zu den in Abb. 747 gezeigten Flaschen für Schweizer Weiss- und Rotweine und einen portugiesischen Rosé. Abb. 746: für einen Walliser Pinot Noir, mattschwarzes Etikett mit Golddruck; Abb. 748: für einen portugiesischen Rosé; Abb. 749: für einen Walliser Weisswein – das Etikett zeigt St. Joder, früherer Bischof von Sitten und Schutzheiliger der Walliser Winzer. (SWI)

**750** Flaschengestaltung mit Traubenornament aus Glas und Etikett für einen Rosé. (JPN)

**751** Etikettgestaltung für drei verschiedene *Frascati*. (ITA)

**744** Trois étiquettes couleurs (style art nouveau) pour des vins blancs et rosé. (USA)

**745** Bouteilles et étiquettes pour un grappa tessinois et une eau-de-vie aux herbes. L'étiquette à gauche représente une distillerie de grappa (d'après une vieille gravure sur bois), l'étiquette à droite est exécutée dans la manière des vieilles peintures paysannes. (SWI)

**746–749** Trois étiquettes pour les bouteilles reproduites sous fig. 747 pour des vins vendus en Suisse. Fig. 746: pour un Pinot Noir valaisan, noir mat avec typo dorée; fig. 748: pour un rosé portugais; fig. 749: pour un vin blanc du Valais – l'illustration représente Saint Joder, l'ancien évêque de Sion et le patron des viticulteurs du Canton du Valais; un autre vin (v. fig. 747) est une cuvée du 500e anniversaire de la Bataille de Grandson. (SWI)

**750** Bouteille avec ornement de grappes en verre et étiquette pour un vin rosé. (JPN)

**751** Etiquettes pour trois vins blancs du *Frascati*. (ITA)

752

## Packaging / Packungen
## Emballages

ARTIST / KÜNSTLER / ARTISTE:

752, 753 Paul Davis
754 Advertising Designers/H. Lee Hooper
755, 756 Annonsbyrån Ericson & Co AB
757, 758 Keith Bowen
760 Hermann Rastorfer

DESIGNER / GESTALTER / MAQUETTISTE:

752, 753 Marvin Mitchneck
754 Carl Seltzer
755, 756 Annonsbyrån Ericson & Co AB
757, 758 Klaus Wuttke/Rod Springett/
John George
759 Rhoda Hunt
760 Hermann Rastorfer

ART DIRECTOR / DIRECTEUR ARTISTIQUE:

752, 753 Marvin Mitchneck
754 Carl Seltzer
755, 756 Annonsbyrån Ericson & Co AB
757, 758 Klaus Wuttke/Rod Springett
759 Rhoda Hunt
760 Hermann Rastorfer

AGENCY / AGENTUR / AGENCE– STUDIO:

752, 753 David, Oksner & Mitchneck Inc.
754 Advertising Designers, Inc.
755, 756 Annonsbyrån Ericson & Co AB
757, 758 Springett Wuttke Ltd.
759 Creative Services, Inc.
760 Visuelles Marketing Rastorfer

753

754

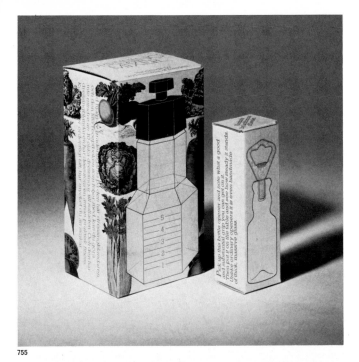

755

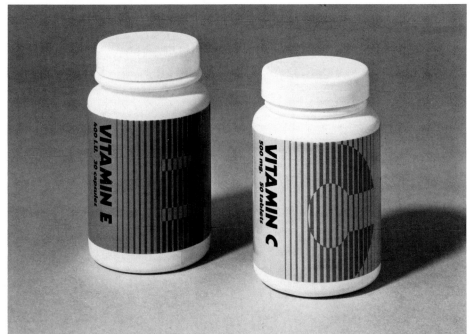

759

756

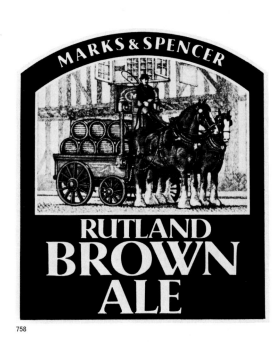

Bisolvon® Linctus

Broncho-Sekretolytikum

90 ml

Boehringer Ingelheim

760

757

MARKS & SPENCER

RUTLAND BROWN ALE

758

**752, 753** Cover design (showing George Washington on his way to his inauguration in New York) and two boxes for *Dutch Masters* cigars from a collection in honour of the Bicentennial. One box shows the first raising of the Stars and Stripes. (USA)
**754** Package for a dietetic ice cream. (USA)
**755** Cartons for a *Lindshammar* salad dressing mixer and bottle opener. (SWE)
**756** Small packages for *Merijal* Finnish pastilles, here with pear and black-currant flavours. Full colour. (SWE)
**757, 758** Carrier pack and label from a range of beers marketed by Marks & Spencer. Label printed white on black, illustration in full colour. (GBR)
**759** From a range of containers for vitamins with colour coding—here light blue/dark blue and yellow/orange. (USA)
**760** Carton for a *Boehringer* medicine against coughs and bronchitis. Colour coding in yellow/brown. (GER)

**752, 753** Detail der Illustration und zwei Zigarrenschachteln, die für die 200-Jahrfeierlichkeiten entworfen wurden. Abb. 752 zeigt George Washington auf dem Weg nach New York zur Amtseinsetzung. (USA)
**754** Verpackung für Diät-Speiseeis. (USA)
**755** Faltschachtel für einen Salatsaucen-Mixer und einen Flaschenöffner. (SWE)
**756** Kleine Packungen für finnische Fruchtbonbons, hier mit Birnen- und Cassis-Aroma. Mehrfarbig. (SWE)
**757, 758** Tragkarton, Flasche und Etikett für dunkles Bier, das von einem britischen Warenhaus verkauft wird. Etikett vorwiegend in Brauntönen, grüner Wagen mit roten Rädern. (GBR)
**759** Dosen mit einheitlicher Etikettgestaltung – hell-/dunkelblau, resp. gelb/orange – für Vitaminpräparate. (USA)
**760** Faltschachtel aus Mikrowell-Karton für ein Broncho-Sekretolytikum von *Boehringer*. Farbkodifizierung gelb/braun. (GER)

**752, 753** Détail de l'illustration (George Washington élu président en route pour New York) et deux boites de cigares créées lors du Bicentenaire. Sur une boîte on voit le premier salut à la bannière étoilée. (USA)
**754** Pour une glace diététique. (USA)
**755** Cartons pliants pour un mixer à sauce à salade et pour un tire-bouchon. (SWE)
**756** Petits emballages de pastilles fruitées finlandaises, ici parfumées à la poire et au cassis. En polychromie. (SWE)
**757, 758** Carton pour six bouteilles, bouteille et étiquette pour une bière brune, vendue par un grand magasin britannique. Etiquette en tons bruns prédominants, véhicule vert, roues rouges. (GBR)
**759** Etiquettes de conception uniforme – bleu clair et foncé, resp. jaune/orange – pour une préparation vitaminée. (USA)
**760** Boîte pliante en carton microwell pour un produit contre la bronchite, avec code couleur en jaune et brun. (GER)

ARTIST/KÜNSTLER / ARTISTE:

763 Centrokappa
764 Urs Maltry
765 Milton Herder
767 Takenobu Igarashi

DESIGNER / GESTALTER:

761, 762 Bruce McIntosh
763 Centrokappa
764 Willy Althaus
765 Gaylord Adams
766 Esther Kurti/
    Alona Degani
767 Yosei Kawaji

ART DIRECTOR / DIRECTEUR ARTISTIQUE:

761, 762 Raymond Waites
763 Centrokappa
764 Urs Arnold
765 Gaylord Adams/Don Flock
767 Tokihiko Kimata/Toshie Sugawara

AGENCE / AGENTUR / AGENCE – STUDIO:

761, 762 Design Group: Design
    Research
763 Centrokappa Srl.
764 Wiener Deville Wälchli
765 Gaylord Adams Design Inc.
766 Esther Kurti & Alona Degani
767 Hakuhodo Co., Ltd.

**761** Range of packaging for the *Design Research* stores. (GBR)
**762** Wrapping paper with logo pattern for *Design Research*. (GBR)
**763** Folding cartons for *Kartell* chairs. (ITA)
**764** Advent calendar in the form of a coloured box with windows to be opened daily. Small gifts can be placed behind each window. (SWI)
**765** Flip-top packet for *Dudes* cigarettes, imitating jeans cloth and zipper. (USA)
**766** Package of four puzzles for small children, made by Orda Industries Ltd. Puzzles in bright colours, plastic storage box. From a range on different subjects, here travel. (ISR)
**767** Carrier bag in blue and white for Citizen Co. Ltd., one of Japan's largest watchmaking companies. Cord in white plastic. (JPN)

761

762

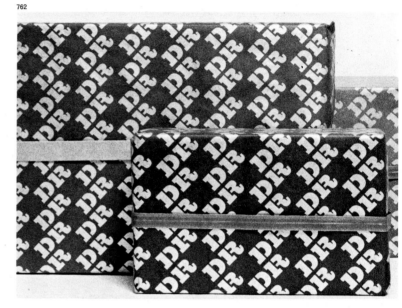

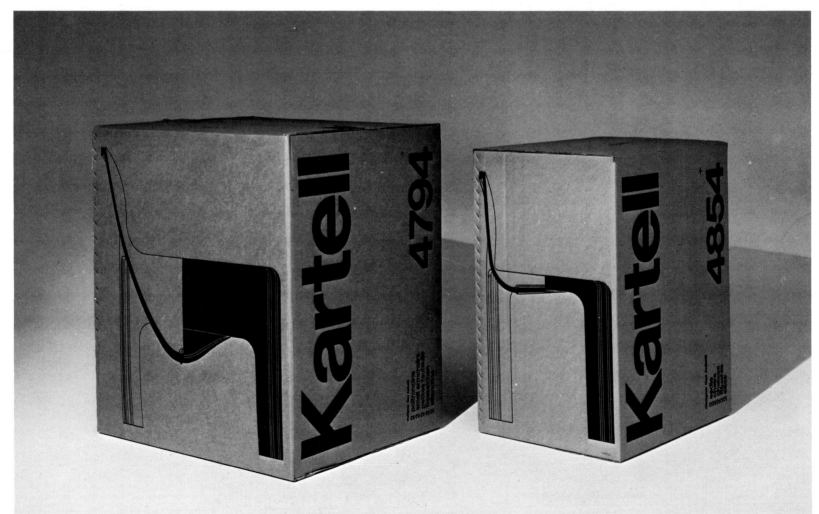

763

764

765

766

767

**761** Beispiele von Packungen und Tragtaschen für das Spezialgeschäft *Design Research.* (GBR)
**762** Einwickelpapier für das Spezialgeschäft *Design Research.* (GBR)
**763** Faltkartons für *Kartell*-Stühle. (ITA)
**764** Kartonhülle für eine Advents-Box aus Kunststoff mit 24 Geschenkfächlein, die gefüllt werden können. Illustration in bunten Farben. (SWI)
**765** Flip-top Zigarettenpackung. (USA)
**766** Aus einer Serie von Packungen – verschiedenfarbene Plastikschachteln mit einheitlich gestalteten, mehrfarbigen Banderolen – mit Puzzles für Kinder. Jede Schachtel enthält vier Puzzles zu verschiedenen Themen, hier Reisen. (ISR)
**767** Tragtasche in Blau und Weiss für Japans grössten Uhrenfabrikanten. (JPN)

**761** Gamme d'emballages réalisée pour les magasins *Design Research.* (GBR)
**762** Papier d'emballage pour les magasins *Design Research.* (GBR)
**763** Cartons pliants pour les chaises *Kartell.* (ITA)
**764** Calendrier de l'Avent sous forme de boîte en couleurs vives avec des fenêtres à ouvrir chaque jour. De petits cadeaux peuvent être placés derrière les fenêtres. (SWI)
**765** Paquet de cigarettes à couvercle basculant. (USA)
**766** D'une série de boîtes en matière plastique contenant des puzzles pour petits enfants. Dans chaque boîte, avec des bandes en papier en couleurs vives, ils se trouvent quatre puzzles consacrés à un sujet particulier, ici aux voyages. (ISR)
**767** Sac en bleu et blanc de l'horlogerie la plus importante du Japon. (JPN)

768

769

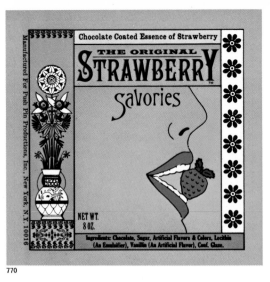

770

771　772

773

774

776

ARTIST / KÜNSTLER / ARTISTE:

768–772 Seymour Chwast
773 Fred Jordan
776 Ford, Byrne & Assoc.
778 Zélio Alves Pinto

DESIGNER / GESTALTER / MAQUETTISTE:

768–772 Seymour Chwast
773 Fred Jordan
774 Kathy Palladini
775 Italo Lupi
776 Ford, Byrne & Assoc.
777 Georg Staehelin

ART DIRECTOR / DIRECTEUR ARTISTIQUE:

768–772 Seymour Chwast
773 Fred Jordan
774 Lou Dorfsman
775 Italo Lupi
776 Ford, Byrne & Assoc.
777 G. Staehelin/J. Robert

AGENCY / AGENTUR / AGENCE – STUDIO:

768–772 Push Pin Studios
773 Fred Jordan Graphic Design
774 CBS/Broadcast Group
775 Studio Lupi
776 Ford, Byrne & Assoc.
777 Pentagram Design SA

**Packaging / Packungen / Emballages**

**768–772** Labels and two examples of the packages from a range of confectionery products used as self-promotion by the Push Pin Studios: candy mints looking like caviar, chocolate-coated coffee beans and chocolate-coated strawberry essence. (USA)
**773** Folding box for a *Kartro* typewriter ribbon. Red and black design. (BRA)
**774** Slipcase and bindings for a CBS Information Guide. (USA)
**775** Carrier cartons for *Stilnovo* lamps. The form and use of the lamps are shown in simple drawings on the cartons. (ITA)
**776** Range of containers for various car maintenance products. The drawings show where they are used. (USA)
**777** Container for a new air freshener using no environmentally dangerous propulsive gas. Blue on white. (SWI)
**778** "Calculators for our time."—"*Sharp* has the same colours as God created." Two self-promotion jigsaw puzzles for *Sharp*, makers of calculators and of colour television sets. (BRA)

**768–772** Etikette und zwei der Packungen aus einer Serie, die von den Push Pin Studios als Eigenwerbung zusammengestellt wurde. Abb. 768: Pushpinoff Caviar – Pfefferminzbonbons; Abb. 769: schokoladeüberzogene «Espresso»-Bohnen; Abb. 770: Schokoladetäfelchen mit Erdbeerfüllung. (USA)
**773** Faltschachtel für Farbbänder. Rot und schwarz. (BRA)
**774** Schuber und Einband eines Handbuches für Presse-Informationen, von einer Fernsehanstalt herausgegeben. (USA)
**775** Tragkartons für *Stilnovo*-Lampen. Form und Anwendungsmöglichkeiten sind in einfachen Zeichnungen dargestellt. (ITA)
**776** Einheitlich gestaltete Packungsreihe für verschiedene Auto-Reinigungsmittel. (USA)
**777** Weisse Kunststoffflasche (blau bedruckt) für einen umweltfreundlichen Raumspray ohne Treibgas. (SWI)
**778** «Rechenmaschinen für unsere Zeit.» – «*Sharp* hat die gleichen Farben, wie Gott sie schuf.» Werbegeschenke, jedes mit einem Puzzle der abgebildeten Illustration. (BRA)

**768–772** Etiquettes et deux boîtes d'une série autopromotionnelle des Push Pin Studios. Fig. 768: Pushpinoff Caviar – bonbons à mente sous forme de caviar; fig. 769: grains de café enrobés de chocolat; fig. 770: tablettes de chocolat fourrées de fraises. (USA)
**773** Boîte pliante pour un ruban de machine. Rouge/noir. (BRA)
**774** Emboîte et reliure d'un guide d'information pour la presse, publié par une station de TV. (USA)
**775** Cartons portatifs pour les lampes *Stilnovo*. La forme et l'emploi des lampes sont indiqués par des dessins simples. (ITA)
**776** Gamme d'emballages de conception uniforme pour divers détergeants pour la voiture. (USA)
**777** Flacon plastique (impression bleue) pour un spray d'ambiance sans gaz propulsif. (SWI)
**778** «Calculateurs pour notre époque.» – «*Sharp* a les mêmes couleurs que Dieu a créées.» Emballages-cadeaux avec des puzzles, distribuées par une entreprise industrielle. (BRA)

775

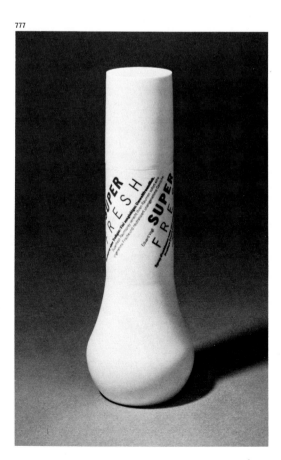

777

778

779

780

783

ARTIST / KÜNSTLER / ARTISTE:

780–782 Norma Epstein

DESIGNER / GESTALTER / MAQUETTISTE:

779 Jack Kellbach/Fred Podjasek
780–782 Janice Goberman
783 Shozo Kakutani
784 Chermayeff & Geismar Assoc.

**779** Packaging range for *Black Tie* cosmetics for men. Real black ties. (USA)
**780** Range of sachets and packages for home freshening products by Estée Lauder, Inc. (USA)
**781** Perfume flacon necklace (jade green bottle, silken cord) and polished metal locket for solid perfume, both marketed by Estée Lauder, Inc. (USA)
**782** Pear-shaped polished metal container for an *Estée Lauder* dusting powder. (USA)
**783** Carrier bag for *Hinodemanju* confectionery. Black on gold. (JPN)
**784** From a range of packages for *Saks Fifth Avenue* stores. (USA)

**779** Packungsreihe für Herren-Kosmetika. Es werden echte schwarze Schleifen verwendet. (USA)
**780** Packungsreihe für verschiedene Artikel von *Estée Lauder*: Raumspray, parfümiertes Schrankpapier und farbig bedruckte Sachets mit Riechstoffen für Schränke und Räume. (USA)
**781** Zwei Anhänger aus einer Reihe von *Estée Lauder*: jadegrünes Parfumflacon und in Silber gefasste goldene Birne, die mit Parfum gefüllt ist. (USA)
**782** Packung und Spraydosengestaltung in Birnenform (aus poliertem zinnähnlichem Material) für einen Puder von *Estée Lauder*. (USA)
**783** Tragtasche einer Konditorei. Gelb und schwarz. (JPN)
**784** Beispiele aus einer Packungsreihe des Warenhauses *Saks Fifth Avenue*. (USA)

**779** Gamme de conditionnements pour des produits cosmétiques *Black Tie* pour messieurs. Avec cravates noires véritables. (USA)
**780** Gamme d'emballages pour divers articles d'*Estée Lauder*: bombe aérosol, papier parfumé pour les armoires, sachets en couleurs pour les chambres et les armoires. (USA)
**781** Deux pendentifs d'une série d'*Estée Lauder*: flacon de parfum vert jade et poire dorée montée en argent, pour du parfum. (USA)
**782** Conditionnement et conception d'atomiseur sous forme de poire (en potin poli) pour une poudre d'*Estée Lauder*. (USA)
**783** Sac en papier d'une pâtisserie. Noir et jaune. (JPN)
**784** Exemples d'une gamme d'emballages du grand magasin newyorkais *Saks Fifth Avenue*. (USA)

AGENCY / AGENTUR / AGENCE – STUDIO:

779 Racila & Vallarta Associates
780–782 Estée Lauder Design Dept.
784 Chermayeff & Geismar Associates

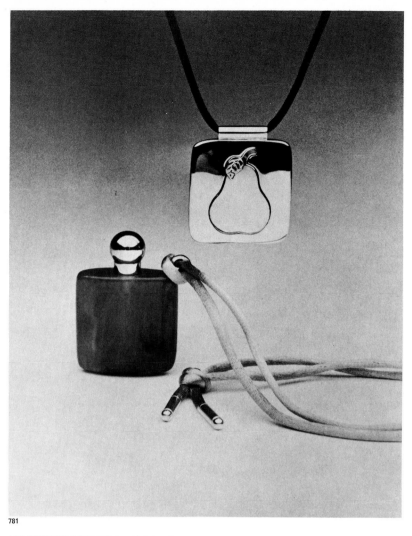

781

782

ART DIRECTOR / DIRECTEUR ARTISTIQUE:

779 Fred Podjasek
780–782 Ira Levy
783 Shozo Kakutani
784 Chermayeff & Geismar Assoc.

**Packaging / Packungen / Emballages**

784

785

## Packaging
## Packungen
## Emballages

787

**785** Range of folding boxes in glossy board, each for three cakes of soap made by Parfumerie Monpelas, Paris. The fragrances shown are verbena, lettuce juice, heliotrope and almond oil. (GBR)
**786, 789** Envelope-like package and point-of-sale display unit for *bant* pantyhose. A window reveals the colour and texture of the goods. (ITA)
**787** Packages from a wide range for *Ribsco* industrial fasteners. Black, white and orange. (USA)
**788** Packages for *Zorba* slips. White symbol on red and green. (BRA)
**790** Boxes in a range of colours for the *Abraham & Straus* department stores, showing the use of the logotype. (USA)
**791** Package from a range for *Bassetti* bed-linen. Blue and silver stripe. (ITA)
**792** Folding boxes from a range for *Crabtree & Evelyn* cosmetics, here a skin freshener and a cleansing lotion. Plants in full colour. (GBR)

**785** Aus einer Serie von Faltschachteln in Glanzkarton. Jede enthält drei Stück Seife der Parfumerie *Monpelas* in Paris in verschiedenen Duftnoten, wie Verbene, Malven, Mandelöl. (GBR)
**786, 789** Hülle und Packung sowie Verkaufsständer für Strumpfhosen. Durch ein ausgestanztes Fenster sind Qualität und Farbe sichtbar. (ITA)
**787** Einheitlich gestaltete Packungsserie für Eisenwaren. Das Design – Schrauben und Muttern – soll auf den Namen der Firma, Rhode Island Bolt & Screw, hinweisen. Orange, weiss, schwarz. (USA)
**788** Packungen für *Zorba*-Slips. Rot-weiss und grün-weiss. (BRA)
**790** Stülpdeckelschachteln eines Warenhauses. Als einheitliches Gestaltungsmotiv wurde das Firmensignet verwendet. (USA)
**791** Verpackung für Bettwäsche. (ITA)
**792** Packungen für Körperpflegemittel. Die Illustrationen auf den Faltschachteln weisen auf die verwendeten Essenzen hin – hier Enzian und Malve mit Honig. (GBR)

**785** D'une série de boîtes pliantes (carton brillant) contenant chacune trois savonnettes de la parfumerie *Monpelas*, Paris. Parfums: verveine, jus de laitue héliotrope, huile d'amandes. (GBR)
**786, 789** Emballage-enveloppe et élément de publicité PLV pour les collants *bant*. Une fenêtre permet de s'assurer du coloris et de la texture des articles. (ITA)
**787** Gamme d'emballages de conception uniforme pour des articles de quincaillerie. Le design – des vices et des écrous – se rapporte au nom de l'entreprise. Orange, blanc et noir. (USA)
**788** Emballages de slips *Zorba*. Rouge/blanc et vert/blanc. (BRA)
**790** Boîtes-cadeaux pour les grands magasins *Abraham & Straus*, utilisant l'emblème en tant que motif de conception. (USA)
**791** Emballage pour des draps de lit *Bassetti*. (ITA)
**792** Boîtes pliantes d'une gamme de produits cosmétiques pour les soins corporels. Les plantes se réfèrent aux parfums, ici gentiane et mauve avec du miel. (GBR)

790

786

788

789

791

792

793

794

795

793 Record cover for a play for children about the adventures of a snowman. (GER)
794 Record cover for two "Punch-and-Judy" stories from a series for children. Bright colours. (SWI)
795 Cover for a recording of bed-time stories for children, from a series in Swiss dialect. (SWI)
796 Cover for a recording of two piano concertos by Mozart. Pastel shades on brown stock. (USA)
797 Cover for a recording of songs by Mose Allison (piano and vocals). Full colour. (USA)
798 Cover for a recording of songs in a romantic and medieval vein. Steel-blue armour. (USA)
799 Record cover for Japanese electronic music. Brightly coloured wiring in the orange. (USA)
800 Cover of an album of music by a Hollywood group drawn from earlier records. Red car, yellow Sphinx. (USA)
801 Cover for a recording of folk music. Yellow bird, green lettering on black. (URU)
802 For a recording by a rediscovered blues singer. (FRA)
803 Cover for a recording of ballet music conducted by Aaron Copland at a 75th-birthday celebration. (USA)
804 Complete record cover for a selection of hits from Sweden. Polychrome on pale blue ground. (SWE)
805 For a recording of carols by a Mormon choir. (USA)

797

798

793 Mehrfarbige Plattenhülle für ein spannendes Hörspiel für Kinder. Von *Ariola-Eurodisc*. (GER)
794 Aus einer Serie von Kinderplatten von *Ex Libris*, aufgeführt von drei Schweizer Kabarettisten. Bunte Farben. (SWI)
795 Mehrfarbige Hülle aus einer Serie von Platten mit Gute-Nacht-Geschichten in schweizerdeutscher Sprache. (SWI)
796 Hülle für ein Mozart-Klavierkonzert. Die Abbildung zeigt den Pianisten/Dirigenten und Mozart. (USA)
797 Mehrfarbige Hülle einer Jazz-Platte mit dem Titel «Mein Geist ist abwesend». (USA)
798 Plattenhülle für Aufnahmen des Jazz-Pianisten Chick Corea. Rüstung in Stahlblau, grüne Landschaft. (USA)
799 Plattenhülle für elektronische Musik aus Japan. Drähte in bunten Farben. (USA)
800 «Vorwärts in die Vergangenheit.» Doppelalbum für eine Anthologie der Gruppe The Firesign Theatre. (USA)
801 Hülle für eine Folklore-Platte aus Südamerika. Schwarzweiss, gelb und grün. (URU)
802 Hülle für eine Blues-Platte. Mehrfarbig. (FRA)
803 Hülle für eine Aufnahme, die anlässlich des 75. Geburtstages des Dirigenten gemacht wurde. Mehrfarbig. (USA)
804 Geöffnete Plattenhülle für die bekanntesten Hits einer Pop-Gruppe. Vorwiegend in Blau und Grün. (SWE)
805 Mehrfarbige Hülle einer Platte mit Weihnachtsliedern, von einem Mormonen-Chor gesungen. (USA)

800

801

793 Pochette d'un disque pour enfants sur les aventures d'un bonhomme de neige. (GER)
794 Pochette figurant dans une série d'enregistrements de guignol pour enfants. Couleurs vives. (SWI)
795 Pochette pour un recueil d'histoires en dialecte suisse allemande pour faire endormir les petits. (SWI)
796 Pochette pour un enregistrement de deux concertos pour piano de Mozart. Tons pastel sur papier brun. (USA)
797 Couverture d'un disque avec des chansons de Mose Allison. En polychromie. (USA)
798 Pochette pour un enregistrement du pianiste de jazz Chick Corea. Armure en bleu acier. (USA)
799 Pochette pour un disque de musique électronique japonaise. Fils en couleurs vives. (USA)
800 «En avant dans le passé!» Couverture d'une anthologie d'un groupe. Voiture rouge, sphynx jaune. (USA)
801 Pochette pour un enregistrement de musique folklorique. Oiseau jaune, typo verte sur fond noir. (URU)
802 Pour un enregistrement de blues. (FRA)
803 Pochette pour un enregistrement de musique de ballet dirigé par Aaron Copland lors de son 75e anniversaire. (USA)
804 Recto et verso d'une pochette présentant une sélection de chansons de la Suède. Sur fond bleu pâle. (SWE)
805 Pochette pour un enregistrement de chants de Noël présentés par un chœur mormon. Couleurs vives. (USA)

802

803

796

799

ARTIST / KÜNSTLER / ARTISTE:

793 Mouche Vormstein
794, 795 Heinz Stieger
796 Milton Glaser
797 Seymour Chwast
798 Wilson McLean
799 Stanislaw Fernandes
800 John O'Leary
801 Fernando Alvarez Cozzi
802 Jean Vern
803 Robert Giusti
804 Hans Arnold
805 James Wood

804

DESIGNER / GESTALTER / MAQUETTISTE:

796 Paula Scher
797 Abie Sussman
798 John Berg
799 Acy Lehman
800 Andy Engel
801 Fernando Alvarez Cozzi
802 Jean Paul Théodule
803 Edwin Lee
804 Rune Söderqvist
805 Roslav Szaybo

ART DIRECTOR / DIRECTEUR ARTISTIQUE:

793 Manfred Vormstein
794, 795 Oswald Dubacher
796 Paula Scher
797 Bob Defrin
798, 800 John Berg
799 Acy Lehman
801 Jorge DeArtieaga
802 Philippe Rault
803 Ed Lee/John Berg
804 Rune Söderqvist

AGENCY / AGENTUR / AGENCE – STUDIO:

799 Stanislaw Fernandes/Solution
801 Imprenta «AS»

PUBLISHER / VERLEGER / EDITEUR:

793 Ariola-Eurodisc GmbH
794, 795 Ex Libris Verlag AG
796, 798, 800, 803, 805 CBS Records
797 Atlantic Recording Corp.
799 RCA Records
801 R. y R. Gioscia
802 Barclay Records
804 Polar Music AB

805

239

806

807

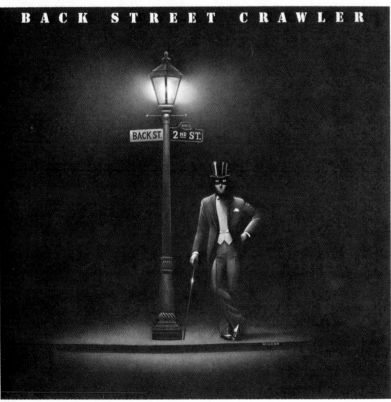

809

810

**806** Cover for a recording by a popular singer. Cerise umbrella, green coat, red title. (JPN)
**807** Cover for a recording of music by the jazz pianist Eubie Blake. Mostly brown shades, pink matchbox, white lettering. (USA)
**808** Artwork for both sides of a record cover. (JPN)
**809** Cover for a recording of songs. Shades of dark greyish green. (USA)
**810** Cover for an album issued for advertising purposes by a Hungarian export organization in the telecommunications field. Purplish camels, orange sand, blue-green sky. (HUN)
**811, 812, 812a** Cover for a recording of New Orleans jazz with the late Louis Armstrong (project). Figs. 812 and 812a show how the two wooden boards open to form a three-dimensional model of a Mississippi steamboat. (SWI)

**806** Mehrfarbige Hülle für eine Single-Platte. (JPN)
**807** Plattenhülle für eine Aufnahme des Jazz-Pianisten Eubie Blake. Brauner Pelzmantel, beige Rauchwolke, dunkler Hintergrund. (USA)
**808** Vorder- und Rückseite einer Plattenhülle. (JPN)
**809** Vorwiegend in düsteren Tönen gehaltene Hülle für eine Rock-Platte. (USA)
**810** Vorderseite eines Doppelalbums, das von einer auf Export spezialisierten Telekommunikationsfirma für Werbezwecke herausgegeben wurde. In bunten Farben. (HUN)
**811, 812, 812a** Vorderseite, halb und ganz aufgeklappte Hülle für eine Louis-Armstrong-Platte (Entwurf). Auf der ganz aufgeklappten Hülle erscheint ein Mississippi-Dampfer mit zwei rauchenden Kaminen. (SWI)

**806** Pochette d'un disque d'un chanteur populaire. En polychromie. (JPN)
**807** Pochette pour un enregistrement du pianiste de jazz Eubie Blake. Prédominance de tons bruns, boîte d'allumettes rose, typo blanche. (USA)
**808** Composition figurant sur le recto et verso d'une pochette de disque. (JPN)
**809** Pochette pour un enregistrement de chansons. Tons gris verdâtre foncé. (USA)
**810** Pochette d'un disque publié en tant qu'élément promotionnel par une organisation hongroise d'exportation d'articles de télécommunication. En couleurs vives. (HUN)
**811, 812, 812a** Pochette pour un enregistrement de jazz de La Nouvelle-Orléans avec Louis Armstrong (projet). Les figs. 812 et 812a montrent les deux panneaux en bois, dépliés à moitié et entièrement, faisant apparaître un bateau à vapeur du Mississippi. (SWI)

ARTIST / KÜNSTLER / ARTISTE:

806 Tadanori Yokoo
807 Thomas B. Allen
808 Shozo Shinoda
809 David Wilcox
810 Kálmán Molnár
811, 812 Robert Metzger

DESIGNER / GESTALTER / MAQUETTISTE:

806 Tadanori Yokoo
807 Ed Lee
809 Abie Sussman
810 Kálmán Molnár
811, 812 Robert Metzger

808

ART DIRECTOR / DIRECTEUR ARTISTIQUE:

806 Tadanori Yokoo
807 Ed Lee
809 Bob Defrin
810 Péterné Zupán
811, 812 Robert Metzger

AGENCY / AGENTUR / AGENCE – STUDIO:

811, 812 Robert Metzger

PUBLISHER / VERLEGER / EDITEUR:

806 RCA Victor Records
807 CBS Records
809 Atlantic Recording Corporation
810 Budavox Telecommunication
Foreign Trading Company Ltd.

**Record Covers**

811

812

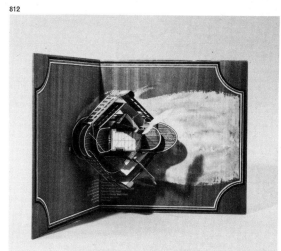

812a

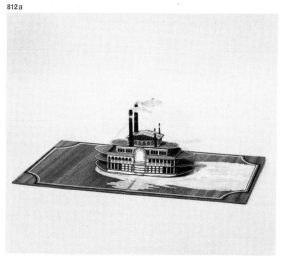

**813** Sleeve for a promotional record of New Orleans jazz issued by the packaging company Container Corporation of America as a foretaste of a concert to be performed at a Frozen Food Show—hence the title "Fire & Ice". (USA)
**814** Cover for a recording of Shostakovich's music for the film *The New Babylon*. (USA)
**815, 816** Two pages from a brochure accompanying a Johnny Cash country music record distributed in Czechoslovakia. Fig. 816 is in black and white. (CSR)
**817** The empty table and the burning toast illustrate the title of one of the songs on this Eddie Harris record. (USA)
**818** An exercise in unreal realism on the cover of a recording by the Don Harrison Band. (USA)
**819** Full-colour cover for a recording of Prokoviev's *Lieutenant Kije*, backed by a Shostakovich symphony. (USA)

**813** Hülle für die neusten Aufnahmen eines Jazz-Trios. Sie wurde von einer Verpackungsfirma als Einladung zu einem von ihr unterstützten Konzert dieser Band an Kunden verteilt. Das Konzert fand anlässlich einer Messe für Tiefkühlprodukte statt, daher auch der Name «Feuer & Eis» (heisser Jazz, kalte Produkte). (USA)
**814** Schallplattenhülle für eine Aufnahme der von Schostakowitsch komponierten Musik zum Film «Das neue Babylon». (USA)
**815, 816** Zwei Innenseiten eines Textheftes, das einer Schallplatte mit Aufnahmen des amerikanischen Country-Sängers Johnny Cash beiliegt. Abb. 816 ist in Schwarzweiss. (CSR)
**817** «Alles, was ich habe, ist Pech.» Der leere Tisch und der angekohlte Toast illustrieren den Titel dieser Schallplatte mit Aufnahmen des Jazz-Saxophonisten Eddie Harris. (USA)
**818** Hülle für eine Aufnahme der Don Harrison Band: irreell wirkender Realismus. (USA)
**819** Mehrfarbige Plattenhülle für Aufnahmen von Prokofieff und Schostakowitsch. (USA)

**813** Pochette promotionnelle pour un enregistrement de jazz de La Nouvelle-Orléans publié par une entreprise de conditionnement en tant qu'invitation pour un concert présenté lors d'une foire de produits surgelés – ce qui évoque aussi le titre «Fire & Ice» (feu et glace). (USA)
**814** Pochette pour un enregistrement de la musique de Chostakovitch composé pour le film «La nouvelle Babylone». (USA)
**815, 816** Deux pages d'une brochure accompagnant un enregistrement de country music de Johnny Cash, distribué en Tchécoslovaquie. Fig. 816 en noir et blanc. (CSR)
**817** La table vide et le toast brûlé devraient illustrer le titre du disque (Tout ce que j'ai, c'est de la malchance). (USA)
**818** Pochette pour un enregistrement du saxophoniste de jazz Don Harrison. Composition de réalisme irréel. (USA)
**819** Pochette pour un enregistrement du *Lieutenant Kije* par Prokofiev avec une symphonie de Chostakovitch. (USA)

ARTIST / KÜNSTLER / ARTISTE:

814 Seymour Chwast
815, 816 Jiří Šalamoun
817 David Wilcox
818 Robert Giusti
819 James Endicott

813

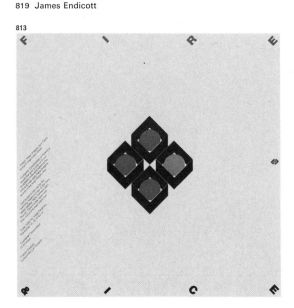

815

814

816

BAD LUCK IS ALL I HAVE / EDDIE HARRIS

817

the DON HARRISON BAND

818

PROKOFIEV **Lieutenant Kije**
SHOSTAKOVICH **Symphony No. 6**
**ANDRÉ PREVIN**
conducting the London Symphony Orchestra

819

DESIGNER / GESTALTER / MAQUETTISTE:

813 Jeff Barnes
814 Ed Lee
815, 816 Jiří Šalamoun
817 Paula Scher
818 Abie Sussman/Bob Defrin
819 James Endicott

ART DIRECTOR / DIRECTEUR ARTISTIQUE:

814 Ed Lee
817, 818 Bob Defrin
819 Marvin Schwartz

AGENCY / AGENTUR / AGENCE – STUDIO:

813 Container Corp. of America
819 Angel Records

PUBLISHER / VERLEGER / EDITEUR:

813 Container Corp. of America
814 CBS Records
815, 816 Supraphon
817, 818 Atlantic Recording Corporation
819 Capitol Records, Inc.

Record Covers
Schallplattenhüllen
Pochettes de disques

820–822

823

824

825

826–828

829–836

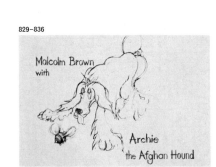

Malcolm Brown
with

Archie
the Afghan Hound

Words and Music by
Evie and Ken Martyne

Singers
Lynn Garner and Noel Cameron

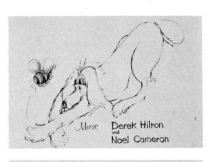

Music Derek Hilton
and
Noel Cameron

Producer
Muriel Young

Director
Dave Warwick

Drawings by
Keith S. Aldred

244

837

838

ARTIST / KÜNSTLER / ARTISTE:

820–828, 839, 840 Anna Farrar
829–836 Keith S. Aldred
837, 838 Christiane Beauregard

DESIGNER / GESTALTER / MAQUETTISTE:

820–828, 839, 840 Anna Farrar
829–836 Keith S. Aldred
837, 838 Christiane Beauregard
841 Thomas Gecan

839

840

**820–822, 826–828** Frames from a *Granada* colour television series of songs for children, here illustrating "Go tell Aunt Rhody" and "Going to the zoo". (GBR)
**823, 824** Two black-and-white frames from "Arrows", a *Granada* pop music programme. (GBR)
**825** Black-and-white illustration for the *Granada* school programme "History around you". (GBR)
**829–836** Frames from an end credit sequence for a *Granada* children's television programme. Dog in black outline, bee in colour. (GBR)
**837, 838** Two frames from a *Radio-Canada* children's television programme. (CAN)
**839, 840** Two frames from the same *Granada* children's programme as in Figs. 820–822 and 826–828, here for "The Old Woman Liko Lived in a Shoe". (GBR)
**841** Title for a television review of folk art in Maryland. Yellow title, green frame. (USA)

**820–822** Sequenz aus einem Kinderfernsehfilm, der im Rahmen der Sendereihe «Eine Handvoll Lieder» ausgestrahlt wurde. Mehrfarbig. (GBR)
**823, 824** Bilder aus einem von *Granada-TV* gezeigten Pop-Musik-Programm. (GBR)
**825** Bild aus einem Film, der im Schulfernseh-Programm von *Granada-TV* gezeigt wurde. (GBR)
**826–828** Sequenz aus dem Farbfilm «Im Zoo», aus einer Sendereihe für Kinder. (GBR)
**829–836** Schlusssequenz einer Probesendung, für eine von der Fernsehanstalt *Granada* realisierte Kinder-Show über einen afghanischen Windhund. (GBR)
**837, 838** Zwei Bilder aus einem Farbfernsehfilm für Kinder. (CAN)
**839, 840** Bilder aus der Titelsequenz zu einem Kinderfilm: «Die alte Frau, die im Schuh lebte». (GBR)
**841** Aus der Titelsequenz für eine Kultur-Sendung über Volkskunst in Amerika. (USA)

841

**820–822, 826–828** Images de deux films télévisés, émis par *Granada TV* dans le cadre d'une série de chansons pour enfants, ici illustrant «Dis-le à tante Rhody» et «Allons au zoo». (GBR)
**823, 824** Deux images en noir-blanc pour un programme de musique pop de *Granada*. (GBR)
**825** Illustration en noir-blanc d'un programme scolaire de *Granada* sur l'histoire. (GBR)
**829–836** Séquence du générique final d'un programme télévisé pour enfants, émis par *Granada*. Lévrier afghan à contours noirs, abeille en couleur. (GBR)
**837, 838** Images d'un programme télévisé pour enfants, émi par *Radio-Canada*. (CAN)
**839, 840** Images d'un programme de *Granada*, diffusé dans le cadre d'une série de chansons pour enfants (voir figs. 820–822, 826–828), ici pour «La vieille qui habitait un soulier». (GBR)
**841** Du générique d'une émission sur l'art folklorique au Maryland. Titre jaune, cadre vert. (USA)

ART DIRECTOR / DIRECTEUR ARTISTIQUE:

837, 838 Jacques Lamarre
841 Thomas Gecan

AGENCY / AGENTUR / AGENCE – STUDIO:

820–836, 839, 840 Granada Television
837, 838 Société Radio-Canada/Section Arts graphiques
841 Maryland Center for Public Broadcasting

PRODUCER / PRODUZENT / PRODUCTION:

820–836, 839, 840 Granada Television Ltd.
837, 838 Société Radio-Canada
841 Maryland Center for Public Broadcasting

**Film / Television / Fernsehen**

842

843

845

846

847–854 →

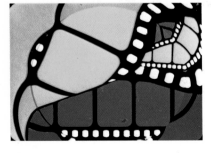

ARTIST / KÜNSTLER / ARTISTE:

842–844 Morton Goldsholl/Tom Freese (Photo)
845, 846 Mark Howard
847–854 Pierre Kohler
855–857 James Quick
858–860 J. Graham Adshead
861–863 John Leech

DESIGNER / GESTALTER / MAQUETTISTE:

842–844 Morton Goldsholl
845, 846 Mark Howard/George McGinnis
847–854 Pierre Kohler
855–857 James Quick
858–860 J. Graham Adshead
861–863 John Leech

ART DIRECTOR / DIRECTEUR ARTISTIQUE:

842–844 Morton Goldsholl
845, 846 George McGinnis
847–854 Hubert Tison
855–857 James Quick
858–860 J. Graham Adshead
861–863 John Leech

246

844

842–844 Frames from the title opener of a film promoting Goldsholl Associates, Inc. (USA)
845, 846 Frames from the titling sequence of a daily film show presented on ABC television. (USA)
847–854 Titling sequence for a cinema programme intended for a young audience, presented by *Radio-Canada* television. (CAN)
855–857 Examples of colour slides accompanying weather forecasts on *Granada* television, here for May (bees), June (cricket) and August (fish) weather. (GBR)
858–860 Colour slides promoting *Granada* television programmes – here a scientific film, a feature film and a midnight mystery. (GBR)
861–863 From a title sequence for a film about John Bull and the Yankees in Britain, shown on *Granada* television. (GBR)

842–844 Aus der Titelsequenz eines Werbespots für eine Agentur. (USA)
845, 846 Bilder aus der Titelsequenz für ein Fernsehprogramm. (USA)
847–854 Aus der Titelsequenz zu einer Jugendsendung des Fernsehsenders *Radio-Canada* mit Filmkritiken und -auszügen. (CAN)
855–857 Aus einer Serie von zwölf Bildern, die in den entsprechenden Monaten zur Ankündigung der Wettervorhersage dienen. Mehrfarbig. (GBR)
858–860 Aus einer Serie von Einzelbildern zur Ankündigung verschiedener Fernseh-Programme. Alle sind mehrfarbig. (GBR)
861–863 Beispiele aus der Titelsequenz zu einem Fernsehfilm in Farbe, der von *Granada-TV* unter dem Titel «Yankees, geht nach Hause» ausgestrahlt wurde. (GBR)

842–844 Images du générique d'un film promotionnel de Goldsholl Associates, Inc. (USA)
845, 846 Du générique d'un programme diffusé chaque jour par la station TV ABC. (USA)
847–854 Séquence du générique d'un programme de cinéma destiné aux jeunes et présenté par la station TV *Radio-Canada*. (CAN)
855–857 D'une série d'images couleur accompagnant les prévisions du temps de *Granada*. (GBR)
858–860 Images introduisant différents programmes télévisés de *Granada* – ici un film scientifique, un long métrage et un policier de minuit. (GBR)
861–863 Plans fixes du générique d'un film en couleurs, intitulé «Yankees, fiche z le camp», présenté par la station TV *Granada*. (GBR)

AGENCY / AGENTUR / AGENCE – STUDIO:

842–844 Goldsholl Associates
845, 846 Image Factory, Inc.
847–854 Société Radio-Canada/Section Arts graphiques
855–863 Granada Television

PRODUCER / PRODUZENT / PRODUCTION:

842–844 Goldsholl Associates
845, 846 American Broadcasting Co.
847–854 Société Radio-Canada
855–863 Granada Television Ltd.

**Film / Television / Fernsehen**

855–857

858–860

861–863

Paper/Papier: Papierfabrik Biberist – Biber GS SK3, blade coated, pure white 120 gm² and Biber Offset SK3, pure white, machine-finished, 140 gm²/Biber GS SK3, hochweiss, satiniert, 120 gm² und Biber-Offset SK3, hochweiss, maschinenglatt, 140 gm²

Printed by/gedruckt von: Seetal Papier AG, Seon (Colour pages/Farbseiten), Merkur AG, Langenthal (black and white/schwarzweiss)

Cover/Einband: Buchbinderei Schumacher AG, Bern/Schmitten
Glossy lamination/Glanzfoliierung: Durolit AG, Pfäffikon SZ